THE LONDON & SOUTH WESTERN RAILWAY

UNIFORM WITH THIS BOOK

A History of the Railways of the Forest of Dean, by H. W. Paar: Part One—*The Severn & Wye Railway*. Part Two—*The Great Western Railway in Dean*

A History of the Narrow-gauge Railways of North West Ireland, by Edward M Patterson: Part One—*The County Donegal Railways*. Second Edition. Part Two—*The Londonderry & Lough Swilly Railway*

The Highland Railway, by H. A. Vallance

The Lynton & Barnstaple Railway, by G. A. Brown, J. D. C. A. Prideaux and H. G. Radcliffe

The West Highland Railway, by John Thomas

The Great North of Scotland Railway, by H. A. Vallance

A History of the Narrow-gauge Railways of North East Ireland, by Edward M. Patterson: Part One—*The Ballycastle Railway*. Part Two—*The Ballymena Lines*

The Cavan & Leitrim Railway, by Patrick J. Flanagan

The Callander & Oban Railway, by John Thomas

The Midland & South Western Junction Railway, by Colin G. Maggs

The Cambrian Railways, Volume I: 1852-1888, by Rex Christiansen and R. W. Miller

The Somerset & Dorset Railway, by Robin Atthill and O. S. Nock

IN PREPARATION

The Cambrian Railways, Volume II: 1888-1968, by Rex Christiansen and R. W. Miller

The London & South Western Railway, by R. A. Williams (Vols II and III)

The London & North Western Railway, by M. C. Reed (three volumes)

The Lancashire & Yorkshire Railway, by John Marshall (two volumes)

An artist's impression of the L & S terminus, Southampton, circa 1840. The early livery is unknown, the colours used here being merely an impression

THE
LONDON & SOUTH WESTERN RAILWAY

Volume I : The Formative Years

by

R. A. WILLIAMS, A.M.Inst.T.

DAVID & CHARLES : NEWTON ABBOT

7153 4188 X

TO MY WIFE

©
R. A. WILLIAMS
1968

Printed in Great Britain by
W J Holman Limited Dawlish
for David & Charles (Publishers) Limited
South Devon House Newton Abbot Devon

Contents

	LIST OF ILLUSTRATIONS	7
1	THE LONDON & SOUTHAMPTON RAILWAY	11
	The need for the line · the Bill before Parliament	
2	BUILDING THE MAIN LINE	21
	Progress under Giles · the fall of Giles · a new regime and better progress · after the opening	
3	THE STRUGGLE TOWARDS THE WEST	48
	Battles for Bristol and Newbury · preliminary moves towards Exeter · powers for an Exeter line · Exeter—central or coast line? · a broken pledge · a few branches	
4	WEST OF EXETER	99
	Cornwall seeks a railway · LSW pawns in Devon and Cornwall · LSW plans thwarted · the first openings in North Devon · a try for Plymouth	
5	STRUGGLES IN THE EAST	120
	A Portsmouth line thwarted and a substitute to Gosport · early relations with the London & Brighton Railway · difficulties over the Portsmouth Railway · intermediate lines	
6	LONDON, WINDSOR AND CONNECTED LINES	158
	Nine Elms and the Metropolitan Extension · the Battersea knot · the Richmond Railway · Windsor line and the Loop · the North & South Western Junction Railway · the Kingston branch · Chertsey, Weybridge, Wokingham and Hampton Court	

7	OTHER LINES OUTSIDE LONDON	183
	The Alton branch · relations with the Reading, Guildford & Reigate Railway · challengers for Southampton · the Somerset & Dorset Railway	
8	THE LSW AND THE SEA	199
	Development of Southampton port and an LSW foothold in France · the railway and steamer services · ships and routes	
9	PERSONALITIES AND POLICIES	215
	Early organisation · finance and audit: the Stovin affair · Archibald Scott: the goods business · the passenger business · amalgamation moves	
10	WORKING THE RAILWAY	227
	Staff matters · the passengers' environment · an operating miscellany · goods trains · the electric telegraph · accidents · maintaining the track · Brookwood Necropolis · royal patronage	

APPENDICES
    1 Arches to Waterloo   251
    2 Company abbreviations   252

AUTHOR'S NOTE   253

BIBLIOGRAPHY   255

INDEX   259

Illustrations

PLATES

frontispiece
An artist's impression of the L & S terminus, Southampton circa 1840

between pages 16 and 17
1 Nine Elms terminus
2 Southampton terminus

between pages 32 and 33
3 Micheldever station, originally Andover Road
4 Weybridge, old station buildings
5 Locomotive, 2-2-2, by Rothwell, side elevation

between pages 48 and 49
6 Locomotive, 2-2-2, by Rothwell, sectional elevation
7 First train on the Bodmin & Wadebridge Railway
8 Rail and stone blocks, Bodmin & Wadebridge Railway

between pages 64 and 65
9 Original engine house at Wadebridge
10 Original workshops at Wadebridge
11 Terminus milestone from Ruthern Bridge
12 Second class tickets, Bodmin & Wadebridge Railway

between pages 96 and 97
13 Bodmin & Wadebridge carriages
14 Beattie tank at Wenford Bridge
15 Crediton station, looking east

between pages 112 and 113

16 Barnstaple station
17 The first Clapham Junction station
18 Colonnaded entrance to Gosport station
19 Remains of Gosport station buildings

between pages 128 and 129

20 Guildford station in the 1860s
21 A contrast in styles, (1) Godalming old station
22 A contrast in styles, (2) Godalming new station

between pages 144 and 145

23 Windsor station
24 Royal waiting room at Windsor
25 Thames bridge at Staines
26 Thames bridge at Black Potts, Windsor

LINE ILLUSTRATIONS

1	Report of first private meeting at Southampton	12
2	First prospectus for a line from Southampton to London	13
3	Design of first rails	23
4	LSW timetable, November 1840	43
5	First advertised service on the Southampton & Dorchester line	63
6	Page from LSW public timetable, August 1860	93
7	Page from LSW service timetable, January 1860	155
8	Shipping advertisements (1)	203
9	Shipping advertisements (2)	204
10	Cabin plan of paddle-steamer *Alliance*	212
11	LSW parliamentary carriage	234
12	Instructions concerning disc signals	237

MAPS

From the prospectus of the Basing & Bath Railway	50
Yeovil	94
Templecombe	194
London & South Western Railway—Portsmouth & Southampton	196
London & South Western Railway—London	198

STATION PLANS

Southampton, c 1847	40
Bishopstoke, c 1865	55
Salisbury, c 1860	90
Guildford, 1848	131
Guildford, 1888	134
Portsmouth, c 1859	148
Nine Elms, 1854	162
Waterloo, c 1871	164

CHAPTER 1

The London & Southampton Railway

THE NEED FOR THE LINE

The seas surrounding and long protecting England from military and political dangers displayed so uncertain a temperament that, early in the nineteenth century, commercial men sought an alternative to sailing vessels for trade between the south coast and London. The route along the English Channel and through the Straits of Dover (the Downs Passage) brought frequent delays from easterly winds which, if prolonged, could close the Passage altogether, while capture or destruction were added hazards in wartime.

After Napoleon's defeat in 1815, various schemes were suggested, including linking canals with existing waterways to create a continuous inland water route. There were also projects for a ship canal, with estimates varying between £4m and £7m, which failed because it was thought impossible to get water to its summit; and a further scheme for a railway from Chatham to Portsmouth, intersected by another between Waterloo, Shoreham and Brighton. Only the link made by the Wey & Arun canal, 1816, and the Portsmouth & Arundel, 1823, succeeded, and shipowners continued their tortuous route.

Credit for a railway from Southampton goes to Robert Johnston, who repeatedly suggested it to Abel Rous Dottin, M.P. for Southampton, by letters commencing in August 1826 and an approach through Mr Le Fevre of Southampton in 1830. On 6 October 1830 Dottin (later chairman of the London & Greenwich Railway) called a meeting at his home, Bugle Hall, Southampton, which fifteen to twenty attended, including Johnston, Le Fevre and Colonel Henderson. The idea was adopted, £400 being raised for expenses and a provisional committee appointed. On 23 October 1830, the *Hampshire Advertiser* published the prospectus of the Southampton, London & Branch Railway Company, capital £1m.

The first survey was made by 'Doswell of Southampton', whose route crossed the Thames between Weybridge and Chertsey, terminating 'somewhere near Paddington'. His report of 19 October

The Hampshire Advertiser
AND
ROYAL YACHT CLUB GAZETTE.

SOUTHAMPTON, OCT. 9, 1830.

SOUTHAMPTON AND LONDON RAIL-ROAD.

A new era is dawning on Southampton, and the march of events is rapidly lifting us over the usual progress of centuries. For several years a rail-road from hence to London has been in contemplation, and often have we heard gentlemen, from the interior of the kingdom, express their astonishment that the inhabitants of Southampton did not take advantage of their incomparable natural position for an entre pôt to our trade in this part of the kingdom: but the damp thrown on all similar speculations, by the ruinous bursting of the many bubble-schemes in 1825, deterred them from bringing forward this great national object. The bright example of the Liverpool and Manchester Railway Company, which has so successfully braved all the apprehensive doubts opposed to it, and which has so far, even in infancy, exceeded the anticipations of the generality of its supporters, has given confidence to Southampton, and opened the eyes of its neighbours to the incalculable benefit that would be derived by the community at large, from a rail-road between this and the Metropolis; and it is with sincere pleasure we announce that on Wednesday last a plan, which had been previously under consideration, was submitted to a most respectable meeting at Bugle Hall, the residence of our much-respected Member, Mr. Dottin, who presided; when a body of directors was elected, and among them are our worthy representatives, Mr. Fleming and Mr. Hoy, with many of the most influential of our merchants and residents, for the purpose of determining the positive practicability of the undertaking, and preparing a prospectus to be submitted to a public meeting preparatory to obtaining the sanction of Parliament. The resolution passed with reference to subscriptions is, that a subscription be entered into for defraying the expense of a survey, and that the amount be allowed to stand as a deposit for shares, at the rate of two pounds for each share of 100l., should the subscribers think proper to become share-holders, on the further shewing of the plan before a public meeting. A liberal subscription was made by the gentlemen present, and books are opened at the different banks. The directors and officers who are appointed give their services gratuitously, until the company is finally established; and so manly and consistent is the preliminary line adopted, that it has acquired a confidence beyond what we have ever before witnessed on speculative occasions. We, indeed, feel fully justified in recommending this measure to our readers as a grand object, fraught with inestimable advantages to the commerce of the kingdom. Looking at the position of our town, on the banks of a fine navigable river, whose entrance is guarded from the Channel sea by the protecting barrier of the Wight, between which and our river is the great rendezvous, in time of war, for our navy and nearly the whole of the trading ships of the kingdom, and is the place of refuge in gales, and during adverse winds, of our East and West Indiamen and other merchant-ships from the eastern ports, in time of peace; reflecting on the vast benefit the merchants would derive from being enabled to get their imports conveyed to London, without being exposed to the serious dangers encountered between the Wight and the river Thames, and that the charges for pilotage and insurance on that part of the voyage alone, would cover the expense of conveying the cargoes from Southampton to London by the railway; and taking into our view the great saving and expedition this line of conveyance would offer to the coasting trade, we see, both in time of war and peace, such strong features of recommendation as admit no shadow of doubt; and, by all we can learn, there is not a line of road of equal extent in the kingdom with fewer impediments, either natural or artificial. As an entre pôt for our commerce, this is not only the best, but, we think we may say, the only port in the English Channel from whence a railway can be usefully effected. Nor do we alone contemplate advantages in the conveyance of merchandize and passengers to the capital and the intermediate towns: we anticipate that Portsmouth, with the eastern counties, and Bristol, with all the western part of the empire, will avail themselves of the incalculable benefit that may be derived herefrom. It is well known that a vast quantity of corn, coals, and other articles, is now conveyed from hence to Salisbury by waggons, and that still greater quantities would be forwarded, were the expense of conveyance sufficiently moderate. We know that Bristol is most anxious to increase that communication which she now has with the Continent, through the medium of her steam-packets. A railway from Bristol to Southampton, through Salisbury, would not only give her all the advantages she can possibly obtain in that view, but would, by the rail-road from Southampton to London, afford her a cheaper and, in in every sense, more beneficial communication with London than she could possibly accomplish by any other line; and, by a branch road to Portsmouth, she would be brought into direct communication with it, and the populous towns around it and in the neighbouring counties, and thus realize those fond and splendid hopes she has so long entertained of a direct intercourse with that part of the Continental and English coasts that are in the British Channel. Our limits preclude us from entering into detail on this important subject, this is, however, but the hour of its birth, and we shall follow it to its maturity with that ardour with which we always support objects of public utility

The *Hampshire Advertiser's* editorial article on the first private meeting at Bugle Hall, Southampton, on 6 October 1830

PROSPECTUS.
SOUTHAMPTON, LONDON, AND BRANCH RAIL-WAY COMPANY.
COMMITTEE.

Abel Ross Dottin, esq. M.P.
James Barlow Hoy, esq. M.P.
John Fleming, esq M P.
Hon. P. B. de Blaquiere.
William Fitzhugh, esq.
Philip Le Feuvre, esq.
Lieut.-Colonel Henderson.
Nathaniel Ogle, esq.
John King, esq.
William Colson Westlake, esq
Rd. Davidson Pritchard, esq
Samuel Le Feure, esq.
Edward Loney Stephens, esq.

THE further civilized men advance towards that degree of perfection of which their faculties are capable, the more they learn of the great laws of Nature, and the more zealously they subject them to their uses.

The uninformed and uncivilized man is satisfied with little, and Jiffe s chiefly from his enlightened brother in the number and quality of his occupations. In proportion as information increases, the practical application of scientific deductions follows, which, while it adds to the power and resources of man, elevates him to a higher intellectual standard, and yields him superior means of happiness.

The oftener men associate, the more frequently opinions are brought to the test of discussion, and the sooner truth is elicited. One method of accelerating the great ends above referred to, is that of giving to men facility and rapidity of communication. Forethought and science point out the means; and we already see how readily the way has been entered upon, and what honour and profit have been derived at Liverpool and Manchester by those who have set the high example.

In every country there are districts particularly calculated for entrepôts, and from which facilities for transporting commodities should emanate. If we examine the Southern coast of our Island, not one spot will be found so well adapted for such an establishment as Southampton. It is well known to be situated at the head of one of the finest and most capacious Rivers on the English Coast, naturally protected from all storms by the Isle of Wight, and defended from all attempts of an enemy by the fortress and naval force of Portsmouth. It has neither rock nor sand to excite alarm; and its Port is sufficiently extensive to contain that portion of commerce to which from its geographical position it is entitled.

The district through which the Rail-way is intended to pass to unite Southampton with London, in no part presents difficulties which cannot easily be surmounted; and large tracts of land, now uncultivated, will thereby become productive and valuable to the proprietors.

This great undertaking will give employment to thousands of labourers. Every parish within range of the work will be benefitted, the Peasantry become more independent, and consequently the poor-rates diminished.

The enterprising merchant will be enabled to appreciate the advantage that will be afforded of escaping the Goodwin Sands, the adverse winds which are known to prevail in the Channel about nine months in the year, and the heavy charges for pilotage, lights, &c.

It is a well-known fact, that London Merchants cannot at present depend on their West India Ships performing more than one voyage during the year, but from Southampton they can always calculate on two such voyages; and while vessels are discharging foreign produce here, outward cargoes may be collected at a trifling charge for carriage, thereby enabling such vessels to be re-freighted immediately, and be despatched sooner than can possibly be done from various other ports.

The advantage that the Fruit Trade will derive by the landing of such cargoes at Southampton needs no comment: the Importers must be fully sensible of the incalculable benefits to be derived therefrom. Other cargoes from the Mediterranean, as well as from the Wine districts of France and Portugal, will also derive advantage from terminating their voyage at Southampton.

The London market may, by this means, be abundantly supplied with fresh Fish from the English Channel, thus giving encouragement to a large and meritorious class of men, as well as keeping up a nursery for the naval service, and obviating an objection which has been started to the introduction of Rail Roads, as tending to the injury of our coasting trade.

The extensive shipments to the Islands of Jersey and Guernsey will be transmitted by the proposed Rail-way, and the rapidity and cheapness with which the Merchants and Traders of those Islands must ensure their entire support. The supplies of goods to the Isle of Wight are also very considerable, and will afford, through the Southampton Rail-way, a great source of revenue.

In fine, the projected communication will open a means for avoiding danger, delay, and expense; and goods landed or shipped at Southampton may at once be despatched to their respective destinations. Southampton is allowed to be the place best adapted for communication by Steam conveyance with Havre de Grace, the first commercial port in France. The traffic already established between these places is very considerable, but when the contemplated perfection of the Seine Navigation, or the Rail Road from Paris to Havre, shall have been effected (and there is every reason to believe one or the other will be speedily realized,) the advantages that must ensue will indeed be important.

The calculations already before the Committee, founded upon careful investigation of the quantity of goods and number of passengers now proceeding along the line of the intended Rail-way, justify the conclusion that the Capitalist who may embark in this undertaking will derive an ample return for his investment. No allusion is here made to the great prospective advantages arising from the expected increase of traffic; they are, however, deserving of the very highest attention.

Prompted by the foregoing considerations, the Committee of Investigation have undertaken to superintend the adoption of preliminary measures in the formation of the proposed Company;—have caused a survey to be made; and, from the assurance of support received from the highest Commercial and other quarters, it cannot be doubted that a sufficient capital will be promptly subscribed to ensure an early application to Parliament.

It is not intended to conceal, that objects like those in view, must, to a certain extent, interfere with existing interests; but, if the perfection of science requires a departure from arrangements which can no longer meet the wants and demands of society, let it be fully understood, that a principle of mutual conciliation, acted on with the liberality which should characterize every important change, will ensure its being so made as to afford general satisfaction. The experience already reaped from the Liverpool Rail-way, demonstrates that the hostility which was there so strongly manifested has not only subsided, but is converted into active and generous co-operation.

The Committee of Investigation invite a Public Meeting (of which due notice will be given) to take into consideration the foregoing statements, with a view to establish a Company to carry this great National object into immediate effect.

It is proposed that the intended Capital of the Company be ONE MILLION STERLING, divided into shares of One Hundred Pounds each.

Books are now open at the Banks of Messrs MADDISON and Co. and Messrs. ATHERLEY and Co for receiving Subscriptions, which Subscriptions will be hereafter allowed in the payment of Shares in the proportion of Two Pounds deposit for each Hundred Pound Share, in case the Subscribers think proper to become Shareholders.

A List of Subscribers will shortly appear
SOUTHAMPTON RAIL-WAY COMMITTEE ROOMS,
No. 79, HIGH-STREET.
October 21st, 1830.

First prospectus for the railway from Southampton to London, 21 October 1830—*Hampshire Advertiser*, 23 October 1830

1830 was cautiously received and Henderson, a Royal Engineer, hardly considered it a survey but 'merely a perambulation'. The committee, deciding to consult an established engineer, sent Henderson to London, where his brother officers recommended James Walker, or Francis Giles, former pupil of Rennie and co-surveyor with him for canals. Finding Giles was not only engaged on the Newcastle & Carlisle Railway, but as engineer to the Basingstoke Canal had become well acquainted with their country, the committee invited him to survey the line, and in 1831 appointed him as engineer. During 1830 he simply explored the country generally, looking at routes of seventy-three miles *via* Guildford and Farnham and seventy-eight miles *via* Basingstoke. From earlier surveys he had made for other purposes, he strongly urged the committee against entering London north of the Thames, as it wanted to, and interfering with property. 'Nearly from the commencement I decided upon recommending the entrance to take place at Nine Elms, Battersea.'

A well-attended public meeting at Southampton Town Hall on 26 February 1831 unanimously decided on promoting a company. The resumed meeting on 6 April heard Henderson, elected chairman of the committee on 5 April, describe the prospects of the line in partnership with the projected docks at Southampton, which now formed part of the scheme. His task was heavy, for much of the route lay over sparsely-populated heathland, and but for Winchester with 8,000 population, no important towns would be served. Basingstoke was a small market town; Aldershot military camp did not exist; and Southampton, with 19,000 inhabitants, was a port of poor reputation.

Henderson calculated a population around 135,000 within ten miles each side of the proposed line, consuming about 135,000 chaldrons* of coal annually. A necessity of life to rich and poor, if carried by railway at an average charge of 6s and supplied to the central parts at 33s to 40s, it would save the inhabitants about 20s a chaldron and yield a gross revenue about £40,500.

The poor family consuming a bushel a week would save 6d a bushel: a most important benefit. Middle-class families using five, ten and fifteen chaldrons annually would save £5, £10 and £15 respectively and, with railway shares worth £100, £200 and £300, their saving on fuel would equal five per cent of the sums invested. This, with a dividend of two per cent from the carriage of coal, would yield a total of seven per cent from fuel alone.

The Colonel claimed this reasoning equally valid for sugar, teas,

*a measure, thirty-six bushels, for coal.

groceries and other articles alien to the district, and that the railway would also provide rapid and cheap transport and shipment for all local produce.

As for motive power, 'I consider that two locomotive engines, making two trips a day each, will be sufficient for passengers at the opening of the railway'. The engine *Samson* had hauled over 100 tons net between Liverpool and Manchester in about two and a half hours at a fuel cost of 20s, and one such engine on the Southampton line could haul 3,000 passengers in two trips, allowing fifteen persons to the ton and assuming they could be stowed. However, he allowed 300 passengers to two engines at two trips each and assumed the use of only one-twentieth of the power. Three freight locomotives would be sufficient, each making one daily trip and hauling annually 31,300 tons, or 93,900 in all.

Henderson relied on 'Captain Stephens' ' report showing 100,000 persons annually using passage vessels at Southampton, from whom the Colonel expected a railway revenue of £50,000 at fares averaging 10s. Stephens estimated 30,262 tons of freight passed annually through the district, producing £63,273 carriage charges. With greater speed and safety, and at one-third the cost, rail would be preferred and tonnage increased. 40,000 tons of foreign fruit entered Britain, and assuming two-thirds reached London by their railway, Henderson expected a revenue of £26,666, conservatively quoted at £20,000. He submitted a table of traffic estimated to produce £120,000 net profit annually, claiming it was so reasonable that 'I have no fear of having my statement controverted'.

A railway 60 ft wide would need 566 acres, but assuming 650 at £100 each, to allow for warehouses, etc, land would cost £65,000: yet this five times exceeded the value of the poor heath to be crossed. Cost of construction estimated at £1,200,000 was justified by recent contracts for a line through difficult country at £14,000 per mile. They expected theirs to be £10,000, but at the higher figure it would cost only £1,092,000, plus £43,000 for contingencies.

Henderson considered the docks and railway 'so intimately connected and of such paramount importance to each other, that the one without the other would be unproductive'.

> When I take into consideration the geographical position of our port, with all its local advantages, its facility of entrance and exit, its safety from the elements, its protection from an enemy, and its adaption for commerce . . . . when I can pronounce professionally on the facility and economy with which the docks can be constructed at Southampton . . . . and when I contemplate the great advantages which such works will yield to shipping, by offering them

a safe asylum, by relieving them from the dangerous passage through the Downs, and of capture by an enemy .... I confess I cannot comprehend how such manifold and manifest advantages can fail to produce their hitherto unvaried results.

If we consider the present deplorable accommodation which is afforded to shipping in our port, it becomes a matter of astonishment that shipowners should allow their vessels to approach it at all: and we need not be surprised to hear the masters of such vessels remark that, instead of being called on to pay port charges, the owners ought to be paid for coming hither. But a brighter day is dawning for Southampton; and it is to be hoped that the clouds which have for so long hung over her commercial horizon will soon be dispersed. Though nature has been prodigal of her favours in forming our port, man has, hitherto, done little to improve those gifts. Let us resolve that this supineness shall not disgrace our day .... let us show that we have enterprise and intelligence enough to avail ourselves of those manifold advantages which nature has presented to us; and we shall soon see stately piles of buildings, docks, quays, and basins, crowded with countless shipping, take the place of those unprofitable and unsightly mudbanks which now surround our town, and mar the scenery of our beautiful river.

Of the national importance of the undertaking, one of its warmest supporters has said, 'if your docks and railways are not carried into effect, more value in shipping and merchandise will be lost to England in the first two years of a war than would suffice to pave your railway with gold instead of iron, and to face your docks with silver instead of stone'. The works would not, said Henderson, be completed in less than three years.

This meeting also being unanimous, the Southampton, London & Branch Railway & Dock Company was formed, with capital of £1,500,000 in shares of £20. A further meeting on 7 September 1831 approved the rules adopted until the incorporating Act was obtained. Meetings to enlist support were held at various other places, including Winchester on 8 November, Basingstoke 9 November, and Kingston 'a day or two after'.

The first appointed directors and officers were:—

DIRECTORS: George Henderson (*Chairman*), Robert Johnston (*Deputy Chairman*), William Fitzburgh (*Trustee*), Robert Sheddon, Philip Lefevre, John Storey Penleaze, John King, William Colson Westlake, Edwin Godden Jones, Richard Davidson Pritchard, Samuel Lefevre, William James Lefevre, Samuel Raymond Jarvis.

TRUSTEES: John Fleming, John Masterman, Abel Rous Dottin, James Barlow Hoy.

SECRETARY: Edward Loney Stephens. TREASURER: Hon Peter de Blaquire. SOLICITOR: John Barney.

STATIONS—1

(1) *The austere terminus in Nine Elms Lane, Battersea*

STATIONS—2

(2) William Tite's station of 1840, known as Southampton Terminus when closed to passengers in 1966

An early choice of route being important, the directors decided on a survey immediately sufficient capital was subscribed. Giles made the survey in 1831 and plans were deposited, but nothing further was done, for the directors were persuaded by Sir Thomas Baring M.P. not to seek the Act in the 1832 session but to allow potential proprietors time to consider carefully before subscribing. This delay, during which the directors watched the fortunes of the London & Birmingham Bill through Parliament, enabled the latter to distinguish itself as the first railway out of London, and made it easier, if not actually possible, for the eventual birth of the Great Western Railway.

After a meeting at the City of London Tavern on 23 January 1832, chairman Sir Thomas Baring, the prospectus of the Southampton & London Railway was published, showing the capital as £1,000,000 in £50 shares, the docks portion of the scheme having been dropped for separate development. Prospective annual gross revenue was £155,949 6s 8d, expenses £55,150 15s 4d, leaving £100,798 11s 4d net. Parliamentary and construction costs were estimated at £1,033,414, based on Giles' figures, and repairs and maintenance £23,000, or £300 per mile annually.

By then, committees of management had been appointed in London and Southampton, chaired respectively by Sir Thomas and Henderson. The company's offices in those places were at 81 Lombard Street and 5 High Street, changing by 1833 to 46 Lothbury and 7 Portland Street.

THE BILL BEFORE PARLIAMENT

Giles re-surveyed in 1833, and on 5 December a further prospectus was published, raising the prospective net income to £263,451 8s 6d. Eventually, in the 1834 session, the Bill reached Parliament, and evidence before the Lords committee lasted from 26 May to 2 July, presided over principally by, at first, the Earl of Malmesbury, and then the Earl of Radnor. Charles Fowler, architect of Covent Garden and Hungerford markets, confirmed the suitability of Nine Elms as the terminus, on its own account and in relation to the metropolis. The site has most commonly been described as 'low and marshy, studded with windmills and pollard trees and Dutch-like in appearance'. Fowler said the only buildings to be demolished were 'some sheds belonging to a stonemason's yard', and two 'old houses built of wood, and of very inconsiderable value'. On leaving the terminus, the line would pass 'over pasture

B

land at first, then through two grounds of market gardeners, and some arable land, and another market gardener's ground ... till it reaches the rising ground towards Wandsworth'. At Battersea, it passed the end of Sleaford Street.

Giles described his line from Francis & White's wharf at Nine Elms as crossing an embankment not more than 25ft high:

> through Battersea Fields to a lane leading from Clapham to Battersea, to a public-house called The Falcon, thence it gets to the London and Portsmouth road, where it passes under it; from thence across the Wandsworth Common to the back of some residences, afterwards across the river Wandle above Wandsworth, thence by the south side of Lord Spencer's park at Wimbledon, afterwards through the low lands, and over that land formerly called Surbiton Common, but now enclosed, till it gets to a point called Surbiton, opposite Kingston.

It crossed Woking Common, five or six miles from Guildford, came within eight to nine miles of Farnham and fifteen to sixteen of Newbury, traversing fairly level ground until, after passing through Basing and to the north side of Basingstoke, a branch would leave for Bath and Bristol. The bend of Basingstoke would start to climb the north-west corner of the Hampshire Downs to the line's summit at a tunnel under Popham Beacons, 593 ft. Descending to Winchester and through the chalk downs, it would enter the Hampshire Basin on a gently falling gradient to the shore at Southampton. Earthworks would be heavy, but no really outstanding engineering features would be necessary. The gradients proposed by Giles are shown in Table 1.

TABLE 1

Miles from Nine Elms	Gradient (1 in-)	Rising or falling	Remarks
0 - 5	550	Rising	—
5 - 19½	—	Level	—
19½ - 28½	300	Rising	—
28½ - 33	—	Level	—
33 - 44½	920	Rising	Basingstoke, with total rise of 275 ft from Nine Elms
44½ - 50½	300	Rising	Popham tunnel reached
50½ - 53	—	Level	Summit of line, 378ft above tideway at London
53 - 64	300	Falling	—
64 - 68½	194	Falling	—
68½ - 72½	500	Falling	—
72½ - 76½	750	Falling	—

Embankments, using 14,000,000 cu yd of materials from the 16,000,000 to be removed from cuttings, would slope two to one in clay or sand and one-and-a-half to one in chalk. Cuttings would be two to one in clay, one-and-a-half to one in sand, and one to one in chalk. Soil was to be moved equally to each side of the line, for spreading on the completed slopes to take grass seed. The deepest cutting, at St George's Hill, Weybridge, would reach 116 ft, a project upon which the opponents of the Southampton line and the ill-fated Basing & Bath Railway, as well as Giles' personal enemies, expended their most violent attacks.

At Nine Elms, engines would not cross Nine Elms Lane (a well-trafficked parish road), but horses would draw wagons to the wharf, 100 yd away, which had a 30-yd frontage and covered an area approximately 30 x 80 yd.

Other engineering evidence for the promoters was given by W. C. Milne and W. Linley, while George and Robert Stephenson, Isambard Kingdom Brunel, the unorthodox and later distinguished engineer of the Great Western, Joseph Locke, William Gravatt, Joseph Gibbs, G. Hennett and H. R. Palmer gave evidence for the opponents.

Many witnesses were called to prove the need for the railway. Captain George Elliott, RN, described Southampton as an ideal harbour; Captain Cornelius Cater, RN, described delays in the Downs sometimes lasting three months, and supporting evidence came from a tide surveyor of Customs, a Merchant Service captain, and a Lloyds surveyor. Lieutenant-General Sir James Willoughby Gordon, Bart, KGCB, the Quarter-Master General, claimed Southampton was suitable for troop embarkations and the railway advantageous for this purpose.

Agricultural products loomed large among potential traffics. About 6,000 cattle and 50,000 sheep and lambs came to London markets annually from Hampshire, Wiltshire, Dorset, Somerset, Devon and Cornwall, plus about 3,446 tons of country-killed meat. It was claimed that driving animals caused loss of weight and value, while quickly-transported carcases would not only fetch more, but the health and cleanliness of London would be improved by reducing the 'nuisance of slaughter houses'. Even the Torbay Fishery would benefit, the harbour master of Brixham giving evidence of improved market prospects if its catches were railed at Southampton for London.

Evidence was given, based on a census taken at Basingstoke, Farnborough and Kingston, and the Somerset House stage-coach office records, that over 100 coaches passed daily in the direction of the proposed railway.

The committee found the preamble proved, and on 25 July 1834 the Bill for making a railway 'commencing at the River Thames, at or near Nine Elms in the parish of Battersea in the county of Surrey, to the shore or beach at or near a place called the Marsh in the parish of Saint Mary in the town and county town of Southampton', received the Royal Assent. It was known as the London & Southampton Railway.

The Act contained 217 sections and two schedules. Section 14 protected the Wandsworth inhabitants, where a large cutting through St John's Hill might interfere with their water supply. The company was to 'well and effectually puddle' the works, rendering them watertight, the practical difficulties of which were to make this an onerous duty to discharge.

Section 102 required each of the fifteen authorised directors to hold at least twenty shares, and Section 103 named the first board of the incorporated company as follows:

Peter Boyle de Blaquire
John Easthope
George Henderson
John Hibbert
Ambrose Humphreys
William Edmund Jerningham
Edwin Godden Jones
John Wright
John King
James Mackillop
John Storey Penleaze
Robert Sheddon
James Whitchurch
William Colson Westlake
Robert Williams

It is interesting to note that, in view of subsequent events, the failure of the Act to stipulate the gauge of the railway created a precedent which, it is said, enabled Brunel to introduce the 7-ft gauge with all its repercussions on the Great Western Railway.

CHAPTER 2

Building the Main Line

PROGRESS UNDER GILES

Having secured its Act, the company had to wait until 31 January 1835 before legal formalities were completed to enable it compulsorily to acquire land. Nevertheless, these were not idle months. On 11 September 1834 Colonel Henderson left the board to become general superintendent for £1,000 per annum and a rent-free house at Lavender Hill, Battersea, while next day the directors settled the terms of Giles' appointment and fixed his salary at £1,500, plus £500 expenses, to date from 1 September 1834. The engineer asked for three assistants to supervise the works. The first, based at Kingston, was to be responsible for London to the west of the river Wey, the second, at Frimley, for the Wey to Hook Common, and the third, at Basingstoke, for Hook Common to the western end of the proposed tunnel at Popham. These appointments were not made until 12 June 1835, when Thomas Dodd, William Lindley and Samuel Giles were engaged, at salaries of £200, £500 and £300 respectively, the first exclusive and the last two inclusive of expenses.

Giles reported to the board on 23 October 1834 that contracts were let for earthworks and bridges; the line was set out from London to Basingstoke and near Winchester, and excavations were under way in the parishes of Winchfield and Elvetham on land secured from co-operative owners. Within two years, twenty miles of line out of London would be in use, he had promised, and the whole work would be completed in three.

It appears that work was first started on Monday, 6 October 1834, on Shapley Heath, near Winchfield, by the contractors Treadwell, who were engaged for the section between the Wey and Basing, and on Shapley Heath the first sod was turned by Mr Bainbridge, a local landowner more sympathetic than many of his kind, who had given without charge sufficient land to build a road across his estate. In the same week another contractor, Robert Stannard, was ready to start at Battersea, but Giles directed him to Wimbledon, Kingston and Merton, 'the labourers being there obtainable at cheaper prices than in Battersea'.

The directors authorised contracts for 6,000 tons of wrought-iron rails, 15 ft long and 50 lb to the yard, 'of the form denominated parallel rails' (as distinct from fish-bellied rails), 1,000 tons to be delivered every two months. The price was £7 18s 6d a ton. The engineer intended laying these directly on wood sleepers 8 ft long, spaced 3 ft apart measuring centre to centre. Wood was chosen because of the high cost of bringing stone to the area, where trees were plentiful. The sleepers were to be 9 in in diameter cut in two from circular pieces, preserved by the Kyanizing process (the invention of Dr J. H. Kyan [1774-1830], using mercuric chloride) and laid with the round sides uppermost and the bark removed. Chairs of 15 lb were to used at the joints, otherwise the rails were to be secured to the sleepers with ⅝ in bolts. The road was to be ballasted with material excavated from St Georges Hill, Weybridge.

Giles' method was to employ a number of small contractors working concurrently at various places on the line, the company supplying them with materials and paying them weekly on account. The Lords committee considering the Bill had questioned him on this.

Q Have you found that mode of contracting is much cheaper than contracting with large capitalists?
A It throws the whole work into the competition of real working men, without paying a high price for the use of capital.
Q Is that a more economical mode of doing the work?
A Most undoubtedly.
Q Have you found that the work can be executed in that manner as well as in the other?
A I have always found it so; it depends very much upon the inspection and arrangement of the engineer himself.

Giles had his critics, whose opposition seemed justified when a number of contractors, having little capital and been asked for no security, completed the easiest parts of their sections and stopped work for more money before going on with the more difficult parts. The company had to choose between giving way or delaying the works and, as for Giles, the failure of his scheme ultimately cost him his appointment.

The company had power to make calls up to £5 per share, with at least three months between calls, and on 24 October 1834 the first general meeting, at the City of London Tavern, approved an immediate call of £3 to finance intensive works planned for the coming winter. At once the company's opponents opened a campaign to discredit it before public and shareholders. One wit foretold it would be used only to convey 'parsons and prawns—the one from Winchester, the other from Southampton', and the line thus dubbed is still known, though without the taunt intended by its early critic. Advertisements and paragraphs appeared in newspapers, and countless anonymous circulars were distributed, saying the line could not be finished in the time promised

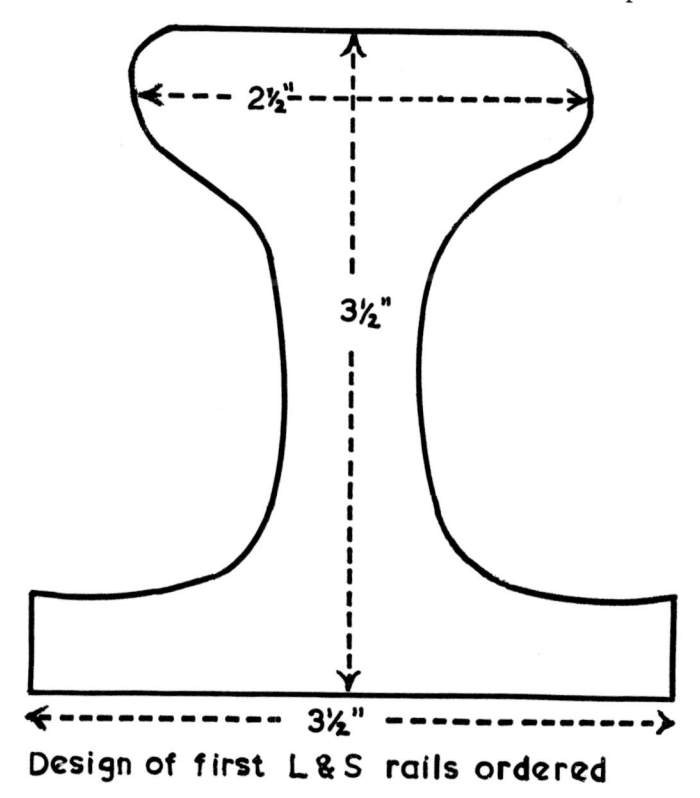

Design of first L & S rails ordered

and that the cost would exceed all estimates. An advertisement in the *Manchester Chronicle* demanding an investigation into the line was meant to discourage local subscribers, but another, postmarked in London and received by a Glasgow newspaper, was not published but handed over to Henderson by the editor.

In his book, *A Royal Road*, Sam Fay blamed coaching interests and the promoters of the Great Western Railway for the attacks. The former seem to have been slow in considering the new form of transport as a serious threat to their livelihood but, suddenly realising their danger, they launched their attack and so added to the opposition of the GWR whose Bill for a line from London to Bristol had been thrown out of the Lords in the same session as that in which the L & S had obtained its Act of incorporation. The story of the struggle between the two companies is told later, but here it is important to note the GWR found reason to attack the Southampton line as being the first step towards a branch planned to leave it near Basing for Bath and thence to Bristol.

With their main criticism aimed at construction costs, the critics could take advantage of George Stephenson's personal dislike for Giles, which stemmed from the time the first Liverpool & Manchester Bill was before Parliament. That eminent engineer planned to build across Chat Moss, a notorious bog, and of course eventually succeeded, but Giles helped defeat him in that session by saying 'no engineer in his senses would go through Chat Moss if he wanted to make a railway from Liverpool to Manchester'. This was one of Stephenson's most serious setbacks, and he was probably prompted by feelings of retaliation rather than sound judgment when he said that in Giles' cutting through St Georges Hill 'the whole wealth and strength of the company would be for ever buried'. He had given evidence against it before the Lords committee in 1834, criticising such a depth of 116 ft in a sandy soil. '. . . if the water comes down in torrents, it will bring the sand along with it; and if the sand gets upon the railroad it will cease to be a railroad.'

The attacks grew in ferocity until, at the beginning of 1835, it was said that to admit being connected with the railway was to choose between being thought a fool or a rogue. The Lancashire proprietors, who held half the shares and had formed their own committee the year before, met at the Royal Hotel, Manchester, on 5 January 1835 with Thomas Cooke in the chair, and urged the shareholders to stand firm. They had investigated the allegations aimed at the company and could say that 'in every instance of importance, not only have the objections been found invalid, but the result has been more strongly to confirm their opinion of the stability of the undertaking, and of the great advantage which will ultimately result to the shareholders.' They considered that the work would be finished in the time originally fixed by the engineer, 'unless some unforeseen obstacle occurs'.

As to cost, they did not think the estimates would be exceeded sufficiently to affect the company's prospects. Thus heartened, the shareholders stood fast, but faint hearts were heard when, on 31 August 1835, the GWR secured its Act at the cost of the L & S Basing & Bath Bill. Stop the works and abandon the whole project, was the cry! Again it was the Lancashire men who showed spirit, and they urged the directors to push on with increased vigour and begin fresh openings where possible.

From Lancashire also came William Reed, who on 30 January 1835 was appointed secretary at £600 per annum, plus £200 for the secretaryship of the Basing & Bath Railway. When the latter project was lost, his salary for L & S duties was increased to £800. The appointment was to have taken effect on 25 March 1835, but he actually took office on 27 February, just before the shareholders met. He succeeded Richard Heathfield, who held office from 12 September 1834 until resigning in the following January.

Several board changes were announced at the February 1835 half-yearly meeting. The Hon P. B. de Blaquire, J. Mackillip, J. S. Penlease and R. Williams went out, they and Colonel Henderson being replaced by John Watkins Drew, Vincent Eyre, John Lewis Eyre, Simon M. Gillivray and Henry Weymouth. The proprietors voted £500 per annum for directors' expenses, eighteen months later increasing this to £1,000 as more befitting the fifteen men on the board. This increase was retrospective to February 1836.

Progress on the line was not spectacular. By 31 August 1835, four miles of line were formed, earthworks begun at twelve major places, some minor stations started, and several bridges built. At Shapley, for instance, men worked in two shifts; 3.0 am to noon and noon to 9.0 pm, making an eighteen-hour day less forty minutes break during each shift for meals. Men received between 3s and 4s daily, and boys in charge of horses 10d a day. Horse-drawn wagons of 3¼ cu yd capacity were used to convey the spoil, and twenty were being filled each hour. The company possessed or had agreed land for thirty miles of line without once needing to go to a jury, and the two locomotives delivered were to be used on earth removals as soon as enough track was laid. Orders had been given to start work on Popham tunnel, but the committee of management had second thoughts, and in October 1835 sent Giles and Henderson to inspect the site. The result was a report to the directors recommending a deviation one and a half miles west of the authorised line, which, although involving heavy excavations would avoid tunnelling altogether and still preserve the gradients at 1 in 250. Deviation being decided on, Giles and Henderson opened negotiations in December 1835 with the landowners concerned, but not until the 1837 session was the authorising Act obtained. Meanwhile, work started between Southampton and Winchester, and when only the portion from Basingstoke to Winchester remained uncompleted, passengers were temporarily conveyed by road between those places.

When the shareholders met again on 19 February 1836, not quite ten miles of line had been built. To justify this poor result, the directors said it included some of the heaviest cuttings and, reckoning from 31 January 1835, i.e., twelve months and nineteen days, they claimed to have completed more than any other railway in the time, conveniently forgetting the work of the preceding three months and twenty-six days. Agreement had been reached with landowners for another deviation, this time at the controversial St Georges Hill, as a result of which the depth would be reduced to 45ft and the excavations from 3,800,000 cu yd to 1,000,000. At the Southampton end of the line the directors had secured six and a half acres of 'very valuable land' for the terminus, near the river Itchen and adjoining the proposed docks. It had been purchased 'for a nominal consideration by the liberal and unanimous vote of the Corporation and Assembled Vestries of Southampton', but three years later, when the company wanted another one and a half acres for access roadways, the liberal attitude of the corporation was missing and it hesitated so long that the company was forced to bring the matter before a jury ere its powers for taking land expired. At the hearing, it described the ground as common land, but the jury decided it was possible building ground and awarded a purchase price of £1,000, in addition to which the company had to pay between £400 and £500 costs. The directors reacted bitterly, alleging that if the land were building ground it was the railway that made it so. The whole affair must have caused some soul-searching in Southampton, for Mr Buchan, a resident, said the jury's findings were against the feelings of the town, the award was preposterous, and 'the respectable part of the town were disgusted with the matter altogether'.

THE FALL OF GILES

Giles' reign as engineer was nearing its end, and the first rumbles of discontent were heard at the half-yearly meeting on 30 August

1836. There was then little to report to the shareholders, but the directors made what they could of the twelve miles of line completed since the last meeting, the work started by David Mackintosh, contractor, between Southampton and Winchester, and the negotiations completed for the Popham deviation, for which they now asked approval for an application to Parliament. Mackintosh had also contracted for bridge centering between London and the Wey, and for erecting buildings at Winchester. What they could not do was give any hope of fulfilling the engineer's promise, but could only expect to open the line between London and Kingston in the spring of 1838, Southampton to Winchester in the same year, Kingston to Basingstoke by the following spring, and the remainder during 1839.

Naturally, the shareholders were not satisfied, and one of them, Mr Lynn, speaking with the utmost politeness, criticised the poor progress and suggested Giles and Henderson were not giving all their time to the undertaking. The chairman, John Easthope, together with Giles, blamed the nationwide increase in railway construction for their difficulties. Demand for labour made it hard to get efficient workmen, and they, finding their services at a premium, gave less work for their money and became unmanageable. The first contractors had failed and been replaced on the same terms, but their successors were seeking higher payments because of rising costs, and their applications were being considered.

On the second point, Easthope sprang to Henderson's defence, saying he was quite certain the Colonel was not otherwise employed, but as for Giles he left him to answer for himself. He had 'twenty times over implored Mr Giles not to take too much upon himself at a time'. Giles agreed he was only giving three-quarters of his time to the line, and the rest to schemes he claimed were closely connected. He was, in fact, surveying the projected Portsmouth Junction Railway between Bishopstoke and Portsmouth, besides being engineer to the Southampton Docks Company, which had obtained its Act that year. He did not think it necessary, but if the proprietors insisted he would give these other schemes up. He was not, however, pressed to do so, and for the moment the meeting seemed satisfied.

In the following December, Giles and Henderson wrote informing the directors that bad weather had seriously damaged cuttings and embankments, and suggested further work should proceed slowly during the winter rather than incur heavy costs in restoring them. To this the directors agreed, and thus progress was further delayed. Now the prophecies of the critics seemed to be coming true, and public confidence decreased; the shares depreciated on the market, while directors and proprietors alike felt anxious concerning Giles' methods. The Lancashire shareholders, unable to contain themselves any longer, sent Thomas Cooke, Robert Garnett and William Hill to meet directors from London and Southampton and thoroughly inspect the line. Starting at Southampton on 12 December 1836, and accompanied by Giles and Henderson, they proceeded to London, examining all the works on the way. As a result, the Lancashire men found the general plan more promising, potential traffic more extensive, and engineering difficulties less than they had anticipated, but they were definitely dissatisfied with the engineering skill and management. They were even more critical of finance. Giles' original estimate for the line was £894,874, plus £105,126 for contingencies, but his amended estimate of November 1836 was £1,507,753 without contingencies. They agreed that rising costs of materials, land (for which the original estimate of £65,000 was ultimately exceeded by over £200,000) and labour were beyond his control, but his other figures showed signs of omissions, indicating that even the amended estimate would be exceeded. Finally, they criticised Giles for using small contractors, saying it 'was admitted by all but himself to be a failure, and it was evident to all but Mr Giles that works executed in that manner, exclusive of uncertainty as to their completion, would in reality cost more than those for which an adequate price should be paid to responsible contractors.'

To complete the line, the directors intended raising additional capital of £500,000, so, taking their chance, the Lancashire deputation virtually issued an ultimatum. They pronounced Giles' amended estimate as insufficient authority for raising further capital, and said the difference between his estimates would stop them relying on any estimate he made. They demanded that his figures be confirmed by another experienced engineer, but even then, should Giles still remain in office, they would recommend their constituents to supply no additional capital, and 'for their own part the members of the deputation signified their determination not even to pay up the remaining instalments of the original capital, but forthwith to divest themselves of all interest in the undertaking and to make the necessary sacrifice for so doing, whatever it might be'.

The directors had no choice. They knew the Lancashire shareholders would act on their deputation's advice, and without their co-operation the necessary capital could not be raised nor the railway completed. The directors therefore made two unanimous decisions. First, they engaged Joseph Locke to inspect the line and present an acceptable estimate for completing it. Secondly, they decided to dismiss Giles. These resolutions were explained to the engineer, who accepted them and resigned, but to spare his feelings and professional reputation they were not entered in the minutes: instead, on 13 January 1837, it was recorded that 'Mr Giles having intimated that it would be inexpedient for him to devote the whole of his time to the business of this railway, resigned his appointment of engineer, which resignation the directors accepted'. His salary was continued for six months, for no other duty than his assistance and evidence in carrying through Parliament the Bill for the additional capital and the Popham deviation.

Locke was then appointed engineer and brought a fresh and invigorating air to the undertaking. Son of a colliery manager and an old pupil of George Stephenson, he came to the Southampton line from the Grand Junction, where he had proved himself an efficient engineer and sound administrator. Strong-willed, tall and of excellent physique, his energy was unbounding, as his less agile and exhausted assistants found when following him from point to point along the works.

Even now Giles' activities were not over. Had he accepted the position and the easy withdrawal prepared for him, the true circumstances of his resignation would never have been recorded. But Giles was an unpredictable man, though perhaps his subsequent actions sprang from a feeling of resentment. Almost immediately he contradicted Locke's instructions to the workmen, an indiscretion which the directors leniently overlooked. Then the Bill for the additional capital passed the Commons without opposition, but at the Lord's committee it was 'deemed indispensably requisite to produce the Deed under hand and seal, binding the subscribing parties to supply additional capital of £400,000'. Far from giving support, Giles now astonished everyone with a proposition to that committee 'for executing the line only partially with the present capital and with a single line of rails', a scheme so decidedly disapproved as to endanger at once the adoption of a report adverse to the Bill.

The embarrassed directors were now forced to prepare a plan

making it possible for the shareholders to subscribe the additional capital, and public meetings in London and Manchester unanimously approved it. Giles was present when the court of directors adopted it, but after again trying to press his single-line scheme he finally agreed to take his entitlement of new shares. He was also present on 8 May 1837 when the proprietors unanimously approved the plan for issuing them. An explanatory circular was sent to all shareholders, including Giles. The plan, briefly, was to create 16,000 new shares of £25, each attracting the same dividend as an original £50 share. Existing holders were entitled to a rateable proportion of new shares, and any not so taken were to be offered to them in addition to that proportion, and the balance, if any, to the public. Existing holders were not required to make any payments on new shares until six months after the amendment Act.

Giles replied to the circular on 12 May 1837 as follows:

> I beg to decline taking any new shares in the London & Southampton Railway, and which I do from the feelings I entertain of the injurious tendency which the measures of raising shares at a depreciated value will create to the capital of the company, and at the same time of the probable effect that it will have in deterring subscribers from promoting the South-Western and Portsmouth Junction Railways, the Southampton Docks, or any of the works which is to contribute to the trade of the London & Southampton Railway.
>
> I am aware of the great difficulty of raising money at this time, but to do so in the way proposed will, I fear, entail upon the company still greater difficulties in obtaining money necessary for completing the railway.
>
> The plans however which appear to me open to the company for obtaining an Act this session, are:
>
> First, to limit the amount to be subscribed for in shares at par to the sum necessary to complete the railway, say, £200,000 with power to borrow one third more—the calls upon these shares not to be made until the powers of the present Act for raising money are exhausted. I hope that the influential proprietors of the railway will be induced to subscribe for shares to the amount of £200,000—on these terms, and that Parliament will so pass the Bill—a measure which I for one will support by taking fifty or more shares, as I feel a strong confidence in the adequacy of return, providing all the money which is to be expended in executing the railway be raised at par.
>
> Secondly, if Parliament should not grant the Bill upon the above terms, I beg to express my opinion that it will be better to defer the Bill until next year, except so much of it as will give the company powers for extending the time for buying land to one or two years hence. Then to complete the line from London to Basingstoke and from Winchester to Southampton without delay out of the

original subscription and the one-third million to be borrowed under the present Bill. The returns upon the trade to these parts will soon afford means for paying the interest upon this one-third million and by that means avoid, in a great degree if not altogether, any additional canker upon the original capital by paying interest out of capital. It was always considered that the returns upon the line from London to Basingstoke would be very much more profitable than from any other part of the line and that this part would in itself produce a full return upon one million, a strong reason why this undertaking should not be depreciated.

I have seen Sir Thomas Baring, and Mr Ordu, Lord Bolton's agent, they both dislike this business. Sir Thomas said that in taking shares for his land he should of course only give credit for them at their depressed value—and Mr Ordu complains that Lord Bolton's shares which he has received at par for his land to the amount of £3,000 will now be reduced to half that value. Mr Ralph of Winchester is also much opposed to the creation of £25 shares, but I believe would take some at par. These are serious considerations to which I feel it my duty to call the attention of the directors, for I cannot but apprehend that Parliament will object to sanction the creation of new shares at an under value of the old shares unless all the proprietors acquiesce in it. Upon this point, however, I beg to recommend that the best advice be immediately taken.

I am, dear sirs, yours very truly,
(signed) FRANCIS GILES.

The directors were now angry with Giles, and alarmed at his unauthorised approach to influential landowners and shareholders. Either of his two suggestions, if adopted, could spell ruin to the undertaking. His conduct belied his letter of 6 December 1836 when he said, 'if it be your desire that I should retire from the concern, I am willing to do so, but in that case I beg to assure you that I shall ever be anxious to render it my professional services, and to promote its interests to the utmost of my powers'. Now that he had shown himself an opponent of the only measures which would save the railway from the difficulties caused by his inefficiency, the directors felt it their duty to record these facts, and resolved 'that the officers of the company do take the necessary steps for compiling a report of the state of the works, the finance, the traffic and all other matters connected with the undertaking in order that it may be printed for distribution among the proprietors previous to the general meeting to be held in August next'.

Following this board meeting, Easthope lost no time in calling on Sir Thomas Baring, whose interest and co-operation had been invaluable to the company from its start. The record of the interview is brief but indicates that Easthope explained the directors' intentions in raising new capital and agreed on arbitration should there be any difference on the share value of Sir Thomas's land, which was vital to the Popham deviation. Lord Bolton's solicitor demanded payment in money instead of shares as agreed, but the directors insisted on adhering strictly to the agreement.

A NEW REGIME AND BETTER PROGRESS

The Act authorising the new capital and the deviations was obtained on 30 June 1837. Four calls of £5 were payable in 1838, on 20 January, April, July and October, with a final one on 21 January 1839. The last call of £5 on the original shares was made on 20 October 1837, and became payable on 12 November 1837, the previous calls having been as follows:

Each £50 share		Date of call	Payable on
Deposit	£2	—	—
1st call	£3	29 October 1834	28 November
2nd „	£5	10 April 1835	1 June
3rd „	£5	9 October 1835	10 November
4th „	£5	25 March 1836	16 April
5th „	£5	8 July 1836	1 August
6th „	£5	10 October 1836	5 November
7th „	£5	13 January 1837	11 February
8th „	£5	14 April 1837	11 May
9th „	£5	14 July 1837	12 August

Five deviations were authorised: three minor ones between Woking Common and Farnborough, Southampton and Otterbourne, and near the Southampton terminus. The two important deviations were between Walton Common and Byfleet, going north of the Parliamentary line to avoid St Georges Hill cutting, and at Popham. The Popham deviation was over eight miles long, leaving the Parliamentary line at East Oakley to take an elliptical course through the parishes of Ash, Overton and Micheldever, rejoining the original route at Weston Colley. Tunnels were not completely avoided. The first, at Litchfield, was to be 590 ft long; two at Popham would have a total length of 1,800 ft, including 390 ft in open section; and one at Wallers Ash, outside the limits of the deviation, would be 1,470 ft. This was infinitely better than the Parliamentary route, where the tunnel would have been just over a mile long, through the parishes of North Waltham, Steventon and Popham, passing under Trinleys Wood to Blackwood. Present-day official lengths of the tunnels vary slightly from the

STATIONS—3

(3) Originally Andover Road, now Micheldever. A survivor of the L & S severely styled country stations, showing the level canopy which surrounds four sides of the simple structure

(4) Old station buildings at Weybridge, now staff rooms and a restaurant. Present booking office and entrance are to the left of the picture

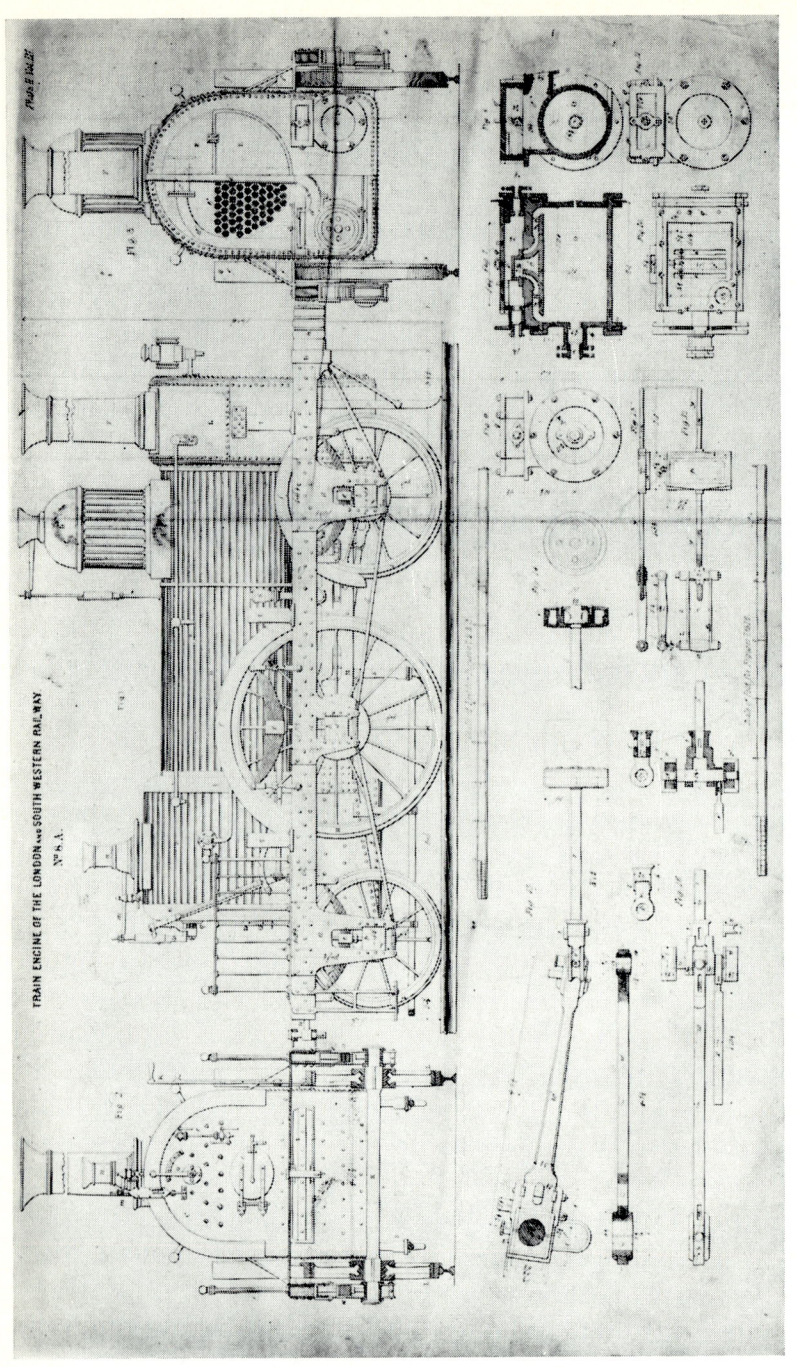

(5) 2—2—2, as supplied by Rothwell & Co, side elevation

figures above, i.e., Litchfield 198 yd, Popham No 1 265 yd, Popham No 2 199 yd, and Wallers Ash 501 yd.

The report the directors had decided on was urgently necessary to dispel doubts created among the shareholders, and to investigate potential traffic three persons were engaged: Messrs Pare, Lacy and Chaplin. Pare was unknown to the directors, but recommended as having had considerable experience in estimating railway traffic in the north of England. His estimates of gross revenue were:

	£	s	d
Passengers and small parcels	269,416	15	4
Goods and livestock	58,124	3	4
Total	327,540	18	8
Less expenses	124,680	1	9
Net revenue, being nearly 12 per cent on capital of £1,700,000,	£202,860	16	11

His calculations were based on observations on the Basingstoke canal and at nine places on the Southampton and Portsmouth roads. Census-taking in those days had its difficulties, and he remarked that 'with respect to those travelling by stage vans and waggons, it may be safely stated that not one half of them could be observed'. Lacy, of Manchester, an 'extensive mailcoach contractor, who is well acquainted with the country to be affected by the Southampton Railway', confined himself to passengers and estimated a gross revenue of £118,177. Chaplin, whose report was favoured, calculated existing passenger traffic at £123,824 2s 8d, parcels at £20,253 9s 0d, a total of £144,077 11s 8d at railway prices. Assuming passenger traffic would double and parcels remain the same, his estimate of coaching department revenue was £267,901 14s 4d.

At the half-yearly meeting on 8 August 1837, the directors said these reports justified them in stating the following prospective revenue:

	£	s	d
Present traffic at railway prices	245,260	16	7
Prospective traffic	157,393	6	8
	402,654	3	3
Costs, expenses, etc.	154,788	5	1½
Nett annual income	£247,865	18	1½

C

During this year William James Chaplin formed a closer association with the company. He was principal partner in the coaching firm of Chaplin and Horne, reputed owners of 64 coaches, 1,500 horses and some hotels; but it seems he had subscribed to the L & S from its beginning, for 'William Chaplin' paid the deposit on his shares on 13 February 1834 and his name appeared with those proprietors listed in Clause 1 of the Act. Doubtless anticipating the future transport pattern, he disposed of his coaching assets, save those sufficient for railway business, and substantially increased his railway holdings. On 8 May 1837 the board elected him a director, the minute stating that this was on the recommendation of the special general meeting held that day. The report of that meeting makes no mention of Chaplin, but when the directors met on 26 April 1837 they had resolved to recommend to the special general meeting that Chaplin be elected to fill the seat vacated by the late William Coulson Westlake. He attended his first board meeting on 19 May 1837 (the day Giles' letter was first considered by the directors) and joined the committee of management on 11 August 1837.

Locke's report to the August meeting of proprietors was of great improvements in the works, with the hope of opening the line to Woking Common on 1 May 1838. His first step had been to dismiss the small contractors on the remaining fifteen miles from Wandsworth to the Wey Navigation, replacing them by Thomas Brassey who, although yet on the threshold of his career, was to become the greatest of the contractors. He gained universal fame as a reliable, efficient, trustworthy and kindly man, heading a veritable army of workmen who built railways all over Britain, on the Continent, and in America, India, Australia, etc. Brassey, who received decorations from a number of countries, remained a lifelong friend of Locke.

From the Wey to Basingstoke, contractors remained unaltered, but now had to provide their own materials. The Basingstoke to Winchester contract, including the Popham deviation, went to Brassey, while McIntosh remained between Winchester and Southampton. Locke predicted opening to Basingstoke by spring 1839, and the remainder by the following spring. Under Giles, work had been poorly supervised, but Locke's allocation of supervision to the assistant engineers had immediate effect. Work proceeded with energy, any laxness by contractors being promptly dealt with. Henderson was required to report monthly to the directors on the state of the works and all other important matters.

The army of navvies had now entered Sir Thomas Baring's country, and he showed great concern for their welfare. He created a 'benefit society' for them, his substantial donation being augmented by Brassey and others. Sir Thomas suggested to the L & S board that as so many navvies were receiving treatment at Winchester County Hospital, it should donate something to that institution. The directors voted £100, and recorded in the minutes that if this should entitle one of them to become a hospital governor, the chairman should accept the post. They also 'resolved, that the sum of ten guineas be paid to Sir Thomas Baring, being the cost of a frame used in conveying men injured on the works to the hospital'.

With expanding railway activities throughout Britain, prices of materials had risen. Rails soared to £14 a ton, which the L & S refused to pay. In July 1837 it fell,, and 11,000 tons were bought at an average of £8 14s, bringing purchases within 2,000 tons of total requirements at reasonable figures. 63-lb rails had replaced the 50-lb originals, in turn to be superceded by 75-lb rails before the completion of the line.

By February 1838, work was progressing well, except that prolonged winter frost had prevented the laying down of rails, and it was hoped to open to Woking Common as promised, or by 1 June at the latest. In anticipation of the opening, Samuel Davis was appointed in March 1838 as superintendent at Nine Elms for £200 per annum.

At last the opening was in sight. On Saturday, 12 May 1838, an experimental trip was made from Nine Elms to Woking Common by a party including the directors; the Earl of Carnarvon; Lord Adolphus Fitzclarence; about a dozen Members of Parliament; Joseph Locke; and Moss, Chairman of the Birmingham & Liverpool Grand Junction Railway, etc. According to the *Railway Times*, 'the day was one of the finest; the atmosphere serene and clear'. The down journey took forty-five minutes, and 'so smooth and easy was the transit, so utterly undisturbed by even the slightest shock or jar, that if the eyes were closed it was difficult to imagine oneself in motion at all'. After a 'handsome and liberal repast' the party returned to Nine Elms in forty-three minutes, and at a banquet at the Clarendon Hotel were joined by the Duke of Sussex. Presided over by Easthope, the gathering was in festive mood, exchanging mutual congratulations and drinking to future success.

On 19 May 1838 a second party of directors and friends left

Nine Elms at 1 o'clock, proceeding rapidly to Ditton Marsh, then slowly to Woking Common because of an engine boiler leak. An 'elegant collation' was taken on Woking Heath in specially-erected tents, and the party, 'after heartily responding to the toast of "success to the railway", resumed their places in the carriages' for an uneventful return trip taking sixty-one minutes.

The line opened to the public on 21 May 1838, trains leaving Nine Elms daily at 8 am, 10 am, 1 pm, 3.30 pm and 6 pm; and from Woking Common at 7.30 am, 10 am, 1 p.m., 3.30 pm and 7 pm. On Sundays, down and up trains started at 7 am, 9 am, 5 pm and 7 pm. First and second-class passengers only were carried, at the following fares from Nine Elms:—

	Timetable mileage	1st Class s d	2nd Class s d
To Woking Common	23	5 0	3 6
Weybridge	17½	4 0	2 6
Walton	15½	3 6	2 3
Ditton Marsh	13	3 0	2 0
Kingston	10	2 6	1 6
Wimbledon	6	1 6	1 0
Wandsworth	3	1 6	1 0

Omnibuses conveyed passengers between Nine Elms and:—

Spread Eagle, Gracechurch Street
Cross Keys, Wood Street
George and Blue Boar, Holborn
Universal Office, Regent Circus, Piccadilly
Swan with Two Necks, Lad Lane
White Horse, Fetter Lane
Golden Cross, Charing Cross

The London & Westminster Steam Boat Company took passengers along the Thames to and from Nine Elms and Dyers Hall Wharf, Upper Thames Street, and Hungerford Market.

During the first twelve weeks, earnings were:

	Passengers carried	Daily average	Receipts £ s d
First four weeks	29,127	1,040	3,085 18 11½
Second four weeks	31,585	1,128	3,755 0 8
Third four weeks	33,083½	1,181	4,218 17 7½
Totals	93,795½		11,059 17 3

No goods or livestock had yet been carried.

Nine Elms station was a practical, unpretentious, rather low affair. From Nine Elms Lane a multi-arched entrance gave access to booking and other offices, beyond which two platform faces were separated by the tracks they served. In such austere surroundings the company's first experience of race traffic, in the week following that of the opening, was almost catastrophic, as described in Sam Fay's *A Royal Road*.

> For the first few days passengers flocked from all over the countryside, and patronized the line for the mere novelty of the thing. Epsom races occurring in the following week, the company advertised their intention of running eight trains to Kingston on Derby Day, for the accommodation of the racing public. To the utter astonishment and alarm of officials arriving at Nine Elms station early on the morning of that eventful day, a crowd of about 5,000 persons was found at the station gates. Several trains were despatched but still the throng increased, till at length the doors were carried off their hinges, and amid the shrieks of the female portion of their number, the mob broke over the booking-counter, leaped through the windows, invaded the platform and rushed pell mell into a train chartered by a private party. Finding resistance useless, the officials sent for the Metropolitan police, and at twelve o'clock a notice was posted on the booking-office window announcing that no more trains would run that day. The company's first experience in the conveyance of race passengers cannot be described as a very successful one; it is evident, however, that they were not discouraged, for a few weeks later they were found advertising trains to Woking for Ascot races. The second venture appears to have been conducted as well as the few wheezey locomotives at their command would permit.

In general, however, the company's arrangements were satisfactory. The *Railway Times* reported:

> The servants are numerous and expert at their duty, so that no unnecessary delay is occasioned in taking up or setting down, while the confusion complained of on the first opening of other lines, in regard to the booking of passengers, is altogether obviated.

Hitherto, meetings of the board had been at No 1, Adam Street, Adelphi, purchased in 1836 for £2,200, but Friday, 13 July 1838, saw the first meeting at Nine Elms. Meetings of shareholders were not transferred there from the City of London Tavern until 27 February 1839. In 1839, the Adam Street property was sold, together with the house at Lavender Hill, Battersea.

Work beyond Woking Common proceeded rapidly but not without difficulties. When the company had gone before Parliament for its Amendment Act, clauses had been introduced into the Bill by the Basingstoke Canal Company, which the L & S did not resist for fear of losing the Act, and so it was that Section 21 compelled the railway to build a bank along the top of its embankments near the canal, sufficiently high to prevent the canal company's horses from seeing the engines. Where the railway was 25 ft above the tow-path, the bank was limited to 4 ft in height: it was to be 'planted with a close furze hedge'. Section 22 required the railway to build a brick wall between 6 and 8 ft high, (or such other fence or embankment approved by the canal company) when the railway was built on or below the level of the tow-path. The canal company insisted that this was to avoid fright to its horses, even though locomotives had used the line during construction without the wall and without affecting the horses. To avoid these needless works, the directors offered their cost to the canal company, but were refused in lieu of a better offer. The L & S therefore started the walls, and the canal company served notice that if before their completion trains ran on the opened line, injunctions would be sought. Nevertheless, the opening to Winchfield and Hartley Row, thirty-eight miles from Nine Elms, took place on 24 September 1838, and brought to the railway the majority of coaches going to and from the south and south-west of England. The directors' preliminary trip took place on Monday, 17 September 1838, when the inspection of the works was followed by dinner with the local gentry at the Wellesley Arms, Murrell Green.

By 27 February 1839, 1,400,000 cu yd out of the total earthworks of 3,200,000 remained to be removed between Basingstoke and Winchester, reduced to 680,000 by 7 August 1839. Meanwhile, on 10 June 1839, the line was opened from Winchfield to Basingstoke and from Southampton to Winchester, leaving only the eighteen intervening miles to be completed. Again, the directors and their friends celebrated the occasion at Winchfield, where 'an excellent *dejeuner a la fourchette* was provided at a cottage in the immediate vicinity of the station, to which about sixty ladies and gentlemen sat down'.

Southampton was not really quite reached, for trains stopped temporarily at Northam Road and the permanent terminus, designed by William Tite and built by Nicholson for £10,498, came into use only when the entire line opened in 1840. Meanwhile, the engine *Pegasus* operated trains to and from Winchester.

When the proprietors met in August 1839, they heard receipts had trebled within six months, traffic between Winchester and Southampton especially having exceeded all expectations. The dividend of 15s announced had, however, been earned chiefly from the extended opening to Winchfield. The bad weather had played havoc with the slopes and repairs were costly, but winter 1839-40 brought more rain than within living memory, the average from

September to January being exceeded by fifty per cent. All recently-constructed railways suffered, but the Southampton line with its unusually high embankments and deep cuttings more than many. Officers and men spent successive nights of toil keeping the line open, and the engineer estimated that £50,000 would be needed to repair slips between London and Basingstoke. At this time Locke became involved in a dispute with Easthope and emerged with a moral victory. Fearless and able though the chairman was, he had, unfortunately, an overbearing manner and assumed the role of dictator, interfering with the running of the various departments. Like others, Locke resented this. In November 1839 Locke had informed the board that slips on embankments in clay districts were recurrent and could be expensive, and suggested they be flattened out. He supplied the required estimate, and over two weeks passed before this necessary action was authorised. He was told that in future cases of urgency he might take action after approaching the chairman or deputy-chairman for approval. The matter would then come before the board at its next meeting. This instruction was embodied in a resolution.

On 25 December 1839 an extensive slip in Goldsworth cutting blocked one road and endangered the other. Martin, an assistant engineer, and his men battled all night and to noon next day, and seemed partly successful. However, continuous rain made it necessary to get an engine and materials from Nine Elms, and thence Martin went. On arrival, he was surprised to find Locke, but when the engineer refused to sanction his efforts until the chairman or his deputy had been informed and authority obtained, Martin promptly sought out Easthope, explained the situation and his intention to attempt a remedy. Easthope immediately regretted Locke's refusal to approve steps which he knew were necessary to keep open the line, and supported Martin's actions. He denied that the engineer was barred from taking action, saying the board only intended to secure its proper supervision and, in emergency, the engineer should immediately take such steps as he thought necessary, reporting them to the chairman or deputy as soon as convenient. When such report could safely precede action, it should do so.

On 10 January 1840 the directors carefully framed this instruction in a further resolution, sending a copy to Locke, who had meanwhile addressed them this letter:—

> However much the chairman may lament the course which I felt it my duty to take on the occasion referred to, I can assure you that

it was equally painful to me to feel myself unable in consequence of that resolution to render those services to the line of which I knew it stood in so much need. That extraordinary measures and precautions were required is, I think, clear from the report which at your request I had the honour to address to you on the preceding day, viz, the 28th November. In that report I described to you the state of the works and the measures it might be necessary to take to protect them. I asked authority from you to guard against fresh contingencies and gave you an assurance that your orders should be carried out with the utmost possible economy. To this request the resolution in question furnished a reply.

Locke protested at the suggestion that he had failed in his duty, and insisted on his explanation being recorded in the minutes, refusing to withdraw even though approving of the second resolution. At the next half-yearly meeting the chairman publicly acknowledged the efforts of the officers in keeping the line open.

On Monday, 11 May 1840, the line was opened throughout to Southampton station which, though restrained in grandeur, far surpassed Nine Elms, as if proclaiming this railway was Southampton-born and London merely its outpost. The structure. which still exists, is here illustrated. At 4.30 am twenty-one empty carriages hauled by *Mars* and *Chaplin* reached Southampton from London, and at 6.30 am the first up passenger train departed. Directors and friends left Nine Elms at 8.0 am, and on arrival at Southampton at 11.30 am the train of thirteen first-class carriages, hauled by *Venus* displaying the 'Union flag from its green and gold back', was welcomed by a deputation from the town, which invited the occupants to fix a day to return as guests at a public dinner. This they could not do, for the chairman and several directors were prevented from attending the opening by another body of Southampton citizens, the Northam Bridge Company, who were that day at the Vice-Chancellor's court seeking an injunction to stop the railway within a mile of Southampton terminus. The affair started on 13 March 1839, when Thomas Clement, secretary to the bridge company, wrote demanding a bridge be built over the Northam Bridge Road by the railway, and offering two counsels' opinions supporting its claim. The demand was rejected after obtaining two more counsels' opinions, but ultimately the L & S directors gave way and the bridge was built. Easthope told proprietors on 29 August 1840 that the affair had cost them £4,000 in legal expenses, but they had succeeded against the attempt to stop the railway, for this he believed was the object and not the securing of the bridge.

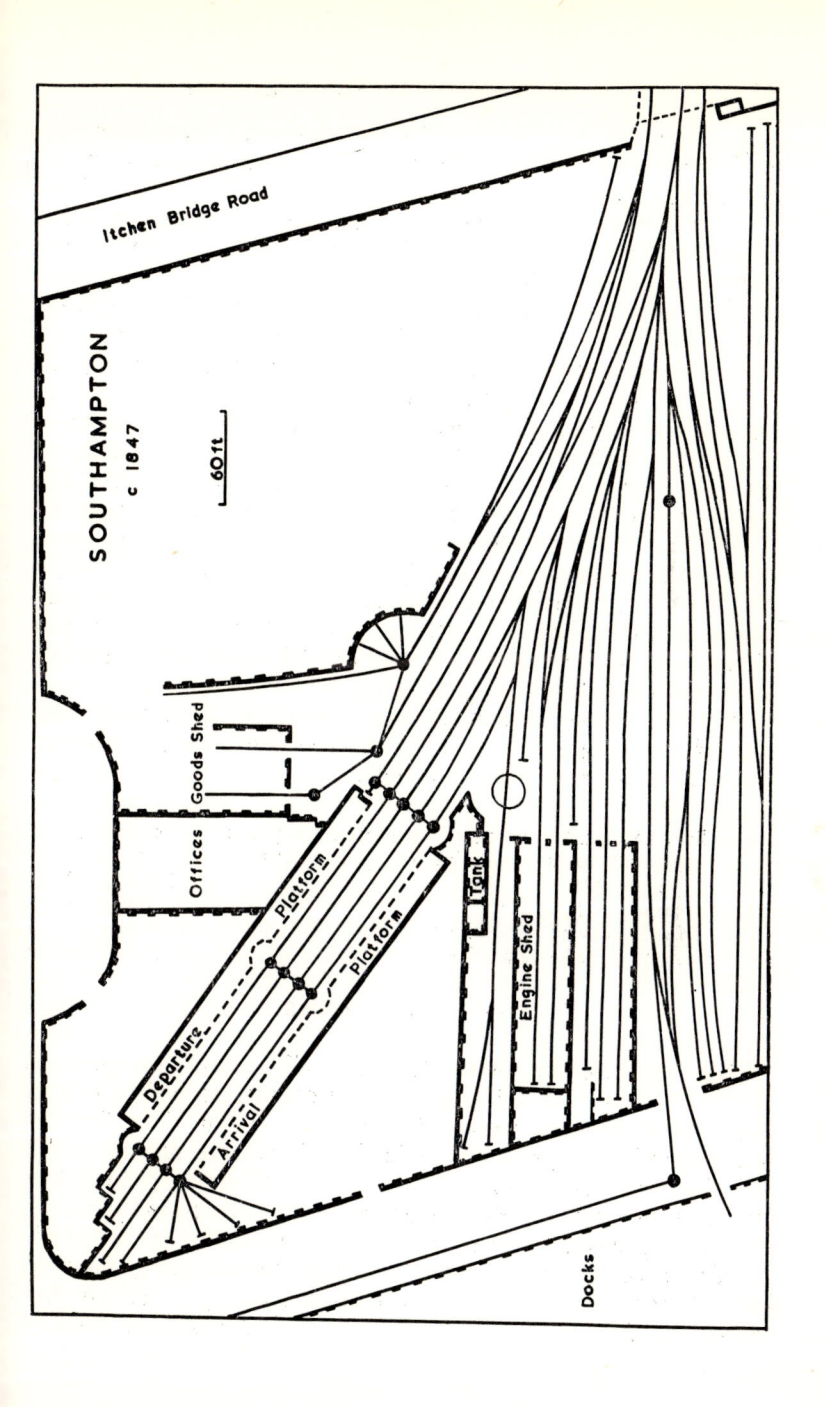

SOUTHAMPTON
c 1847

60 ft

Itchen Bridge Road

Goods Shed
Offices
Departure Platform
Arrival Platform
Tank
Engine Shed
Docks

To return to the opening, after two hours at Southampton the party withdrew to Andover Road station as the guests of Brassey in 'marquees amply set forth with delicate viands and rare wines', while the labourers feasted from a roasted ox and an unlimited supply of strong beer. The day's only casualty was a dog decapitated by the 10.0 am up train near Itchen Bridge Road, though an engine proceeding to the 'water station' at night ran through the gates at Northam while the keeper was absent.

Southampton did play host to the directors, on Saturday, 20 June 1840, when 600 persons sat down to dinner in a large tent on the Royal Victoria Archery Ground. Distinguished guests included the Duke of Sussex, Lord Palmerston, the Duchess of Inverness, and the French ambassador. Richly lined with striped silk, and arranged to give the utmost comfort, their carriages set out from Nine Elms at 10.30 am, reaching Southampton three hours later. Before returning early to London, the ambassador replied to the toast to his health and promised his personal support to the Paris and Rouen line, in which the LSW was much involved. (See Chapter 8). Other toasts and speeches followed, and the party arrived back at Nine Elms just before 8.0 pm.

The cost of the line had, of course, exceeded all estimates, and the following figures are the last detailed ones shown in Reports and Accounts on 25 February 1843.

	£	s	d
Main line. Expenditure obtaining Parliamentary powers	41,965	14	0
Land and compensation, law charges, valuing, surveying, etc.	293,042	4	1
Premises at Nine Elms	7,461	14	6
Construction of way and works	1,176,556	12	9
Surveying and engineering	32,887	6	3

AFTER THE OPENING

The timetable for almost the first full service throughout is reproduced. The L & S, like other early companies, had to feel its way into the new world of railway operating. The first inexperienced employees were trained by Davis, the superintendent at Nine Elms who, with a few porters, had left a northern line to come to the L & S. He was an Irishman, and unfortunately he had a temper which often let him down. In April 1840 one of his incidents was with a coachman whose vehicle was being conveyed by rail for part of its journey until the extension of the line extinguished it altogether. Such men naturally disliked railway

BUILDING THE MAIN LINE

companies, and this one threatened Mr Davis's life. In July 1845 he was requested to resign his position, and he went to the quiet of a country station as agent. He resigned from the service at Chertsey in January 1851.

At first, passengers booked at an open counter, receiving paper tickets, stamped with destination station and date of journey, which were torn from books having five to a page. The change

LSW timetable, November 1840

to card tickets invented by Edmondson was not ordered by the board until 25 April 1845, with concurrent alterations to the counter to allow only one passenger to book before each clerk at a time. An agreement with Edmondson was sealed on 20 March 1846.

An intending passenger was given a leaflet containing regulations for working the line. This forbade his opening a carriage door or alighting without assistance from the staff, and told him the guard would blow a whistle to warn trespassers when the train approached curves or habitations. Having booked, he could board a train if there was room, and passengers travelling farthest took priority. Losing a ticket meant paying the fare from the station whence the train started, while smoking brought removal from the premises with forfeiture of the fare.

Even first-class passengers had unlit carriages until lamps were authorised in December 1841. Sideless second-class carriages exposed their occupants to all weathers, while third-class passengers, not carried until the line opened throughout, travelled in open trucks attached to goods trains, an arrangement over which the board soon professed to have qualms.

On 26 February 1842 Garnett, now the chairman, announced:

> I would also take this opportunity of noticing the alterations which we have made in favour of the third-class passengers. We felt and thought that it was a prevalent opinion that the goods trains were not so secure from danger as the passenger trains, and therefore we adopted a third-class conveyance by an early train in the morning which gave the industrious poor not only a greater chance of security, but also encouraged them for rising early in the morning and travelling to London cheap, which could not fail to be productive of considerable benefit. In adopting this plan, our paramount feeling was that of ensuring their security and their comfort.

What Garnett failed to say was that this had been forced on the company by the Board of Trade, after some pertinent correspondence had passed on the subject.

The earliest first-class carriage, resembling a collection of stage coaches on a frame, gave a frightening journey by present standards, and the *Railway Times's* enthusiastic writer doubtless remembered the stage coach it displaced. Hastily built by inexperienced persons, the first models soon needed improvements, including stronger springs, while exposure to weather through lack of carriage sheds did not help.

Buffing gear, of course, was very crude. From January 1843 a luggage van separated the engine and the first carriage of every train, and not until November 1842 did the board instruct John Viret Gooch, locomotive superintendent and brother of Daniel

Gooch of the GWR, and Joseph Beattie, carriage and wagon superintendent, to settle a uniform height for engine and carriage buffers.

Porters at first had fustian jackets with arm badges, and chocolate-coloured caps, until in 1841 dark corduroy was introduced and two jackets were provided annually with number plates on the collars.

Policemen outnumbered other staff and wore swallow-tailed, chocolate-coloured coats, dark trousers and tall hats with leather crowns. They acted as signalmen, ticket collectors and watchmen, and until the opening to Basingstoke were stationed at frequent intervals along the line.

The guard received a waybill showing the numbers and destinations of passengers of each class from each station. Five minutes before each train left, a large bell rang from a terminal roof, hand bells being used at other stations. On 17 September 1841 it was ordered:

> .... that with respect to the starting the trains at the stations after the bell has been rung, the trains shall not start until the guard shows a white flag or lamp to the engine man, and that he shall see that the passengers are seated and the doors of the carriages closed before he shows his flag.

Six weeks later this was amplified:

> ... upon all occasions of the starting a train, the same is not to be put into motion until at least half a minute has elapsed between the ringing the bell, the guard seeing that all the passengers are in the carriages and taking his seat, when he is then to give the signal for departure, and that upon no occasion shall a train be started without both guards being in their seats, and the signal is not (to be) given until they have taken their places.

Guards wore chocolate-coloured frock coats with dark trousers, changed in 1841 to scarlet coats, lace collars and silver buttons. In May of that year, they were designated first and second class, the former being distinguished by belts. The guard's seat was on the roof of a first-class carriage, where he worked a crude brake 'consisting of a shaft or rod underneath the carriage, attached to the brake blocks, with a connecting rod running up to the guard's seat'. Sam Fay described the man's miseries:—

> In summer or in winter, by day and by night, through tunnels and cuttings the guard occupied this exposed position; and it not unfrequently happened that in bitter winter weather friendly hands

were needed to lift this gorgeous but invaluable official from the seat to which he had become frozen.

Mail-train guards for a time were luckier, until on 11 November 1843 three carriages were damaged by thrown stones, the result being 'that in future the guards sit outside the carriages instead of in the closed box, and that they be provided with coffee at the Woking and Basingstoke stations'.

Discipline was severe everywhere, but greatest in the locomotive department, where minor carelessness to gross negligence was punished by fines, confiscation of pay, dismissal or prosecution. Drivers were undoubtedly heroes of the day, and one such gallant, returning to Woking after taking the 5 o'clock down mail on 4 March 1839, stopped by a cottage and took up two young ladies for a footplate excursion. Not profiting from the light punishment of a 40s fine and a reprimand, he was dismissed shortly after for assisting a passenger to avoid paying his fare by carrying him on the tender.

Two accidents throw interesting light on early operating methods. On 14 August 1840, the 10 o'clock luggage train from Southampton stopped after six miles, being too heavy for the engine. The train being divided, the engine took the front portion on and the guard was ordered to go back a mile with a flag, to warn the next train, He, however, sent a boy, who had not gone 100 yd before the 11 o'clock mail with thirty first-class carriages came up, 'propelled by two engines for the sake of expedition'. The 'conductor' saw the vans before the flag, but emergency action did not prevent a collision, with injuries to passengers.

The 1.30 pm mixed train from Southampton, with eighteen carriages, arrived late at Nine Elms on 17 October 1840. While its two engines were being detached, the 3.0 pm fast train arrived and ran into it, having received a white instead of a red signal on that misty night. Material damage was slight, but a female passenger subsequently died. Evidence before the coroner concerning procedure showed that an arriving train stopped at Nine Elms before 'the points', the locomotive was detached and a rope fixed to the carriages, which were drawn forward under the covered way for passengers to alight. A driver said if one train ran late, station clerks would warn the driver of the next to 'go a little easy', but were he driving a mixed train between Basingstoke and Woking Common with a fast overtaking him, he would cross to the other line at the first station, even without orders.

Signal lights were described as, red for 'danger', green for 'caution', and white for 'all right'. The Nine Elms signal was a revolving lamp with one red and one green, and two white lights opposite each other. Joseph Woods, Gooch's predecessor as locomotive superintendent, testified that engines carried red lamps for attaching to carriages at night, and a small hand lamp 'turned backwards' on each tender, for use when trains were delayed or stopped by accidents.

The jury's verdict was accidental death, with a deodand of £300 on the engine *Eclipse*, and the accident prompted the locomotive, way and works committee to recommend on 23 October 1840 that 'in all cases where a train passes a station without stopping within a quarter of an hour after that which immediately preceded, the policeman shall exhibit the green light'. Two weeks later, it

> .... recommended to the court of directors that lamps for the trains be kept at the different stations, and that no train which does or may travel in the dark be suffered to depart without a lamp. That the agents at the termini be responsible for this duty being performed, and the guards for keeping them fixed upon the last carriage during the transit of the train.

CHAPTER 3

The Struggle Towards the West

BATTLES FOR BRISTOL AND NEWBURY

The 'Branch' in the company's title of 1831 was from Basing to Bath and Bristol, and to form the junction the Southampton line took the longer way round the 'great bend of Basingstoke'. Thus would the English and Bristol Channels be united, and both with the Metropolis.

Preliminary correspondence began in 1830, and on 23 January 1832 a prospectus appeared. In April 1832, Henderson went to Bristol, seeing several influential persons in promising discussions, including Phillip John Miles, Vincent Stuckey, Alderman Camplin, Messrs Fry, Harford, Jones and Robert Bright. Harford suggested William Brunton as engineer, and in May 1832 Bristol supporters published a prospectus. However, with political unrest still simmering over the rejected Reform Bill, Henderson left Bristol.

On 11 July 1832 L & S promoters decided to get powers for the Southampton line before presenting a Bristol Bill, and so encouraged Bristol citizens, including Harford and Jones, to launch independently in 1833 the Great Western Railway from Bristol to London, Bright becoming chairman of the Bristol committee. Being short of capital, the GWR presented in 1834 a makeshift scheme to link the cities by terminal railways connected temporarily by canal. On 25 July, the Lords threw it out. while the opposing L & S got its own Act in that session.

Awakened by GWR activities, L & S Bristol-line promoters resolved at Basingstoke on 16 July 1834 that ' "the Basingstoke and Bath" be forthwith formed . . . . that Messrs Giles and Brunton be appointed engineers, and that the necessary steps be immediately taken for raising the subscriptions and completing the capital'. The provisional committee included Henderson, Easthope, Lord Bolton, C. S. Lefevre, and the Hon P. B. de Blaquire. During July 1834, meetings at Devizes, Trowbridge, Bradford, Newbury and Hungerford approved the Basingstoke decision and formed local committees.

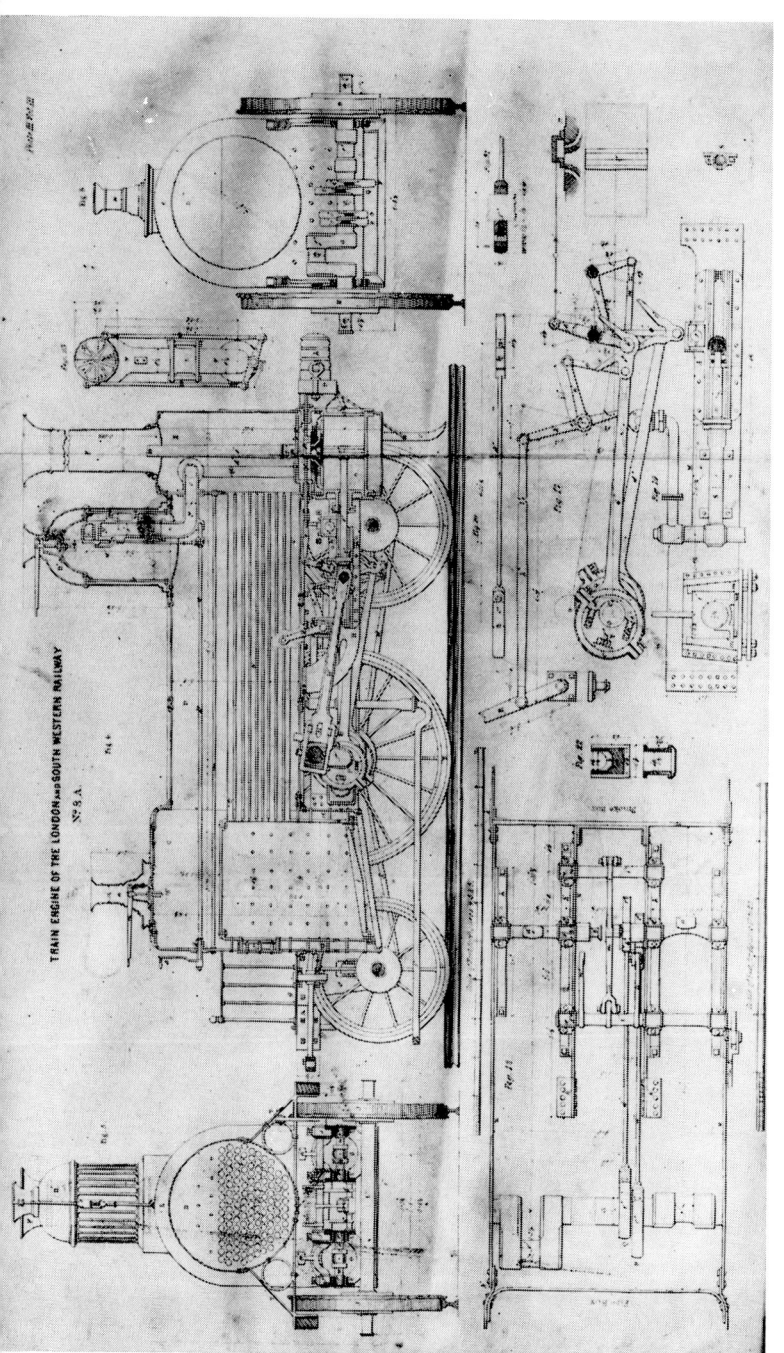

LOCOMOTIVES—2

(6) 2—2—2, as supplied by Rothwell & Co, sectional elevation

BODMIN & WADEBRIDGE—1

(7) *First train, drawn by the Camel, crossing Pendévy Bridge, 30 September 1834. Note the Omnibus prominent among the wagons*

(8) *Parallel rail and stone blocks, 1834, showing the method of fixing with 'pins and wedges'.*

Crown Copyright, Science Museum, London

If the promoters saw only sunshine they were disillusioned at a public meeting at the White Hart Inn, Bath, on 12 September 1834, chaired by Sir Thomas Fellowes, KCB. The Hon de Blaquire, claiming personal credit for the branch, explained its advantages and how Nine Elms was ideal for handling Irish cattle, etc, going to a proposed market to serve Lambeth and Southwark. He scorned the GWR for taking its line to London instead of seeking a junction with the L & S, and criticised the exclusion of Newbury and Devizes from its scheme. Just then, Bath and Bristol sympathies were with the GWR whose failure was blamed on the L & S, and de Blaquire was heard coldly, as was Brunton explaining his route and Reed proclaiming the support of Manchester.

The audience, unimpressed, called on Saunders, the GWR secretary, who alleged that the L & S was planning to stop its line at Bath so as to deny Bristol railway facilities unless it surrendered to L & S wishes. He accused the L & S of a 'gross perversion of truth' against the GWR. Enthusiastic cheering followed, with repeated calls for Brunel who, after theatrical reluctance, rose to attack mercilessly the Basing & Bath. He considered its route inferior to his more northerly one (he had earlier rejected it when surveying for the GWR); questioned the soundness of Giles' price of 5d a cubic yard for earthworks against his own of 1s, and in contemporary fashion criticised Giles' use of small contractors. Overwhelming the B & B deputation, the meeting declared support for the GWR against all rivals.

The climate improved at the George Inn, Frome, on 17 December 1834, when de Blaquire addressed agriculturists and hinted at a possible extension through Frome, Bruton and Taunton to Exeter. They promised to urge Members for Somerset and Frome to support it. Concurrently, the GWR successfully sought support for its revised Bristol to London line, by meetings, advertisements, etc.

The Basing & Bath prospectus of 9 February 1835, capital £1,000,000, listed a general committee of eighty-eight (twenty forming the committee of management), including the mayors of Newbury and Basingstoke, Lord Bolton, the Earl of Carnarvon, and many reverend gentlemen. Reed was the secretary. The 106 miles route from London to Bath, claimed to be the shortest, would pass through or near Newbury, Devizes, Trowbridge and Bradford, and by curving between Devizes and Bath, the extension to Frome, Taunton and eventually further westward would be facilitated. There would be two tunnels; at Bradford half a mile, and Claverton Hill, Bath, one mile.

D

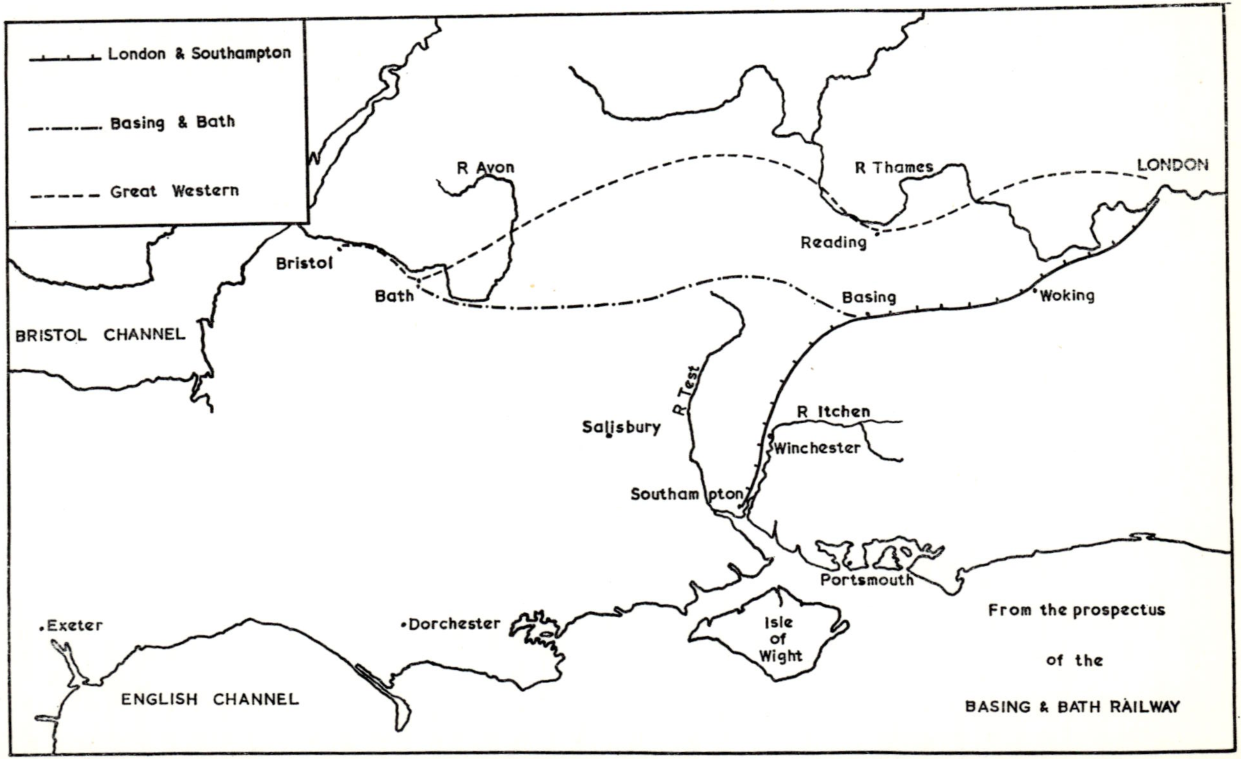
London & Southampton
Basing & Bath
Great Western
LONDON
R Thames
Reading
Woking
Basing
R Avon
Bristol
Bath
BRISTOL CHANNEL
R Test
Salisbury
R Itchen
Winchester
Southampton
Portsmouth
Isle of Wight
Exeter
Dorchester
ENGLISH CHANNEL
From the prospectus of the BASING & BATH RAILWAY

Brunton's route to Bristol from a 'depot' (station) at the bottom of Prior Park, Bath, he described thus:

> From this depot it was proposed, keeping to the south side of the Avon all the way, to go under the road to Lyncombe Hill, passing under the Holloway Road to the South Hayes, under the Wells Road, to the south of Tiverton church, thence to Newton Mill, over the Newton Brook; keeping on the south side of the collieries. From the Mill at Newton it was proposed to carry a viaduct to the north of the collieries, or, if more agreeable to Colonel Langton, to turn the turnpike to the north of the railroad. This embankment would be continued to the Crown at Saltford, where there would be some deep cutting. From thence across the River Chew at Keynsham, a little to the left of the New Mill, on to Brislington, then through the grounds of Arno's Court on to Pile Hill, and lastly, to a depot in Somerset Square, Bristol. At present, the object would be confined to a railway between Basing and Bath.

The junction at Basing would reduce new mileage to sixty-two, minimising property disturbance and capital needs; a benefit, it was hinted, to be passed on to the users. It was intended the completed B & B should merge with the L & S, but no L & S funds would be involved until the B & B got its Act.

The opposing GWR would go 'through or near to Slough, Maidenhead, Reading, Wantage, Swindon, Wootton Bassett, Chippenham and Bath, and thus intersect the south of England from east to west, in the manner of a main trunk, calculated to send branches to each district, north or south'. Brunel chose this northerly route for its easier gradients, a superiority which proved the greatest weapon in the GWR attack. Indeed, when the B & B party were championing their line against the GWR before a Lords Committee, they tried overcoming this obstacle by pleading that, because up gradients would neutralise downs, their own Bath line would be level. The chairman retorted that if this were so the highlands of Scotland would be ideal for railway building.

The revised GWR Bill, now including branches from Chippenham to Bradford and Trowbridge, reached Parliament in 1835, where the Commons committee accepted its easier gradients against L & S opposition and rejected the rival B & B. The GWR Bill had its first reading in the Lords on 27 May, the second being due on Wednesday, 10 June. Despairing B & B promoters wrote to Benjamin Shaw, the GWR chairman, on 6 June, offering to surrender their project if the GWR would adopt their line from Bristol to Basing in lieu of its own. On 8 June, before the GWR could consider its answer, the B & B lithographed and circulated copies of its letter among GWR shareholders and members of the Lords, hoping to induce rejection of the Bill. Shaw refused the offer on 12 June, and one week later the Lords committee began a forty-days hearing. On 31 August 1835 the GWR got its Act, leaving the L & S to console itself by expecting that 'new and unlooked-for income will be derived by the construction and junction to other lines, which are in contemplation to various parts of the Southern coast of England'. Vainly had it proposed to the GWR a joint line to London from Basing or a junction at Frimley. The two companies now concentrated on building their parallel lines from London, the GWR opening throughout on 30 June 1841 with Brunel's unorthodox gauge of 7 ft.

Calm lasted until the summer of 1843, when Newbury inhabitants, whose prosperity had declined since the GWR and LSW had opened, approached the latter for a branch from Basingstoke which would connect them with London, Winchester, Southampton and Portsmouth. Chaplin, now LSW chairman, considered Newbury to be GWR territory and suspected 'they were coquetting with us merely to enable them to make better terms with our neighbours'. He abruptly dismissed their spokesman, the Reverend Ashworth, but publicly apologised when he realised their sincerity. In September 1843 Newbury asked again, revealing that besides Lords Carnarvon and Craven heading the landowners and commercial men interested, the Duke of Wellington, an old LSW critic of Stratfieldsaye, near Basingstoke, was also sympathetic.

Chaplin was now tempted, for a way through the broad-gauge barrier to the prosperous industrial north would promote trade and feed the growing docks at Southampton, and a Newbury branch could be extended through Swindon to Birmingham, about 157 miles from Southampton or forty-five less than through London. Thus discussions in October 1843 produced the Basingstoke, London & Southampton Railway, whose sixteen miles of single line the LSW would rent. In 1844 a Commons committee approved it and rejected a GWR Bill for a Pangbourne to Newbury line. Despite strenuous GWR appeals, the LSW Bill passed the House with a large majority, but when the Lords threw it out, honours were even.

On 15 June 1844, Charles Russell, now GWR chairman, wrote to Chaplin suggesting a mixed-gauge joint line from Basingstoke to the GWR between Pangbourne and Reading, seventeen miles, with an eleven-mile branch to Newbury to give that town two routes to London, plus openings south through Basingstoke and north through Oxford. The Oxford Railway Company's broad-gauge

THE STRUGGLE TOWARDS THE WEST

line from Didcot to Oxford, opened on 12 June 1844, was meant eventually to reach Rugby and Worcester. With the London & Birmingham seeking a narrow-gauge line from Rugby to Oxford, and another planned through the Trent Valley from Rugby to Stafford to shorten routes to Ireland and Lancashire, Russell argued that his proposed joint line, completing a chain of communication to the north, would benefit the LSW more than its contemplated forty-five mile line to Swindon. The LSW refused, alleging that Russell's line would encourage Newbury traffic to go to London via the GWR, besides creating such a detour between Southampton and Newbury as to kill trade between them by raising carriage charges above those to London.

Battle now recommenced, the LSW surveying from Basingstoke to Didcot, and through Newbury, Hungerford and Marlborough to Swindon, seeing from the latter a possible outlet north through Gloucester and the Birmingham & Gloucester Railway. The GWR promoted lines from Reading to Basingstoke and Newbury (the Berks & Hants), extending the Newbury prong to Hungerford.

The Regulation of Railways Act, 1844, was companion to a required preliminary examination of new schemes by a board of five—the 'Five Kings'—Earl Dalhousie being chairman, with Samuel Laing, (future LBSC chairman), G. R. Porter (economist and a founder of the Statistical Society), Captain Coddington (later general manager of the Caledonian Railway), and Captain D. O'Brien the members. During September 1844 that board told Chaplin that Newbury to London traffic belonged to the GWR whose Berks & Hants line it had approved, subject to an equal-rate clause for LSW protection. Immediately the LSW asked the London & Birmingham to co-operate with a narrow-gauge line from Basingstoke through Newbury, Didcot and Oxford to Rugby, the LSW guaranteeing it south of Didcot, the L & BR to the north. The L & BR agreed, subject to Board of Trade approval. The LSW decided that, were the line approved, it would not extend its proposed western line from Newbury beyond Marlborough; but should the Board of Trade encourage traffic by Gloucester to Birmingham, it would go to Swindon and abandon the Didcot branch.

The *London Gazette*, 31 December 1844, reported Dalhousie's board against LSW schemes in the territory dividing it from the GWR, so with further struggles there being futile, the LSW sought peace with its rival. Newbury was only one disputed area, and to understand the agreement reached we must study events in the other territories it covered.

PRELIMINARY MOVES TOWARDS EXETER

The fair city of Exeter, whose favours included the key to the south-west peninsula, had long attracted both her suitors. L & S earliest designs had foundered with the Basing & Bath Bill, but reappeared in 1836 with a prospectus for a South-Western Railway from the Southampton line between Basingstoke and Winchester, to reach Exeter as directly as possible and perhaps extend to Plymouth and Falmouth. This L & S brainchild never matured, and 1 May 1844 saw the Bristol & Exeter's broad-gauge line enter the city, giving the GWR a through route from Paddington. LSW hopes were not extinguished, but its immediate target now became Salisbury, to which a 21 miles 57 chains double-line branch from just north of Bishopstoke station was authorised by Parliament on 4 July 1844, capital £240,000. Dividends of six and seven per cent were expected, and though local subscriptions were encouraging, the LSW had decided to make the line itself for, by linking Salisbury with Southampton and Portsmouth, it furthered its policy of cultivating shipping interests at those ports by tributaries embracing the maximum country.

Passing through Chandlers Ford and Romsey, the line was to terminate near 'Smith's Close, otherwise Fowlers Croft' at Milford, east of Salisbury by the turnpike road to Southampton. Work was to start at once, but luck ran out. First, unusually obstructive landowners delayed the company taking the property. Then, despite earlier experiences, it did not engage the reliable Brassey but sought tenders, accepting Hoof and Hill, small contractors of little capital, whose price was about £18,000 below any other. The delay with land made completion impossible during the early summer of 1846 as the contract specified, so Locke obtained authority to offer the contractors an additional £1,000 if the opening were made on 10 August 1846. The incentive was insufficient, for their difficulties increased by having to compete for labour with farmers engaged in harvesting.

Locke resisted ruining the contractors by enforcing the time limit, or the farmers by enticing their men with high wages, and further delay preceded a winter of weather changing repeatedly from frost to thaw. The works, though not heavy, involved treacherous material which became continuously waterlogged. Earthworks sank during the thaws, carrying away completed brickwork; they became solidly irreparable during frost. Opening was

BISHOPSTOKE
(Eastleigh)
c 1865

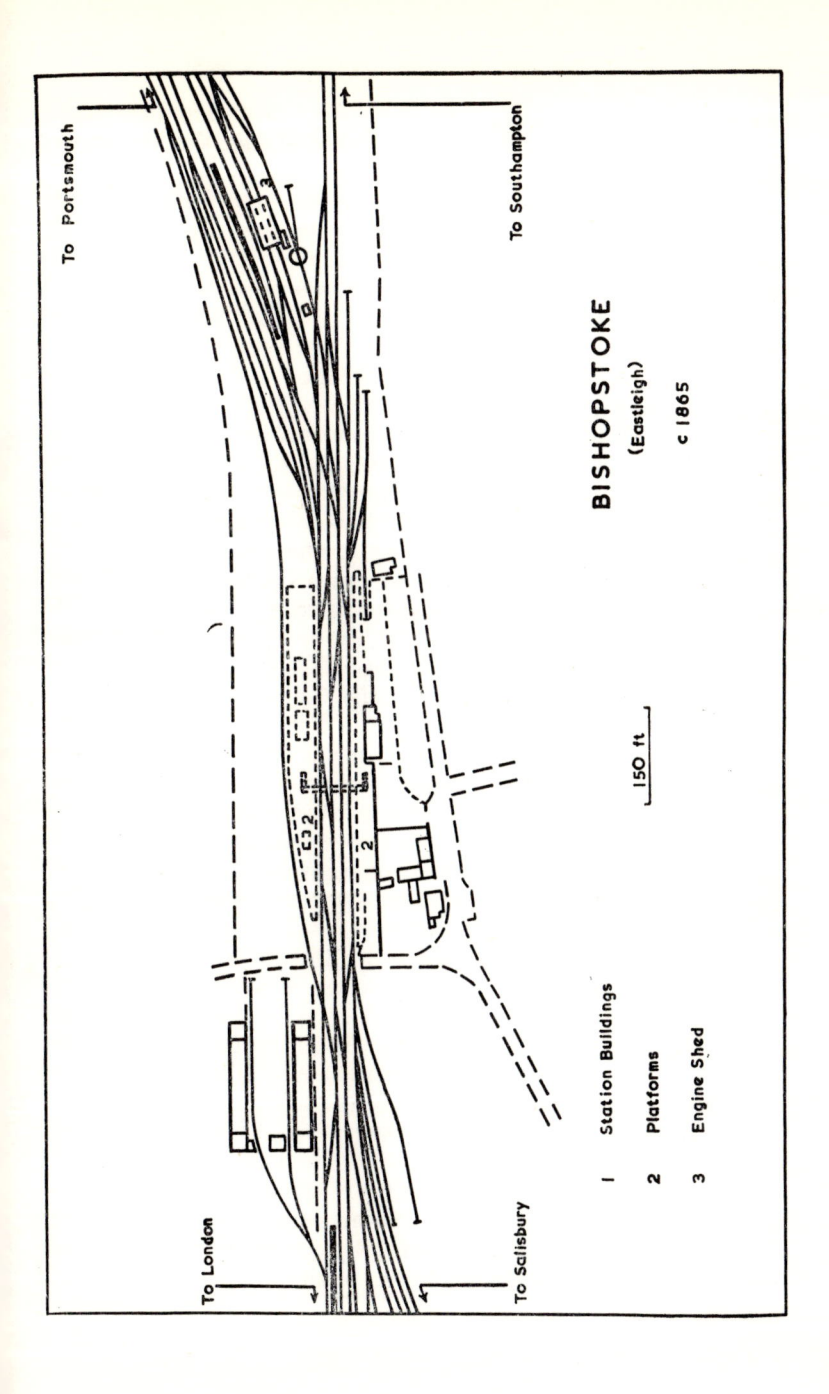

150 ft

1 Station Buildings
2 Platforms
3 Engine Shed

To Portsmouth
To Southampton
To London
To Salisbury

postponed until October, then November, then December, until, to meet Salisbury's pressing needs in that winter, the line opened for coal and goods on 27 January 1847.

At 11.25 am that day, the sight of smoke from the approaching engine provoked deafening cheers from over 2,000 Salisbury citizens gathered to see the railway enter their city. A few minutes later the six-coupled goods engine *Rhinoceros*, No 52, arrived, driven by Naylor who usually drove the LSW royal train, and hauling twenty-three heavily laden 'carriages', three of them containing fifty tons of coal for distribution to distressed persons, with another fifty tons coming on the next train.

The opening had been set for 25 January, but repairs were not completed to an arch which collapsed on 22 January about four miles from Salisbury. This was unfortunate, for on 25 January Salisbury elected Chaplin its M.P., honouring him with a public dinner in the town hall that evening at which he rose amid cheers to promise his best exertions for the town's prosperity.

The Bishopstoke branch opened for passengers on 1 March 1847, but the delay cost the company £6,000 in compensation to those shareholders who had lost dividends. Passengers might now reach Salisbury from Nine Elms by five daily trains with connections at Bishopstoke. There were four daily up trains, and two each way on Sundays. The fastest journey from London was 3 hr 50 min, fares being 15s single and 24s return, first class; 10s 8d single and 18s 6d return, second class. Third-class passengers paid 7s for a five-hour journey. Four daily and two Sunday trains each way connected for Gosport or Southampton, while on Salisbury market days a second-class carriage was attached to the goods train from Southampton at 6.00 am.

Salisbury, however, had long wanted a direct London line. In 1839 Easthope had promised LSW assistance, although vowing he and his colleagues, after their experience with the Southampton line, 'would never undergo the toil of constructing another railway'. That help had been sought in 1840 by a Salisbury deputation including the Hon Sidney Herbert, and Messrs Brodie and Wyndham, all M.Ps, who proposed a twenty-two miles branch, almost entirely through chalk, from the Southampton line at Hook Pit, near Winchester, which Locke estimated would cost £600,000. The LSW promised to try and find one-third when Salisbury had raised two-thirds of the capital and borne all preliminary expenses, which Brodie interpreted as sharing the profits when the risks had passed.

THE STRUGGLE TOWARDS THE WEST

Increasing railway developments compelled Chaplin to change his 1842 policy of sitting back and leaving provincial towns to construct branches. By 1844 he was explaining how railway capital, by going to ironmasters, mechanics, labourers, etc, would cause financial expansion and produce new railway investors.

> Now if these are sound views, and the expenditure of money in railways does not reduce its circulation in this country, we have a right to assume our neighbours, right and left, will be entering on our frontiers, with an intention of sapping the foundations of our trade, and I am sure you will expect us to do our duty, by being on the alert to fix our standard at the very limits of our territory, and to turn to profits, as far as possible, all our intermediate space.

Consequently, a special meeting of proprietors on 7 December 1844 had recommended the Hook Pit line be built in addition to the Bishopstoke branch, which it would join at Mottisfont and shorten the London journey by eight miles.

Meanwhile, on 2 February 1844, Charles Castleman, a Wimborne solicitor, had put to the board his proposed line between Southampton and Dorchester, and had sounded LSW intentions beyond Salisbury. He was told 'that if hereafter any circumstances should arise so as to lead to an extension of the proposed Salisbury branch, he should be informed thereof'.

Castleman and his supporters met at Southampton on 9 May 1844 and appointed Captain Moorsom their engineer who, in turn, engaged Pare to probe traffic prospects. Moorsom rejected the proposed direct route as useless for intermediate towns and involving considerable earthworks and tunnels. He recommended going via Redbridge, south of Lyndhurst, through Brockenhurst, Ringwood, Wimborne, near Hamworthy church, Poole, and Dorchester, with perhaps branches later to Lymington and Christchurch. Gradients would not exceed 1 in 200, save a short 1 in 100 stretch between Poole and Wimborne, where a pilot engine would be stationed. There were two possible entries to Southampton, i.e., the route of an abandoned canal and a short tunnel, joining the LSW at Fareham Road bridge, or, by the western shoreline to the pier, with a quay tramway to the LSW station. A Weymouth extension from Dorchester, although desirable, would present difficulties. Moorsom preferred an eight miles direct atmospheric line over the hills, to the 'alternative of tortuous deviations or expensive tunnelling' for locomotives. Estimated construction costs were £450,000, plus £104,000 for the Weymouth extension.

The LSW board agreed that Chaplin might subscribe as a provisional committee member, but when his name was used to identify the LSW with the project he withdrew, warning the promoters not to count on LSW support. During September 1844, Castleman wrote seeking LSW assistance in a tone causing the latter to ask whether he was seeking to restrict the LSW from extending its own line beyond Salisbury to Yeovil. Castleman confirmed that such a pledge should precede negotiations. Whatever his ambitions towards Exeter, such a dictatorial attitude towards the powerful LSW was astonishing; besides which the LSW could not have agreed without yielding its proposed through Cornwall line (see Chapter 4) to the GWR. A few days later Castleman reached agreement with the GWR which leased the Dorchester line at three and a half per cent. 'Castleman's Corkscrew' or the 'Watersnake', as the winding route was dubbed, would now be broad gauge.

Alarmed by this development, the LSW immediately promoted the Salisbury & Dorsetshire Railway, to leave the Bishopstoke branch at its junction with the Hook Pit deviation and go down the Avon valley to Fordingbridge, south-west to Wimborne, and then parallel to Castleman's line to Dorchester. Its 125-mile route from London would be twelve less than that of the Corkscrew, and a Poole branch and Weymouth extension were contemplated.

Chaplin complained bitterly of GWR activities:

> From Bath and that quarter, down to Salisbury, our neighbours are surveying the hills to Dorchester and Weymouth, with the evident intention of withdrawing the Weymouth and Dorchester trade from our line . . . . It is our legitimate country, it is in our traffic tables: and I think their going as far as Bristol out of the way towards Exeter, must have told us long ago they did consider it was ours, and that it was for us to occupy it . . . . Gentlemen, I should have observed, there is some difficulty always in defining the title in a new country or a new undertaking; and I have no doubt that that will apply in this western district, where we shall be deemed, as at Newbury, aggressors. That was a neutral country; it was entirely disregarded and left: but the moment we responded to the application of the locality, we were termed aggressive. I dare say it will be the same in the west of England; but it will occur to you that, about 130 years after Christ, the Romans found a way through, and laid it down for us; therefore I think that going far enough back to define a title for a line of country which will exclude us altogether from the epithet of aggressors.

The GWR scheme causing offence was the Wilts & Somerset Railway, from the Bristol line near Corsham via Melksham, Trowbridge, Westbury, Warminster and Wilton to Salisbury, thence to

THE STRUGGLE TOWARDS THE WEST

funnel traffic along the Bishopstoke branch to the south coast. Branches to Bradford, Devizes and Frome were planned. Its second prospectus in 1844 renamed it the Wilts, Somerset & Weymouth Railway and extended the Frome branch through Yeovil and Dorchester to Weymouth, with a Bridport branch. From the Bristol & Exeter, a branch to Sherborne via Yeovil was planned.

The LSW, being persuaded by Sherborne, Yeovil, Shaftesbury and Dorchester citizens to extend the Bishopstoke branch their way, decided on a line to Taunton through Shaftesbury and Yeovil. Its minute of 2 August 1844 reads:

> ... it appears that the distance between Salisbury and Taunton is about sixty-six miles, of which five miles would be traversed by the Bristol & Exeter line, leaving sixty miles to construct at an estimated cost for a single line of about £15,000 per mile. The Court were of opinion that it is highly desirable to cultivate this extension and to continue it to Taunton or Exeter.

With a Dorchester and Weymouth branch, this line was judged more valuable than the Corkscrew, but another minute, of 30 August 1844, says:

> Mr Locke produced maps explanatory of the country which he had recently surveyed and reported that a line to Exeter would be most difficult and almost impossible from the nature of the country, and after considerable discussion it was unanimously recommended that the Salisbury line should be extended to Yeovil for the present, with a branch from Yeovil to Dorchester, and another to Warminster, having its continuation to Exeter open for future consideration.

Unconvinced that the Romans had marched west to survey for the London & South Western Railway, the 'Five Kings' on 31 December 1844 announced in favour of the broad-gauge Berks & Hants, Wilts & Somerset, Bristol & Exeter branch to Yeovil, and the Corkscrew. They rejected the LSW-promoted Basingstoke & Didcot Junction, Salisbury & Dorsetshire, Hook Pit Devation, and the Salisbury & Yeovil lines. Their reasons, published on 28 February 1845, came from a conviction that the district could support only one of the two great but basically opposed schemes. The LSW central trunk line from east to west was to have been fed by branches from north and south, while the GWR sought criss-cross lines over the area bounded by its main line to the north and the Corkscrew to the south. Though the LSW route from London was shorter, the GWR offered a better service between the local towns (many of which the LSW ignored) and better communication with Bath and Bristol, whence much of the district's traffic flowed. The 'Five Kings' were swayed, too, by local preference for the GWR, and the military advantages of the coast line in national defence doubtless played their part. However, the Wilts & Somerset scheme had been approved only after its promoters had promised to submit in the next session a scheme to improve the circuitous route from Salisbury, Warminster, Bradford and places north of Yeovil towards Bath and Bristol.

Having publicly abandoned its rejected schemes, the LSW on 16 January 1845 signed its agreement with the GWR, both companies pledging not to promote opposing lines in the district settled by Dalhousie's report, 'unless under such a completely altered state of circumstances as would induce the Board of Trade to consider the principles which have guided them in that report as no longer applicable', and then only with that Board's approval. An important paragraph read:

> In the above agreement reference has been had more especially to extension lines from Salisbury or Dorchester competing with the Great Western (including its branches) and the lines now sanctioned on the one hand, and to extension lines from Basingstoke competing against the South-Western Railway (including its branches) and the coast line to Dorchester, on the other.

To compensate it for not going beyond Salisbury, the LSW was allowed to lease the Corkscrew for £20,000 annually and half the net profits, and the Southampton & Dorchester was naturally a third party to the agreement.

The GWR-sponsored Bills passed easily through Parliament in 1845, but the LSW board was confident Dalhousie would recommend that Basingstoke should be a junction between the gauges and allow the LSW to construct any necessary extension thence towards Salisbury. Soon, instead of only their seventy-seven miles original line, LSW trains would be working over 240 miles, 'comprising the London, as well as the local traffic of the district, whereof London, Basingstoke, Salisbury, Dorchester, Weymouth, Poole, Portsmouth, Chichester and Guildford may be considered the important outstations through which must flow the traffic of a yet wider range.'

The Southampton & Dorchester Act succeeded on 21 July 1845, capital £500,000, and authorised the lease to the LSW, which might appoint four of the twelve directors. The single line would now be narrow gauge, with bridges, etc, built for doubling when gross receipts of three consecutive years exceeded an average of

THE STRUGGLE TOWARDS THE WEST

£65,000. Capital would then be increased by £180,000. A branch from Turland Farm, Hamworthy, to the Ballast Quay at Poole was included, while at the Dorchester junction with the broad-gauge Wilts, Somerset & Weymouth, the company was to provide facilities for interchange of traffic and 'to provide and lay down upon any part, not exceeding eight miles of the Southampton & Dorchester Railway, adjacent to Dorchester, additional rails . . . . to enable engines and carriages constructed for the gauge of the said Wilts & Somerset Railway to pass along such part of the Southampton & Dorchester Railway'. This strange section meant the mixed gauge ending abruptly in mid-country eight miles east of Dorchester, probably only to balance Board of Trade power, under Section 29, to require mixed gauge on the WS & W between Dorchester and Weymouth.

Southampton inhabitants had complained of empty hotels and business at a standstill since the LSW had arrived there, because passengers were whisked from trains to ships instead of lingering awhile in the town as in coaching days. Thus Section 33 found its way into the Southampton & Dorchester Act, obliging the company to build a station at Bletchynden Terrace near the town centre and to stop ample trains there, though the line terminated at the LSW station. Chaplin, however, regarded attempts to force passengers into the town as levying a 'discreet tax' on them. Today, Bletchynden station thrives as Southampton Central, while the original LSW station, Southampton Terminus, closed to passengers in 1966.

Under the Act, consent of the Commissioners of Woods and Forests was necessary before New Forest land was taken, and they, not wanting the railway to touch the forest at all, pressed a very hard bargain after only engineering difficulties stopped them forcing it round the coast. Consequently, the company had to deviate southwards between Eling and Brockenhurst, leaving Lyndhurst two miles from its station, Parliamentary powers being obtained on 2 July 1847, a month after opening. With this setback Peto, the contractor, anticipated a long delay in finishing, but once it was resolved he was offered £5,000 bonus to complete the works by 1 May 1847. The LSW agreed to wooden bridges being built for speed, and to finance their subsequent conversion to embankment or brick. Double track was installed from Southampton to Redbridge.

On 25 May 1847, a beautiful, balmy spring morning with a gentle south-west breeze off the shimmering Southampton Water, an experimental train of three carriages, a horse-box, and three trucks of signal apparatus for distribution to each lodge and station, left Bletchynden at 5.30 am and arrived at Dorchester at 10.30 am, returning in three hours. Legal clouds had gathered, however, and in *Fotheringham v Southampton & Dorchester Railway*, heard during May 1847, the plaintiff sought to restrain the defendants from making Bletchynden station where they had begun it on land called King John's Pond, alleging that it infringed his agreement with the company. It should, he claimed, have been erected at the end of Bletchynden Terrace, out of sight of Kings Bridge House. Work on the station consequently stopped, but when the town council discovered the line was to be opened without it, the mayor and town clerk were ordered to London to secure an injunction to stop the Corkscrew opening until Section 33 of the Act had been complied with.

Two Southampton & Dorchester directors got wind of this and immediately guaranteed a temporary station and platforms 'till that at King John's Pond can be proceeded with, and on Monday morning (30 May 1847) they took Mr Purkis's premises at Bletchynden Terrace, known as Ivy House, for two years, to use as a station'. Purkis did not get his house back until 1850, and Bletchynden station proper was built, apparently opening that year just east of where the Central station today stands.

The line was publicly opened on Tuesday, 1 June 1847, but from Bletchynden because during the previous Sunday night the tunnel between that station and the LSW terminus failed. During May, the town council had had doubts about its safety and consequently had not re-opened the public road above it. The trouble stemmed from the disused canal tunnel which crossed the railway tunnel obliquely and about a foot below it, approximately beneath London Road. The canal tunnel had been properly dealt with at the point of junction, but Peto had agreed with fearful owners of property above to fill the canal tunnel solid with rubble. This damming up prevented drainage from the canal tunnel, and the accumulating water, seeking to escape, saturated the clay on which the railway tunnel stood until it could no longer support the weight. Omnibuses linked the stations during repairs until, after Board of Trade inspection by Captain Coddington, a mail train went through on the night of 5/6 August 1847 and normal service began on 6 August. Actually, the first passengers travelled with directors, engineers, etc, on a test train which passed through on 29 July 1847 to meet the 11.0 am train for London.

The incident had caused confusion on opening day, and a public dinner was postponed. On that morning, a notice on Ringwood station doors announcing postponement of the opening was hastily removed when a train arrived at 10 o'clock, and thereafter traffic partly commenced. The dinner was held on 8 June at the Crown Inn, Ringwood, presided over by John Mills, the deputy-

LONDON AND SOUTH-WESTERN RAILWAY.

On and after Monday, June 7th, 1847, the trains are intended to run as follows:—

DOWN.

Class.	From Nine Elms at	From Southampton at	Arriving at Dorchester
1st and 2nd	....	7 45 a.m.	10 50 a.m.
1st, 2nd, and 3rd	7 30 a.m.	12 35 p.m.	3 40 p.m.
1st and 2nd	9 0 a.m.		
1st and 2nd	11 0 a.m.	2 50 p.m.	5 45 p.m.
1st and 2nd (Exp)	12 30 p.m.		
1st and 2nd	3 0 p.m.	*6 20 p.m.	9 40 p.m.
1st and 2nd (Mail)	8 50 p.m.	12 30 p.m.	3 30 a.m.

UP.

Class.	From Dorchester at	From Southampton at	Arriving at Nine Elms
*1st, 2nd, and 3rd	7 15 a.m.	11 0 a.m.	1 50 p.m.
1st, 2nd, and 3rd	11 10 a.m.	3 0 p.m.	5 50 p.m.
		4 0 p.m.	8 0 p.m.
1st and 2nd	3 40 p.m.	7 0 p.m.	10 35 p.m.
1st and 2nd (Mail)	10 5 p.m.	1 15 a.m.	4 25 a.m.

* This is third Class between Dorchester and Southampton only.

On SUNDAY, commencing June 6th, 1847.

DOWN.

Class	From Nine Elms	From Southampton	Arriving at Dorchester
1st and 2nd	....	7 45 a.m.	10 50 a.m.
1st, 2nd, and 3rd	7 30 a.m.	1 35 p.m.	4 40 p.m.
1st and 2nd			
1st, 2nd and 3rd	10 0 a.m.	6 30 p.m.	9 40 p.m.
1st and 2nd (Mail)	8 50 p.m.	12 30 a.m.	3 30 a.m.

UP.

Class.	From Dorchester	From Southampton	Arriving at Nine Elms
1st, 2nd, and 3rd	7 15 a.m.	....	....
1st, 2nd, and 3rd	12 10 p.m.	4 0 p.m.	8 0 p.m.
1st and 2nd	6 0 p.m.	....	....
1st and 2nd (Mail)	10 5 p.m.	1 15 p.m.	4 25 a.m.

By Order,
P. LAURENTZ CAMPBELL, Secretary.

Advertised service for the opening of the Southampton & Dorchester line—*Hampshire Advertiser*, 5 June 1847

chairman. After the usual toasts, reminiscences and mutual congratulations, especially to Castleman, the 'original promoter', the party enjoyed a gay evening.

A head-on collision on 27 September marred the opening year. While the last down train was negotiating points at Wool, two carriages and the guard's van were derailed. A messenger rushed to Wareham for help, where in the excitement the stationmaster understood the up mail was involved and ordered out the contractor's 'muck engine'. Meanwhile, back at Wool, the down train had been rerailed and left for Dorchester, where on its arrival the up mail departed towards Southampton and met the 'muck engine' in a deep and curved cutting at Worgret, 1½ miles from Wareham. Casualties were fortunately light. Though the 'muck engine' was forced under the mail engine, both drivers escaped, but one stoker was concussed and buried in coke, the other losing some toes. The Press urged the company to hasten installation of the electric telegraph, for which posts had been erected as far as Ringwood.

During construction, the LSW had complained that unsuitable materials were being used. In November 1847 Peto took a three-year contract to maintain the track, which was so bad that by June 1848 severe wear to locomotive wheels on irregular curves was causing concern. Nearly all platforms were too short, but their extension to 250 ft began in 1858, concurrent with doubling.

A LSW board minute of 29 June 1848 says:

> .... at Beaulieu Road, the building of a station was enforced by the Woods and Forests without any adequate requirement on the part of the public, as is fully proved by the fact that the money taken has been barely sufficient to pay the wages of the people employed at the station. It is the duty of the directors to endeavour to obtain leave to suppress the station altogether, and in the meantime to confide it to the care of some responsible man and his wife.

The Commissioners refused to agree, so the board decided that Parliamentary trains only would stop there. In September 1859 closure was again ordered, but the platform was to remain for the use of the Duke of Bucclough. Now local inhabitants successfully protested, and local opposition also defeated efforts to close Redbridge to passengers in June 1859. However, the Beaulieu Road victory was short lived: passenger trains ceased calling there from 1 March 1860.

The Southampton & Dorchester obtained powers on 2 July 1847 for branches (1) at Eling to a quay on Southampton Water, (2) from Brockenhurst to Lymington, and (3) from Moreton to Melcombe Regis, Weymouth, where it would join the expected Wilts, Somerset & Weymouth. Landowners' opposition caused suspension in the Lords of a Blandford Bill until the next session. The salt works at Lymington had offered the LSW 250,000 tons of traffic annually when that branch was completed, but lean times

BODMIN & WADEBRIDGE—2
(9) *Original engine house at Wadebridge*
(10) *Original workshops at Wadebridge*

BODMIN & WADEBRIDGE—3

(11) *Terminus milestone from Ruthern Bridge indicating 4 miles, 1 furlong, 5 chains, 10 yards from Wadebridge*

(12) *Second class tickets, (left) pink, dated 1856 and signed by E. T. Liddell, superintendent of the line, and (right) white, undated but initialled by him*

succeeding the railway mania killed most of these projects, though a Lymington branch was independently promoted in 1856 and Blandford was later served by the Dorset Central. The Eling branch (or Tramway) was leased to Sir John B. Mills to build, and opened for freight probably in April 1851.

The Act of 22 July 1848, which authorised the amalgamation of the Southampton & Dorchester with the LSW. appointed Sir John Mills to a specially-created seat on the LSW board (Castleman did not become a LSW director until 31 May 1855), and the Southampton & Dorchester ceased to exist on 11 October 1848.

After vainly seeking Board of Trade permission to delay it, the LSW doubled the line and the second track opened as follows:

Redbridge	to Beaulieu Road	1 August 1857
Brockenhurst	to Christchurch Road (later Holmsley)	1 August 1857
Ringwood	to Wimborne	1 October 1857
Beaulieu Road	to Brockenhurst	1 September 1858
Christchurch Road	to Ringwood	1 September 1858

This completed thirty-six miles from Southampton to Wimborne, but Dorchester citizens wanted doubling throughout and urged the Board of Trade in 1860 to order it. The LSW sought to double instead an equal portion of its newly-opened Exeter line, to gauge the effect on the Dorchester line before completing the latter. The Board of Trade insisted that the Dorchester line be finished, and double track reached Wool on 1 June 1863 and Dorchester on 1 August 1863.

Dorchester station layout looks strange, for it was planned with extension to Exeter in mind. On 20 January 1857, with powers renewed on 31 July 1854, the WS & W reached Weymouth, being mixed gauge from Dorchester. Through narrow-gauge trains which now ran from Waterloo reached WS & W lines by a sharp single line curve which left the Corkscrew just before Dorchester station. Trains crossed that junction into Dorchester station, then reversed over it before moving forward again round the curve. During 1878 the curve was doubled, and in 1880 a new platform was built alongside it for down trains only: up trains from Weymouth to the Corkscrew negotiated the curve and junction and reversed into the original Dorchester station, as they still do at the time of writing. The WS & W Act included another section for the eight broad-gauge miles along the Corkscrew. Passengers from London to Dorchester also had the inconvenience of going first into Southampton terminus, then coming back and round the left-hand

E

curve and on via Bletchynden. On 2 August 1858 advertised services started round a new curve completing the triangle and giving direct access to Bletchynden, which was renamed that day Southampton West End (or West) and became the new changing point. The journey from London to Dorchester by express was now fifteen to twenty minutes shorter.

POWERS FOR AN EXETER LINE

The triple agreement was short-lived. On 14 March 1845, Chaplin's board received overtures from Andover residents for a line from Basingstoke to Salisbury through their town, and Locke was asked to survey it. Being quite open, the board told the GWR of its intentions, whereupon Russell wrote to Chaplin on 28 March protesting at this 'infraction of the contents of the agreement', which would divert traffic from lines approved by the Board of Trade. Chaplin rightly replied that the agreement 'did not extend to any line which the South-Western company might propose to make from Basingstoke by or near Andover and Whitchurch to Salisbury', and suggested Board of Trade arbitration. That body insisted this was beyond its jurisdiction, though it privately admitted to Chaplin its opinion that the LSW was not prevented from making the line.

Meanwhile, Andover residents became impatient and formed a London, Salisbury & Yeovil Railway Company, which met at Andover Town Hall on 29 March 1845 and heard Giles explain the route from the LSW at Worting through Whitchurch, Andover and Salisbury to Yeovil. Locke was present and denied that the LSW intended abandoning its own line, though he had to admit he was surveying only to Salisbury. The LS & Y, however, had contacted the Exeter, Yeovil & Dorchester promoters, whose prospectus of 3 March 1845 described a line from Yeovil to Exeter, with a Dorchester branch, serving Crewkerne, Ilminster, Chard, Bridport, Beaminster, Axminster, Honiton and Ottery St Mary. The LS & Y saw itself part of a 165-mile narrow-gauge line from London to Exeter, the shortest route by about thirty miles. Nothing would stop it building about forty of the seventy-five new miles, not even GWR or LSW activities, and should the Exeter, Yeovil & Dorchester falter, it would immediately form a London, Salisbury & Exeter Company.

The LSW directors were trapped. The LS & Y intruder threatened the advantages gained by the agreement with the GWR, and this was not all. Feeling that even the LSW extension to Salisbury was uncertain, the LS & Y added a Wimborne, Poole and Dorchester branch from Salisbury and negotiated with promoters of a line from Manchester to Poole via Salisbury to incorporate it in their scheme.

Fearing for its prospects should all this succeed, the LSW decided to throw in its lot with the LS & Y, EY & D, and the Cornwall & Devon Central companies which, together, could make one line from London to Lands End. Before announcing this, it was necessary to escape from the agreement with the GWR, and opportunity came in October 1845.

When considering the WS & W Bill, Parliament had indicated the importance it attached to a direct line to the west, and in 1845 the GWR took steps to promote that direct line, actually reaching agreement with the Bristol & Exeter Company. When B & E proprietors refused to endorse it, the GWR proceeded alone with a scheme to extend the Berks & Hants line from Hungerford to Westbury, and promoted an Exeter Great Western Railway to leave Exeter by Ottery St Mary and Honiton to Axminster, where one line would diverge to Yeovil via Crewkerne and another via Charmouth to Bridport. Between Westbury and Yeovil, through trains from Paddington to Exeter would use the WS & W.

Immediately these plans were announced the LSW acted. On 30 October 1845 Morgan, the secretary, protested to Saunders that 'this large disturbance of the scheme of railways settled for the district' violated the agreement and so completely altered circumstances as to nullify the principles behind Dalhousie's report. His board therefore intended seeking Board of Trade reaction to a LSW-promoted line through Salisbury, Yeovil and Exeter to Cornwall. Morgan sent a copy of his letter to Dalhousie and sought a hearing of deputations from both companies for the 'Five Kings' to express their opinion.

Saunders denied a breach of the agreement, but Dalhousie's board evasively replied that it had agreed to arbitrate only when urgently requested by both companies, and that no GWR request had been received. The following paragraph no doubt encouraged the LSW:

> Their Lordships admit that the numerous schemes which have been advertised for supplying railway accommodation through the district referred to in the agreement alter the circumstances in which the agreement was made, but my Lords do not feel called upon to express an opinion whether this alteration of circumstances is

sufficiently extensive to justify a departure from the agreement by one or other of the two companies.

Admittedly, the schemes were numerous. In addition to those described, there were the Bridport & Exeter, or South Coast Junction Railway; Bristol & English Channels Direct Junction Railway; Exeter, Dorchester & Weymouth Junction Coast Railway, etc, for these were days of wild speculation.

Morgan wrote again to Saunders on 7 November 1845, claiming that the state of affairs was now beyond recall even if the parties wished it; that 'it has now become necessary for our directors to act upon their own responsibilities' and 'they have come to the conclusion that, in the present state of circumstances, the London & South-Western Railway Company are at liberty to act in such manner as shall seem best for the interests of this company'.

Three weeks later Russell wrote indignantly to Chaplin, accusing the LSW of 'an unexampled breach of faith'. Recalling negotiations preceding the agreement, he claimed the LSW had then interpreted the phrase 'an entirely altered state of circumstances' as if, for example, 'some extraordinary mass of new population should settle down in the district to constitute a second Manchester, ... a town of very considerable manufacture or trade . . . an event far too remote to be taken into account.' It had, he said, denied that the definition included a new company approaching Yeovil from Cornwall or Exeter.

The Southampton & Dorchester Company, alarmed at renewed threats to its own traffic should the LSW build west of Salisbury, demanded Chaplin's explanation. He replied that unless it permitted a GWR line as injurious to the Corkscrew as the LSW extension to Yeovil, it must consider the LSW action justified, but he soothingly offered to leave to Board of Trade arbitration the amount of extra rent Southampton & Dorchester shareholders should receive.

Quite unappeased, the Southampton & Dorchester complained bitterly at not having been consulted, especially as Chaplin had admitted in 1844 that two western lines could not co-exist on the available traffic. He was reminded that negotiations in 1844 had failed because the LSW refused to pledge itself not to go beyond Salisbury. The Southampton & Dorchester was chiefly angry with the LS & Y-proposed Wimborne branch (whose effects it feared more than that company's Yeovil line) and for which it held the LSW partly responsible. It did not consider the GWR extension a breach of the agreement. So intense were its feelings that, on 7

January 1846, its chairman, Lord De Mauley, wrote to Chaplin complaining strongly of LSW actions and its casual behaviour generally towards the Southampton & Dorchester, including the frequent absence of LSW members from board meetings. This correspondence was later published.

LSW proprietors met on 26 January 1846 and heard Chaplin's explanation; his strong denial of ulterior motive or breach of faith; his complaint that the GWR had not notified the LSW of its intentions, and of its going into a district reserved for future consideration. He thought the LSW had submitted too much to the Board of Trade, especially as Dalhousie's committee had now been overthrown. Agitation had followed its increasing number of decisions against different companies, and Sir Robert Peel himself finally withdrew support.

With the bridle removed and the railway mania now at the gallop, Chaplin agreed some restraint was necessary. 'I fear,' he said, 'that competition will be the ruin of the railway system. unless Government should bring forward some measure to control the direction in which lines are to be made.'

Estimates of the proposed conjoined schemes were:

London & South Western	Basingstoke to Salisbury	£700,000
London, Salisbury & Yeovil	Salisbury to Yeovil	£900,000
Exeter, Yeovil & Dorchester	Yeovil to Exeter	£1,300,000
Cornwall & Devon Central	Exeter to Falmouth and Penzance	£3,000,000

The LSW would take a quarter of each other company's capital and a proportionate share in each management. Each company would seek individual powers, and if all were successful the LSW, LS & Y and C & DC would amalgamate and jointly lease the EY & D.

Louis H. Ruegg, in his fascinating book *The History of a Railway*, described a meeting on 26 March 1846 at Sherborne to support the direct scheme, when the rival gauges were strongly represented. Broad-gauge supporters included Robert Gordon, former Secretary to the Treasury; the Earl of Digby; Sir John Awdrey, chairman of the WS & W; Captain O'Brien, its secretary, and Tucker, Secretary of the Exeter Great Western. The more numerous narrow-gauge party included Crombie, secretary of the LS & Y and later of the LSW; Chapman, LS & Y chairman, and owners of silk factories at Sherborne and glove factories of Milborne Port.

The town hall was densely crammed, and, after considerable delay, it began to be known in the room that there was a split in the local railway committee, and that the meeting might go off. This gave fresh excitement to the feeling in the hall and when, after an hour's delay, the members of the committee struggled through the mass which had overflown the floor and covered the platform, the cheering was tremendous.

On behalf of the Exeter Great Western ... it was averred that it (the broad-gauge through route) could not be more than five miles further from the locality in which the meeting was being held than the line via Salisbury. A part of it, it was said, was actually made (a part of the Wilts & Somerset). It would open up some of the best corn markets in the world and tap the great coal measures of Somerset. It would give communication with the north, and carry them down to Land's End. With cheap coal and communication, north, east, west and south, what more, it was asked, could they want? The meeting enquired the sort of line they were to have, and when it was described as a branch from Sparkford, they indignantly declared "It won't do!" and the continued mention of "the drop line from Sparkford" was received with shouts of laughter. Would that line, it was asked, carry their wheat to Salisbury, or their cattle to London? It was said that the two great companies, the Great Western and the South-Western, were tied by some sort of agreement with the Board of Trade which prevented them entering upon this territory; and amidst loud cheering, Mr Crombie asserted that but for the London, Salisbury & Yeovil Company the Great Western would never have been seen in the district at all.

Narrow-gauge supporters swept that meeting, as they did another soon after at Salisbury; but a meeting at Yeovil resented that town's name being included in a line coming no nearer than Sutton Bingham.

All schemes reached the 1846 session, where the Commons rejected the GWR extension from Hungerford to Westbury on Standing Orders, and the Exeter Great Western on its merits. The LSW fared little better. The C & DC failed on Standing Orders, while the LS & Y and EY & D foundered in the Lords. However, the Basingstoke to Salisbury Bill succeeded on 13 August. Leaving the LSW at Wootton Saint Lawrence, it would terminate at Milford station and 'also near the proposed Salisbury terminus of the Wilts, Somerset & Weymouth Railway abutting on Fisherton Street'.

The Lords committee had liked the Salisbury to Exeter scheme but objected to the details, so the LSW was encouraged to seek its own powers for a revised Salisbury to Yeovil line and offered LS & Y proprietors share for share of new LSW stock. The LS & Y pressed for 50s on each LSW share to be taken as paid, as reward for its keeping the district for the LSW and helping the latter get its Basingstoke to Salisbury Act. It got 25s, plus 30s to come when the

Yeovil Act succeeded, but only because Uzielli, who negotiated for the LSW, exceeded what he had been authorised to offer.

The revised Yeovil line, estimated at £1,000,000, included branches to Shaftesbury and Wincanton, following pressure on Chaplin when he visited the area enlisting support. A cross line from the proposed Southampton & Dorchester branch at Blandford to Bruton, through Sturminster, Stalbridge and Wincanton,, for £400,000 more, was promoted because of GWR surveys for a similar line. The independent EY & D intended trying again, this time with branches to Bridport and Dorchester, Sidmouth and Charmouth (Lyme Regis). The LSW would rent it and subscribe a quarter of the capital, of which £500,000 more was needed, but as many EY & D proprietors hesitated to increase their holdings the LSW agreed to provide the outstanding capital.

These schemes reached the 1847 session, when the LSW also presented a revised Cornwall & Devon Central Bill (see Chapter 4). The GWR again presented the Berks & Hants Extension and the Exeter Great Western, the latter now incorporating a central Exeter station and junctions with the South Devon and Bristol & Exeter lines. The B & E, opposing the Exeter Great Western, sought a branch from its line at Durston to Castle Cary on the WS & W, to shorten the broad-gauge route from the Berks & Hants extension to Exeter. The GWR also sought to link Yeovil with Salisbury, by a line from Compton on the WS & W north-east of Yeovil, to Wilton. During a fifty-three-days battle before the Commons committee, Mr Cockburn's three-days reply for the LSW, involving 11½ hours of speaking, was noted for holding the attention on so dry a subject!

On 2 July 1847 the committee passed the EY & D except the branches. It also approved the Salisbury to Yeovil scheme save the Wincanton branch, but rejected the Blandford to Bruton scheme. The B & E Castle Cary branch succeeded, but the only GWR success was its Berks & Hants extension. *Herapath's Journal* said the blow to the GWR was heavy, 'but we hope they will extract good out of it, as bees do honey out of weeds'.

It being late in the session, the successful Bills were suspended until the next, but premature local celebrations were held, with bells ringing and cannons firing, while at Chard 'the band patrolled the streets playing triumphal airs'.

The year's progress was inevitably clouded by repercussions from the railway mania, a period of financial folly and greed, whose story has elsewhere oft and adequately been told. During its course, the LSW and other sound companies had been forced to launch defensive but otherwise unnecessary schemes, and when the bubble companies had finally burst, with thousands of investors ruined and the economy severely depressed, not only were existing lines starved of traffic but it was virtually impossible to find necessary new capital. Thus the LSW directors, sensitive of greater responsibility, told proprietors on 27 November 1847 they had, in the company's permanent interests, postponed all operations except in districts actually contested. Some shareholders, led by Alexander Hoyes, opposed all further extensions whatever, but a large majority supported the directors.

Proceedings in the Lords in 1848 were rapid. The EY & D Act succeeded on 22 July for a narrow-gauge line from Exeter, Queen Street, to Yeovil, including three branches, (1) to Chard, (2) to Bridport Harbour and (3) from Bradford Abbas to the junction of the B & E branch and the WS & W at Pen Mill, Yeovil. The LSW could subscribe £900,000 of the £1,400,000 capital, and Chaplin, Henderson, Eyre and Uzielli represented it on the board of sixteen.

The Salisbury to Yeovil Act succeeded the same day, capital £875,000, the line to leave the LSW Salisbury extension at Fisherton Street and terminate near Pen Mill turnpike gate, Yeovil, plus a Shaftesbury branch. At Bradford Abbas one branch would link it with the EY & D, another with the WS & W near its junction with the B & E.

In the same session, Acts succeeded for the broad-gauge Berks & Hants extension, and the Castle Cary branch.

The economic depression damped down the gauge war, and many expensively-won powers of both sides simply lapsed. By December 1847, work begun between Basingstoke and Salisbury was limited to an expenditure of £3,000 monthly. This route crossed open, chalk country with no great engineering problems, the heaviest stretch being between Andover and Salisbury where the steepest gradient, 1 in 140, would descend from Porton to the Wiltshire city. Work was concentrated on the Basingstoke to Andover section, but in October 1848, with rising costs and land-purchase prices soaring above estimates, it was found impossible to finish even that by May 1849, the target date. All activities were suspended, despite local protests, though a two-years extension of powers was hopefully gained on 26 June 1849.

The monotonous inactivity of 1848 was broken on 1 November when the GWR's 15½ miles of broad gauge between Reading and Basingstoke opened, giving communication between north and south without touching London, and this became mixed gauge on 22 December 1856.

EXETER—CENTRAL OR COAST LINE?

So far, LSW general meetings had been remarkably peaceful. As Chaplin said, they had never had to resort to formal voting and had scarcely had any division, but in 1849, as the icy winds of depression withered the shareholders' half-yearly dividend from six or eight to a mere three-and-a-quarter per cent, murmurs of discontent arose. Accusations of dishonesty were made against the directors in general and Chaplin in particular; of irregularities in share dealings; of falsifications in the books, etc, with demands for a searching enquiry (see Chapter 9). Ill-feeling came, too, from inhabitants affected by the suspension of the westward through line, who rightly feared economic disadvantages if the district were deprived of an early place in the national railway pattern then being weaved. It was a handicap from which the area has never recovered.

The board had promised not to resume suspended works without first consulting the proprietors, and feelings were divided when the gauge-war lull was broken in March 1850 by the GWR absorbing and proceeding to complete the WS & W, whose works had been suspended, although the Thingley Junction to Westbury section had opened on 5 September 1848. The GWR opened the line to Frome on 7 October 1850 and Warminster on 9 September 1851, but the Frome, Yeovil & Weymouth Railway it formed for the purpose had failed to produce the capital within three months as its Act required, leaving the GWR to find the money.

Determined to keep their through line, residents between Salisbury and Exeter had produced a revised scheme to cost only £1,100,000, and with Locke's advice had got tenders from Brassey, Peto and Betts to build from the LSW authorised terminus at Fisherton, Salisbury to Northernhay, Exeter. Ten miles would be double, but the remaining seventy-nine single with earthworks. etc, for a double line. If LSW co-operation was not forthcoming, the promoters intended negotiating with 'other parties'. Meeting at Honiton and Yeovil on 13 and 14 November 1851, they formed a formidable committee of eighteen, including the Marquis of Westminster; Lords Arundel, Rivers, Ashburton and Bridport; Baronets Edward B. Baker, W. C. Medleycott, John Kennaway and Edward Marwood Elton; Henry Seymour, M.P. and Sidney Herbert, M.P.

LSW proprietors, meeting on 16 December 1851, heard that this Salisbury, Yeovil & Exeter Railway wanted them to provide rolling stock and work the line for twenty-five years, for half the receipts, less half the profits of additional traffic brought to the LSW at Salisbury. The LSW contribution was, in any case, to be limited to a sum assuring the SY & E six per cent on the capital of £1,100,000. The directors recommended acceptance, as this important line would capture the district without hurting LSW shareholders, although they would have to complete the time-expired Basingstoke to Salisbury line for up to £500,000, including rolling stock.

However, some proprietors, including Castleman and Captain Moorsom, were more interested in extending the Corkscrew on narrow gauge to Bridport and Exeter by the new Dorchester & Exeter Coast Extension Railway, and held a public meeting in Southampton on 15 December 1851 in support of it. Next day the LSW met, with the Earl of Morley presiding because Chaplin was ill, and Castleman circulated a paper arguing that the fifty-six-mile Coast line, costing £490,000, would be financed entirely by the D & ECE, whereas the Central line would involve the LSW in finding the capital for the Basingstoke to Salisbury extension which, with the rest of the Exeter line that way, would require £1,500,000. Apart from this, the LSW would own a greater proportion of the Coast line and so receive a larger share of through receipts.

When the chairman moved that the meeting should approve the Salisbury to Exeter extension and co-operate with its promoters, Castleman moved an amendment that a committee should examine both schemes. He stressed the Coast line's role in national defence and warned that the Central line would incite renewed broad-gauge activities. Locke, whose ambition had long been to complete the Central line, said the Coast line was circuitous, and if the WS & W intersected it, traffic would switch to the GWR.

After two shows of hands, the chairman declared the amendment carried and refused a poll. The meeting adjourned until 23 December 1851, when William Reed was chairman. The week-old committee, including Helps, Castleman, Mortimer, Hutchinson, Crowley, East, the Rev Blunt and Serjeant Gaselee, recommended the Coast line as one to enhance LSW property. Of the Central line, it said:

> ... whenever the period shall have arrived at which it may be wise or prudent to promote a "Central Line", that object would be best accomplished by a direct procedure on the part of this company, by which, not only would the capital be raised at the lowest possible

THE STRUGGLE TOWARDS THE WEST

cost, but the construction and management of the line be placed in your own absolute control.

However, it urged early completion of a single line from Basingstoke to Andover, which was already well advanced, and called for friendship with the GWR and all companies. Only the Rev Blunt failed to sign the report, which Helps moved be adopted, whereupon Mr Currie, M.P. moved the following amendment:

> ... that the report of the committee be received, and the directors requested to give the same their full consideration, and also to consider the proposal made today by Mr Locke.

Speaking for the Central line promoters, Locke had promised that if the LSW found half their capital they would find the rest. A show of hands defeated Currie's amendment, but Reed conceded a poll, the result at the resumed meeting on 31 December 1851 being: 4,095 for the motion, 3,125 against. Applause greeted this Coast line victory.

No time was lost in engaging Brassey to finish the Basingstoke to Salisbury as a single line as far as Andover for £74,000, and work began. Well might they hurry, for on 22 November 1851 landowners meeting at Andover had formed the Basingstoke & Salisbury Railway Company to complete the abandoned LSW works. Choice of gauge was delayed, and the prospectus shows there were hopes of converting the Andover & Southampton Canal to a broad-gauge railway and linking the port with the broad-gauge system. This dangerous scheme failed Standing Orders on 7 February 1852.

Following the Coast line victory, the D & ECE promoters had quickly sought working arrangements with the LSW, but their Bill failed Standing Orders in February 1852 and so settled the matter.

LSW shareholders' dissatisfaction with their board was demonstrated during January and February 1852, when Helps, Mortimer and Gaselee challenged Reed, Lacy and the Hon Francis Scott for the seats to which they were seeking re-election. Though Reed was a Manchester man, proprietors there supported the challengers as men determined to close the capital account immediately.

The board was charged with a grave error of judgment in having selected the more expensive Central line during the previous December; with rubber-stamping vital decisions made only by Chaplin, the individual members not troubling to understand the facts and making no effort to close the capital account. Contemporary journals repeated this, and criticised the need to submit candidates' names thirty days before elections, implying that news of vacancies was stifled until new candidates were too late, so that existing directors retained seats for life and showed little vigour in return.

Scott was called 'one of those safe and easily-led colleagues on whom the more robust and astute can rely for an affirmative vote at any time', while Lacy was criticised for 'silence at the late meetings'. Reed was the main target, chiefly for accepting Currie's amendment on 23 December 1851, and then, when it was lost, agreeing to the poll. Truly, he had not impressed by confessing to little knowledge of the problem in Chaplin's absence.

Herapath's Journal, whose namesake proprietor and LSW shareholder opposed the Central line, published on 17 January 1852 a letter from Alex Kay, a lawyer shareholder, furthering the Manchester attack and saying 'the conduct of Mr William Reed, one of the retiring directors, when in the chair, we refrain from commenting on'. Reed replied in the *Railway Times*, scornfully referring to Kay's hearsay evidence, who was absent from the meetings.

The battle continued until voting on 12 February 1852, when a tense meeting heard the Earl of Morley declare Scott, Reed and Lacy elected on a show of hands. A poll was conceded, but their narrow victory was upheld. On 17 August 1852, Gaselee and Mortimer successfully contested two further seats, reducing the Central line majority on the board. In that month, too, the Earl of Morley, who had joined the board in 1846 for the westward extension, felt circumstances had changed and resigned his seat.

The door was still open to the Central line party. On 17 August 1852, the proprietors were told the WS & W intended renewing its powers for a Dorchester to Bridport line, which the LSW would oppose. To counter it, the board recommended that a narrow-gauge line be built from Bridport to Axminster, for which the LSW should contribute £50,000. At Axminster, it could join the proposed Central line, whose independent promoters had now provisionally agreed to the LSW providing £550,000, i.e. half the capital, and with its own rolling stock to work their line between Salisbury and Exeter for fifty per cent of the gross receipts. Independently-held shares would receive four per cent of net receipts preferentially, and LSW holdings would then take three-and-a-half per cent, anything left being equally divided. LSW shareholders were thought likely to receive £28,115 annually, and might purchase the independent shares after seven years.

Moorsom objected to re-opening a question already decided, but Locke headed the Central line's supporters. He had been succeeded as LSW engineer in January 1849 by J. E. Errington, his one-time resident engineer on the Grand Junction, and was now interested as owner of an estate near Honiton, for which constituency he was M.P. Chaplin, now back in the chair, sought authority to, (1) conclude the agreement with the Central (Salisbury & Exeter Extension) Railway Company, (2) assist it to secure its Act in the next session, and (3) promote the Bridport to Axminster line. A resolution was passed, confirming the Central line's importance and instructing the directors, with a committee of shareholders, to seek better terms from the promoters. Moorsom had moved an amendment requiring the committee to consider also a line between Dorchester and Axminster, which Locke agreed to support if 'Bridport' were substituted for 'Dorchester'. Moorsom refused, for this would defeat his objects, but he agreed to put his amendment as a motion, whereupon Locke moved an amendment substituting 'Bridport' for 'Dorchester' and the amendment was carried amid Moorsom's protests that the proprietors had misunderstood the question.

Meanwhile, on 12 August 1852, GWR proprietors had approved the broad-gauge Devon & Dorset Railway to be promoted jointly with the Bristol & Exeter. Leaving Maiden Newton for Axminster, it would then take the familiar route to Exeter through Honiton and Ottery St Mary, with branches to Bridport and Sidmouth.

The LSW committee secured a minor concession from the Central line promoters—four per cent to the LSW, and its report, leaving the proprietors to decide, was accepted on 24 September 1852. It was then resolved that every proprietor be invited to express in person, in writing, or by proxy, his feelings on the subject for consideration at a special general meeting. The board's views were published (an abnormal procedure) as follows:

For the Central line	Against it
W. J. Chaplin, M.P.	Stephen Gaselee
Count Eyre	John Hibbert, Jun.
Colonel Henderson	John Mills
Henry Lacy	Charles Mortimer
William Reed	
Hon Francis Scott M.P.	
Henry Ker Seymer M.P.	
Thomas Smith	
Matthew Uzielli	

The committee's report was circulated among proprietors, with an appeal by Chaplin and suggestions for raising the £550,000 by new preference stock. On 26 October 1852 they voted against the line, and the result of the inevitable poll was announced four days later:

In favour of the line:		Against the line:	
Proxies	11,038	Proxies	10,781
Personal	1,351	Personal	1,829
Total	12,389	Total	12,610

Thus, by merely 221 votes, the Central line was again defeated, and now Chaplin resigned the chair, convinced that he had lost the shareholders' confidence. He agreed, however, to continue until the February 1853 general meeting, but hostility towards him culminated in a personal affront by a new director at a board meeting on 3 December 1852. He immediately quitted the chair and left the room. Though he retained his directorship, the company had lost a wise and valuable leader who, since taking office on 23 December 1842, had led it through perilous days. Ruegg paid him well-merited tribute in *The History of a Railway*:

> Throughout the subsequent struggles for the Central line, Mr Chaplin's figure towers above that of every other person associated with the undertaking. A man of shrewd abilities, with a large capital invested in the business which railways were destined to supersede, Mr Chaplin had not only the sagacity to perceive the coming change, but to prepare to profit by it. He rode on the wings of the storm whilst others were swept away by the blast. The great coach-proprietor became, by easy and rapid gradations, the railway adviser, director, deputy-chairman, and chairman. Tried as perhaps never man—not even railway chairman—was tried before, Mr Chaplin continued steadfast to the end in his appreciation and support of the Central line. He was opposed—bitterly; he was thwarted often; more than once he was undermined in his own cabinet and defeated by his own shareholders; but he never lost faith in the project of a grand, straight, trunk line to the West. Once, smarting under the mistrust of his co-proprietors, he sold out £20,000 of South-Western shares and bought into the opposition line; but he consoled his shareholders by telling them he still held £180,000 of South-Western stock. To his bonhomie, thorough knowledge of men, and aptness in business affairs, was added a facility of expressing himself in forcible Saxon language. His speeches were straight and to the point . . . .'

The Hon Francis Scott succeeded Chaplin to an unhappy term of office. On 14 May 1853 a special train conveying him and other directors killed an employee at Farnham. The coroner's jury verdict was manslaughter, on which charge Scott and the traffic superintendent appeared at Croydon Assizes. The hearing was stopped, the jury being told that the defendants were no more responsible than an ordinary passenger and that the accident had resulted solely from the deceased's inattention.

More pertinently managerial matters equally discomfited him. The Devon & Dorset Bill was making good progress and was to come before a Commons committee in May 1853. The LSW dare not stand still in the face of invasion, and Scott gathered the proprietors on 19 May 1853, urging them to authorise a narrow-gauge extension of the Corkscrew from Dorchester to Exeter, now to cost between £630,000 and £700,000, or to relieve the directors of responsibility by deciding contrarily. They agreed to oppose the Devon & Dorset and promote the Corkscrew extension entirely with LSW capital. A further resolution, destined bitterly to divide the company, read:—

> Resolved, that the directors be accordingly authorised and requested to pledge this company to apply to Parliament at the earliest period for powers to construct such last-mentioned line, and to put such powers into execution, so as to give the district in question the accommodation which such extension will afford with the least possible delay.

Thus armed, Scott fought the Devon & Dorset before the Commons committee and, by pledging the LSW to promote the double-line extension in the next session and to double the Corkscrew throughout, he secured its defeat.

Those who favoured closing the capital account found a champion in Snell, lately an unsuccessful candidate for the board. His circular to the shareholders preceded a meeting he called at Morley's Hotel, Strand, on 3 October 1853, when he accused the board of obtaining the pledge by falsely stating a profit on the Southampton & Dorchester, whereas he alleged it was losing money. This, he said, justified the proprietors breaking the pledge, and he sought sufficient proxies to oppose the scheme at a Wharncliffe meeting. (The Wharncliffe Standing Order of the House of Lords required every extension Bill brought before it to have been approved at a specially-convened meeting by proprietors holding three-quarters of their company's stock.) The Morley's Hotel meeting decided that western extensions would invoke GWR hostility, and demanded a new board which would follow a non-extension policy and make peace with that company.

Scott circulated all proprietors on 15 September 1853 rebutting the charges against the board. Chaplin did likewise on 28 October 1853, declaring he still favoured the Central line but supported the Coast line as the next best thing.

Seeking evidence of the Southampton & Dorchester's alleged losses, Snell's party had inspected the company's books. Their report, claiming to prove their case, published in *Herapath's Journal* on 5 November 1853, alleged that Coleman, Accountant to the Bank of England, and Fowell had examined the accounts and confirmed the losses. Coleman denied this and demanded that Snell should retract it. Scott promptly published this to the shareholders, calling on those misled to withdraw their proxies. He revealed that professional accountants conversant with railway matters had examined the books and would report on 15 November 1853.

A BROKEN PLEDGE

The meeting that day culminated weeks of vigorous correspondence, discussion, charges and countercharges, and the electrified atmosphere needed firm chairmanship. Instead, because the already excited proprietors were stirred to frenzy, the proceedings became the most discreditable in the company's history. The *Railway Times* held Scott responsible for being studiously insulting to the proprietors, aggravating in his conduct, and supercilious in his demeanour.

He said his pledge might be redeemed by building a single line from Dorchester to Cowley Bridge, two miles beyond Exeter, there joining the North Devon and Exeter & Crediton lines. The LSW had invested £160,000 in the latter, and this proposal would secure the benefit of traffic from forty-seven miles of line beyond Exeter.

The ensuing discussion was often in uproar. A proprietor aptly named Puncher, refusing to be put down, declared the Devon & Dorset would have done them no harm, whereas the proposed extension would never pay. The only part of the chairman's speech giving him consolation was his threat to resign, and he hoped he would quickly carry it into execution. He regarded the board as a nest of scorpions, and the sooner they got rid of them the better. Dickinson, who was also a GWR proprietor, claimed that the Wharncliffe Standing Order nullified the pledge, and if the chairman wanted to know how to evade it, he should tell Parliament that the captain was steering the ship on to a shoal of rocks and the crew mutinied and prevented him. This remark provoked great applause.

A poll was demanded on the report favouring the extension and an opposing amendment, and the meeting adjourned until 19 November 1853. The resumed proceedings were well-attended but even worse-conducted. Scott opened by calling for the accountants' report, which cleared the board of Snell's charges and confirmed a profit on the Corkscrew. Protesting shareholders demanded the result of the poll first, whereupon Scott abandoned the report and proceeded to a directors' resolution of that morning denying charges made on 15 November that Bircham, the solicitor, had influenced their proceedings. When Bircham tried to clear himself, loud cries of 'Poll! Poll!' amid general confusion prevented his being heard. Scott therefore announced the poll:

For the amendment		Against the amendment	
Proxies	12,089	Proxies	11,933
Personal	1,825	Personal	1,978
Total	13,914	Total	13,911

Majority for the amendment, 3.

Loud cheering broke out, then Scott, desperately trying to save the day, said the amendment having been carried he would put it as a substantive motion, but Snell's immediate protest prevented further voting. 'Very well,' said Scott, 'This concludes the business before the meeting.' Snell, Henderson and Gaselee forestalled this move, so Scott called on Bircham to defend himself, which immediately caused Gaselee to repeat the charges.

When Beattie (not an engineer) tried to speak on Henderson's motion that the weak and divided board be reconstructed, the meeting tried to drown him. Amid the confusion, a shareholder near Beattie apparently insulted him and both nearly came to blows. Beattie's appeal to Gaselee triggered off fresh disturbance, and Gaselee's and Scott's words were lost as both energetically tried to restore order. Eventually the tumult subsided, when Scott said:

> You are eminently qualified for the management of a great mercantile undertaking. It is useless for you to persist in trying whether by your noise and disorderly conduct you can prevent my enforcing the rules of order. If you think so, you may continue your

clamour, but I will maintain the rules of order, and will stay here till your lungs are exhausted.

A proprietor: 'I have never heard a chairman address a public meeting in that way.'

The chairman: 'And I never saw a public meeting so conducted.'

After Beattie had questioned the competency of the meeting to discuss Henderson's resolution, Scott dissolved the meeting, left the chair and, with other directors, departed. Gaselee promptly took the chair, declared the dissolution illegal and accepted Henderson's resolution, which was carried enthusiastically. Gaselee warned that the resolution might not be legal, but its moral effect would be great. Snell's motion for an adjournment until 7 December 1853 was carried.

The publicity following these events included a *Times* article of 22 November 1853 implying that the directors had interferred with votes to ensure authority for Scott's pledge. Criminal proceedings for libel followed, and William Harrison, the paper's printer and publisher, was found guilty by jury and fined £100. Sober reflection convinced many participants of the damage to the company's reputation and their investments, but when Snell suggested to the secretary that both sides try to reach agreement his olive branch was ignored.

The board itself was badly shaken. Scott, Hibbert, Mills, Seymer and Reed resigned, possibly after contemplating the consequences of breaking a pledge to Parliament, for the proprietors had been unmistakably warned:

> The directors court the fullest enquiry and investigation on all points; and, in conclusion, have only to add the expression of their opinion that if, after a well-considered pledge, a company be at liberty to repudiate a bargain the benefit of which it has obtained, and incur the odium of having misled Parliament and deceived the country, a suicidal act will have been committed and an example set which will go far to put an end to any trust being hereafter placed in public companies.

When the proprietors gathered on 7 December 1853, neither Scott nor his deputy attended and Gaselee presided. Recognising its restricted powers, the meeting dissolved and a shareholders meeting followed. It was told of a Brockenhurst to Lymington branch, promoted by Mr Hutchins M.P., which the LSW had arranged to subscribe to and work before the activities of Snell's committee had caused its withdrawal. The indignant meeting voted against further branches.

When Chaplin presided over the half-yearly meeting on 16 February 1854, his dignity restored reason to the proceedings. He confessed his unexpected return had been proposed by Gaselee and seconded by Mortimer. He asked proprietors not to tell new directors what line to follow at board meetings, but rather to give them their confidence and so add strength to the executive and officers, the latter recently having had nobody to whom they could take their difficulties.

Colonel Henderson and Mortimer retired on rotation making, with the resignations, seven seats to fill. Sir William Heathcote, M.P. for Oxford University, having been asked to select six from the list of candidates and to take the remaining seat and chair, had chosen Captain Mangles, the Hon R. H. Dutton, Colonels Henderson and Luard, and Messrs Hutchins and Mortimer. Despite this unusual procedure, the meeting elected them all. Sir William ended his short chairmanship on 6 April 1854 because of ill-health and Parliamentary duties, and Chaplin was re-elected that day by both old friends and enemies.

Meanwhile, the Central line promoters, whose patience with the LSW had been quite unrewarding, had formed the Salisbury & Yeovil Railway Company, alias, the Central Western Railway. Its prospectus of December 1853 said:

> The necessity to the district of a railway in the direction of the old coach road from Salisbury by Yeovil and Honiton to Exeter has been acutely felt from the time of the opening of the Great Western Railway, which robbed that part of the country of its ordinary means of communication, and supplied no accommodation instead of it.
> The propriety on general grounds of forming such a line has been proved again and again before committees of Parliament, at the instance of a local and independent company, in 1845 and 1846, and by the Great Western and London & South-Western Railway companies in 1847 and 1848. That the public have not been long since in possession of this great and needful accommodation is to be accounted for solely by the opposition of the Great Western, and the simulated friendship of the South-Western Company.
> It has at length become apparent that, whilst the former may no longer be feared, the latter cannot be longer trusted; and it has become the determination of the promoters of the present measure to seek from Parliament powers to carry out this great line of communication in perfect independence . . . asking, and they feel certain that they will obtain, the compulsory acquisition of those equitable rights and privileges against the South-Western Company which it was in vain attempted to secure from them by amicable arrangements in 1851 and 1852.

The immediate object was a Salisbury to Yeovil line, with

running powers over the LSW to London, Southampton and Portsmouth. An Exeter extension would follow, for the LSW repudiation of its pledge came too late to include it in the 1854 Bill.

The Bill was first imperilled on Standing Orders, through an irregularity in published notices. Fortunately, the examiner accepted the newspaper manager's explanation, and Standing Orders were dispensed with.

But worse was to come! When Chapman, deputy-chairman, and Townsend, the solicitor had urged Brassey to invest in the company, he had made three conditions, (1) the LSW should work the line for forty-five per cent of gross receipts, (2) the LSW should pay twenty-five per cent of receipts from traffic the S & Y brought to it, and (3) the LSW should run four through-trains daily each way. Of course, this smells of LSW connivance, but it precipitated negotiations between the two companies and Brassey guaranteed £125,000 of S & Y stock. On 22 June 1854, the Commons proceedings opened with an attack by the line's opponents (including the GWR, then seeking renewed powers to complete the WS & W) on the contract document. There followed the sorry spectacle of subscriber after subscriber, many of small means, being examined and admitting having signed the subscription list, sometimes for large sums, without paying deposits. Edward Nelson, employed by the LSW for 30s weekly, had signed for shares worth £500 and believed the deposit had been paid for him. It transpired that the true subscriber was Brassey, whom the *Railway Times* accused of breach of privilege and constructive perjury, and demanded he be summoned to the bar of the House.

The Commons committee said Standing Orders were meant to ensure the solvency of subscribers, and the examiner was not concerned with who paid deposits. Being satisfied this was not a bubble scheme, it therefore passed the Bill.

During negotiations in April and May 1854, the S & Y had refused the LSW offer not to oppose its Bill if the running powers clauses were withdrawn, yet though the S & Y eyed broad-gauge outlets (it sought powers to lay mixed gauge) the LSW held its obvious route to London. Agreement was bound to come eventually, but recent events suggested caution, and hearing that the LSW intended submitting any proposals to its shareholders instead of reaching a binding agreement immediately, the S & Y ended negotiation. However, the Commons committee had removed the running powers clauses and provided for the companies to make ten-year working agreements and, thus amended, the

Bill passed the Commons on 10 July 1854.

The LSW shareholders met on 22 July 1854 and Chaplin proposed that the amended Bill be approved. He thought the line would increase traffic at Salisbury, but Snell insisted it would be competitive and believed that the S & Y consisted of sham shareholders. His amendment demanded resistance against attempts to get running powers over the LSW.

This time commonsense prevailed. Castleman supported Chaplin, as did Mortimer, who asked the meeting to be as unanimous as the board. The S & Y being forced on them, they must accept it. His appeal to Snell to withdraw his amendment was supported by Gaselee and Puncher. Eventually Snell did so, receiving Chaplin's thanks and hearing Puncher recommend that his reward should be a directorship. On 10 August 1854, his opponent for Sir William Heathcote's vacancy was B. Willcox, a P & O director, but the voting caused such controversy that Snell's election was not confirmed until 31 May 1855.

The S & Y Bill, without LSW opposition, scraped past a time limit in the Lords and received Royal Assent on 7 August 1854, capital £400,000. The first board of nine included Sir William Medlycott, John Chapman, William Wyndham and Alfred Seymour. Seymour became chairman when Sir William declined; Robert Notman was secretary until his appointment on 8 May 1855 as manager, when Henry Wilkes Notman succeeded him as secretary.

Leaving Salisbury near the authorised terminus of the LSW extension from Basingstoke, the forty-mile single line would follow a switchback course, with summits at Semley, Milborne Port and at a 816-yd tunnel at Buckhorn Weston, ending near Pen Stile turnpike gate, Yeovil. A three-furlong branch would diverge from Bradford Abbas to join the WS & W near its junction with the Bristol and Exeter, though this was dropped in favour of the Joint station at Yeovil. The company's seal incorporated the arms of the Rt Hon Sidney Herbert.

East of the S & Y, the London & South-Western (Basingstoke and Salisbury) Act of 4 August 1853 required the portion to Andover to be completed within a year and the rest within three years, otherwise LSW dividends would be suspended. With Brassey as contractor, and good weather favouring work on deep cuttings and high embankments, the single line was finished and publicly opened to Andover on 3 July 1854. On 1 July, a special train from Waterloo took the company's officers and Brassey's friends to Andover to enjoy his renowned hospitality. Brassey continued work on the heavier section to Salisbury, for which another two years extension was given by the LSW Consolidation Act of 14 August 1855, and it opened to Milford station on 1 May 1857.

West of the S & Y, the LSW was not allowed to abandon its pledge over Exeter. The proprietors had never seriously heeded warnings of Parliament's retribution when it received the next LSW Bill, and when such Bill, seeking to re-organise capital, improve stations, etc, came before the Commons in February 1855, the LSW was reminded that the Exeter extension had been omitted. The Bill was referred to the same committee which had accepted Scott's pledge, and it resolved:

> That the committee conceive that the reference of the London & South-Western Railway Bill by the House of Commons to the same committee which sat on the Devon & Dorset Bill in the session of 1853 had special regard to the non-fulfilment of a pledge given to that committee, on the part of the London & South-Western Railway Company, and they regret to find that no provision is made in the Bill now submitted to them for the redemption of that pledge. The committee further desire to intimate to the London & South-Western Railway Company that, in the absence of any satisfactory proposal being made upon this point, they will, in the event of the present preamble being proved, insert a clause, binding the London & South-Western Railway Company to carry out fully the terms of that pledge, on pain of the company's dividends being stopped. And they further desire to intimate that if, from any cause, the present Bill should be abandoned in its course through Parliament, they will consider it their duty to bring the subject before the House, to be dealt with as the circumstances of the case may require.

Faced with this, the directors persuaded the committee to insert instead a clause giving the company the option of promoting an Exeter line in extension of either the S & Y or the Southampton & Dorchester in the 1856 session, when, if its genuine effort were defeated, it would have discharged its obligation. Failing application in 1856, it was to try in 1857, and if then unsuccessful through want of effort, ordinary dividends would be stopped until the passing of an Act or the grant of a Board of Trade dispensing certificate. Five years were allowed for completing the single line, with power to raise £1 m, and the Consolidation Act of 14 August 1855 contained these clauses.

Thus compelled, the directors re-examined both routes, for circumstances differed to earlier occasions. Firstly, the Andover line was open and would soon reach Salisbury; secondly, the S & Y would continue the narrow gauge to Yeovil; thirdly, Bridport, the only important place between Dorchester and Axminster, was again taken by a broad-gauge company, and lastly, the WS & W line to Dorchester and Weymouth would soon be finished. On 16 January 1856 a special meeting of shareholders heard all this, and that the Yeovil route would cost £600,000 compared with £700,000 for the longer and heavier coast line. There would be eight miles of 1 in 80 by the coast, or three on the Yeovil route. The coast line would have to compete for over half its distance, while the Yeovil route, uncomplicated by break of gauge, would be unopposed and give shorter distances to Exeter from London, Southampton and Portsmouth. The meeting therefore approved the Yeovil route and confirmed an agreement with the S & Y.

The Act for this Exeter extension was obtained on 21 July 1856, the authorised line being from the S & Y at Bradford Abbas to Queen Street, Exeter, with a junction near Bradford Abbas throwing a spur to the S & Y line nearer Yeovil to complete a triangle. The stage was now set for a complete narrow-gauge line from London to the west, running much of the way along the route of the old coaches.

The S & Y had watched these developments anxiously. It had had visions of being forced to seek Parliamentary release from its obligations if the LSW had chosen the coast line, but when that threat vanished it gladly reached the agreement mentioned. This required the S & Y line to be completed by 1 July 1859, when the LSW would work it at cost. The S & Y would take twenty-five per cent of LSW gross receipts on traffic which the S & Y brought to the LSW until the Exeter extension opened (provided it travelled ten miles on the S & Y and to or from within ten miles of London). The LSW could at any time take a 1,000 years lease, or purchase the S & Y within three years of its opening for £567,000, or its actual cost with four per cent interest, plus ten per cent bonus. The LSW would take 5,000 S & Y shares with normal dividend, subject to four per cent preference, unless they were previously disposed of. Two LSW directors could sit on the board, and Locke and Errington were to be S & Y engineers until its completion. Proprietors of both companies confirmed these arrangements.

The first S & Y turf was cut in a Gillingham field on 3 April 1856 by Miss Louisa Caroline Seymour, sister of H. Danby Seymour who had succeeded Alfred Seymour as chairman on 29 November 1855. Ruegg records that 'a solid silver spade, a handsomely-decorated barrow, and an elegant pair of gauntlets were presented to the lady'. His description of the scene defies improvement:

In keeping with the bitter elements of turbulent hostility which the Salisbury & Yeovil Railway undertaking had had to encounter, but at this time had seemed to have subdued, were the deluge of rain and the bitter blasts of wind which flung it into the faces of the people who were going to the town of Gillingham to be present at the ceremony of "turning the first sod". It seemed as though, human adversaries having done their worst to impede, Nature had now taken up the work of baffling and obstructing. That fickle Jade, the Weather, whirled sheets of water on our heads, blew garments into ribbons, and cast our speeches back into our teeth. And when the sodden field was left, and the party sought some protection from the bitter elements under a large marquee, Pluvius made his unwelcome way through the canvas, and, crowning insult of all! mingled our wine with water. These would have been trials enough to break the hearts of many men, but the promoters of the undertaking had had too much of the buffeting of adversity to be depressed now; and they simply raised the diluted champagne to their mouths with the quiet remark, "We have had so much cold water thrown upon us before that a bucket or two extra can make no difference now".

Speeches there were, among which that of Henry Ker-Seymer, M.P. for Dorset, summarised past hopes and disappointments.

We proved the case, but never got the line. We were unfortunate. Whenever we got a chance there was sure to be a commercial crisis. The Central line—potato failure! The Central line—money at seven and eight per cent! The Central line—funds at a very low level! The Central line—deficient harvest! The Central line—wheat at £20 a load.

One senses irony in Chaplin's expression of pleasure in attending the first movements of the offspring of the South Western—the child of the west. He toasted 'the landowners on the line'.

Leslie and Davidson successfully tendered £300,000 to construct the single line with bridges, etc, ready for doubling. By July 1856, over one hundred men and seven horses were working at Gillingham, but in November 1856 the contractors' continuing reluctance formally to sign the contract increased the board's regret that Brassey had refused to build the line. However, on 1 October 1857, Leslie and Davidson transferred their contract to him.

The navvies' wild habits prompted local clergy to seek an S & Y subscription towards providing them with a chaplain and scripture reader. Sympathetic, but powerless to divert railway funds, the directors refused, yet had no choice but to pay for additional constables provided by local authorities to quell the men's behaviour near Wilton and Buckhorn Weston.

At Salisbury, the corporation objected to the line from Basingstoke crossing Fisherton Street on the level, so powers to deviate and change levels were secured on 10 August 1857. A bridge would now take that line to an end-on junction with the S & Y, and the station would be west instead of east of Fisherton Street. The S & Y maintained its rights up to that street, against LSW attempts to limit it to 600 yd west and so secure absolute ownership of the station. The deviation created a sharp southward curve, partly to bring the narrow and broad-gauge stations ideally together for interchanging traffic, for on 30 June 1856 the GWR branch from Westbury reached its terminus, also west of Fisherton Street. But for the deviation, the S & Y would have come into Salisbury by mixed gauge on GWR property, but now it rejected a GWR offer to lay mixed gauge between Salisbury and Wilton, and built its line parallel to the broad gauge.

'This day the railway between Salisbury and Gillingham was opened for public traffic.' That S & Y minute of 2 May 1859 conveys none of the excitement of this long-awaited event. Decorated towns, celebrations, and distribution of beef, bread and beer to the sick marked the occasion. That day also, the Milford Junction to Fisherton Junction line opened and Milford closed to passengers, becoming henceforth the freight depot it still is. LSW trains from Basingstoke and Bishopstoke lines now went to the new Fisherton Street station, described by the *Salisbury & Winchester Journal* as having a glass-roofed platform nearly 800 ft long, then the longest in England. On 27 March 1858 at Milford station, the original and apparently wooden buildings, with refreshment rooms, Smith's bookstall and passenger shed (total length about 350 ft), had caught fire and been destroyed within an hour.

In July 1857, under a fresh agreement, the LSW consented to lease the S & Y for forty-two-and-a-half per cent of gross receipts, and to guarantee S & Y debentures up to £133,000. This Parliament approved in 1858, providing 'that within twenty years after the opening throughout for traffic of the Salisbury & Yeovil Railway, the South Western and the Salisbury & Yeovil companies shall commute the yearly rent payable under the lease into a fixed yearly payment'. When the S & Y back-pedalled over settling the terms of the lease, the LSW refused to seal the debentures. This caused embarrassment between the S & Y and its creditors, and forced it to settle the lease quickly in November 1858. It was separately agreed that, until the S & Y was opened throughout, the LSW would work and maintain the twenty-two miles between Salisbury and Gillingham for fifty per cent of gross receipts. A

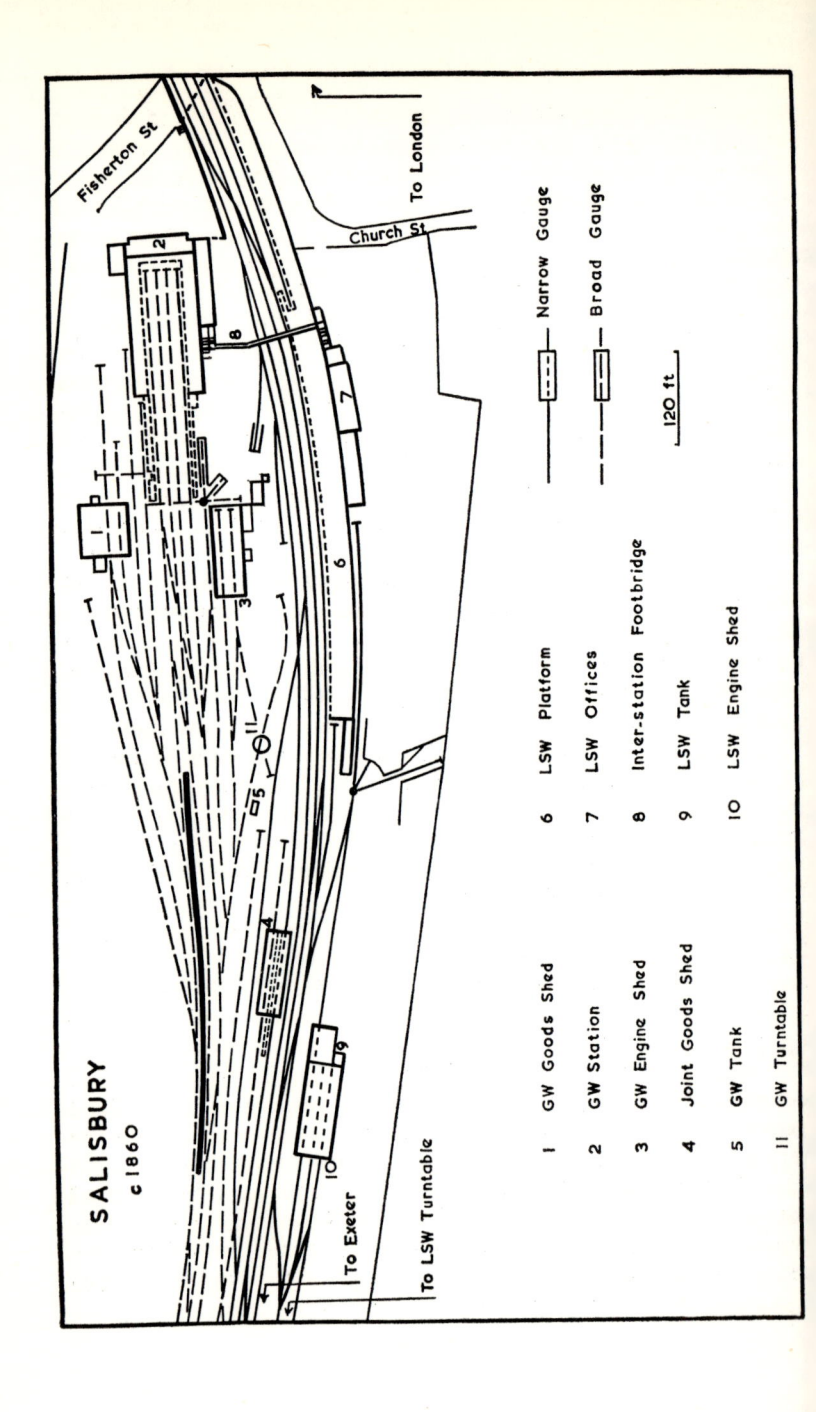

SALISBURY
c 1860

1	GW Goods Shed
2	GW Station
3	GW Engine Shed
4	Joint Goods Shed
5	GW Tank
6	LSW Platform
7	LSW Offices
8	Inter-station Footbridge
9	LSW Tank
10	LSW Engine Shed
11	GW Turntable

Narrow Gauge
Broad Gauge

120 ft

dispute arose when the LSW insisted that this superseded its obligation to pay the twenty-five per cent rebate it had undertaken in 1856 for traffic the S & Y brought to it. The S & Y was earning about £10 per mile per week, 'a rate satisfactory to the directors' but without the rebate it was only sufficient for the interest on the debentures, and the LSW four per cent preference dividend could not be met. Mr Buller, learned counsel, arbitrated and found for the S & Y. Thus the LSW paid the rebate and the S & Y admitted its liability for the preference dividend.

Beyond Gillingham, where heavy work remained, water from the greensand caused trouble in Buckhorn Weston tunnel. By July 1859, with additional shafts sunk to improve drainage, work was proceeding more satisfactorily and at twelve faces. Its official length today is 742 yd. The company had secured powers in 1857 to deviate at Sherborne, and the line reached there from Gillingham, 12¾ miles, on 7 May 1860, an event marked by a general holiday. The final portion to Yeovil, six miles, opened on 1 June 1860, and terminated at the B & E Hendford station until Yeovil Joint station opened on 1 June 1861.

In August 1858, the S & Y had begun negotiations with the B & E for the joint station without LSW knowledge. When the latter found out it protested, but swallowing its indignation it participated, and provisional agreement was reached in June 1859. It was to be on the B & E Durston branch near the town centre, with narrow gauge provided on to Hendford. The LSW board dallied over approving the plans, causing bitter S & Y complaints that non-completion of the station had seriously reduced its revenue. When opened, the new station was warmly welcomed. In Gothic style, it had a central waiting-room flanked by two ladies' rooms, on each side of which were booking-offices and houses for the respective stationmasters. Two platforms were spanned by roofs with longitudinal skylights containing about 15,000 sq ft of glass. All lines and sidings were mixed gauge.

Between Yeovil and Exeter, Taylor, the contractor, worked with 3,000 men, 600 horses and two locomotives on about 150 arches and bridges and 3,000,000 cu yd of earthworks, including 200,000 at Misterton embankment, Crewkerne. Tunnels at Crewkerne, 206 yd, and Black Boy, Exeter, 263 yd, gave little trouble, but that at Honiton, 1,345 yd through the ridge between the Otter and Axe valleys and aproached by a 1 in 80 incline, proved difficult. Work was slowed by water filtering through a vein of sand overlaying the marl.

On 18 July 1860, LSW directors left Waterloo at 8.0 am and were joined *en route* by S & Y colleagues. Just after noon, the special train of twenty carriages, hauled by the *Britannia, Montrose* and *Vulcan*, reached the station at Stoford (Yeovil Junction) and proceeded thence along the new line. Stopping at each gala-infected station, the directors received and answered congratulatory addresses from local dignitaries, often in pouring rain. At 3.0 pm the train reached Exeter, and the long, long bitter years of struggle were over.

The holiday at Exeter that day marked also the Exeter Fair and a total eclipse of the sun during the afternoon. The *Western Times* described the railway's welcome as modest. 'The shops were some shut and some open, flags were put out by some of the citizens, but the display was not general, nor was the feeling enthusiastic.' Sixteen years earlier, the B & E had entered Exeter in triumph, and now the narrow gauge was accepted 'somewhat in the spirit with which a widower bridegroom of fifty-five leads his second love to the altar'. Much to public chagrin, Northernhay was closed because a banquet was provided there presided over by the mayor, though many 'desirable guests' were absent, among them fervent B & E supporters. As rain seeped through the marquee canvas, congratulations were offered to the directors, and the Hon Ralph Dutton, who proposed the toast of 'prosperity to the city of Exeter', paid tribute to Chaplin, whose vision and courage had made possible the day he had not lived to see. Ill-health had forced him to resign the chair on 6 January 1859, and he died four months later. His successor as chairman was Captain Charles E. Mangles.

Locke, who recalled his sixteen years of persuasive struggle for this line, chided the directors for 'the cool way in which they came down for the praise when they did not make the line till they were forced'. This upset Gaselee and other directors, but Captain Mangles only laughed. Unhappily, Locke survived only until 18 September 1860, when he died at Moffat, Scotland, having burned himself out, like Brunel and other great contemporary engineers, with years of unbelievable energy to build his part of Britain's railway network, of which much still remains as their memorial.

Public services began on the Exeter line on 19 July 1860, with three trains each way daily; one to and from Yeovil, and two to and from Waterloo. The full passenger service began on 1 August 1860. On that day also goods services were advertised to start, but

Page from LSW public timetable, August 1860, covering many lines as well as giving the first full Exeter service

apparently did not so until September, probably the 1st. LSW timetables were then published for 1d monthly, and part of the Exeter service of four daily and two Sunday trains each way is here reproduced from the August 1860 issue. By covering the

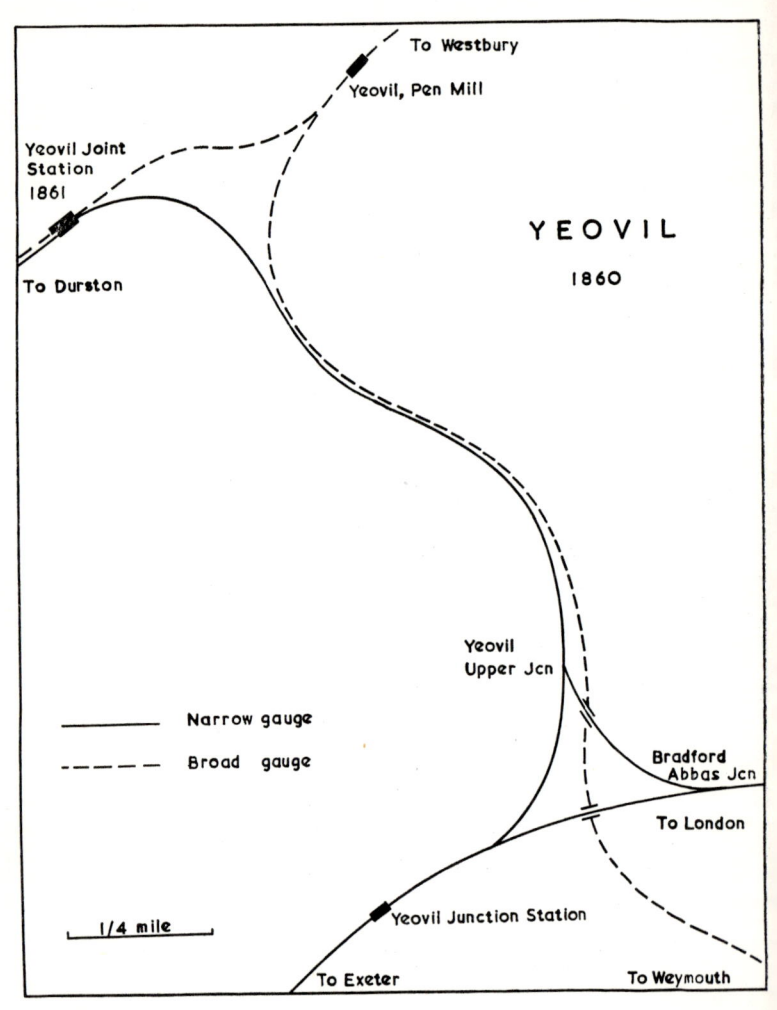

YEOVIL 1860

- To Westbury
- Yeovil, Pen Mill
- Yeovil Joint Station 1861
- To Durston
- Yeovil Upper Jcn
- Bradford Abbas Jcn
- To London
- Yeovil Junction Station
- To Exeter
- To Weymouth

Narrow gauge
Broad gauge

1/4 mile

171¾ miles in 310 min (reduced a year later to 305) the 9.0 am express from Waterloo averaged 33.2 mph including stops, over a route still largely single line. The GWR express was then leaving

THE STRUGGLE TOWARDS THE WEST 95

Paddington at 9.20 am and reaching Exeter at 2.25 pm, including ten minutes at Swindon and at Bristol. Its start to stop average for the 194 miles was 38.2, worse than 1845-9 when the journey was done in 4½ hr. Competition intensified in February 1862, when the LSW introduced a noon express from Waterloo, reaching Exeter in 4¾ hr. The GWR answered in March with the 'Flying Dutchman', departing Paddington at 11.45 am and arriving at Exeter at 4.15 pm, thus restoring, until 1865, the old timing.

The layout at Yeovil in 1860 is shown opposite, and the reproduction from the timetable for that August shows some trains, e.g., 7.30 am from Exeter, stopped at Yeovil Junction before running via the spur to the temporary station in Yeovil, then reversing to go direct to Sherborne via Yeovil Upper Junction and Bradford Abbas Junction. Others, like the 1.5 pm from Exeter, kept to the main line, being fed at Yeovil Junction by a local

TABLE 2
Doubling between Basingstoke and Exeter

			Second line opened
1. Basingstoke to Salisbury	to Worting	to Oakley	1 May 1862
	Oakley	,, Whitchurch	1 June 1866
	Whitchurch	,, Andover	2 December 1867
	Andover	,, Grateley	1 February 1870
	Grateley	,, Porton	1 July 1870
	Porton	,, Salisbury	1 June 1868
2. Salisbury to Yeovil	Salisbury	,, Wilton	2 September 1861
	Wilton	,, Tisbury	1 October 1863
	Tisbury	,, Semley	21 May 1865
	Semley	,, Gillingham	1 September 1866
	Gillingham	,, Templecombe	1 October 1867
	Templecombe	,, Sherborne	1 August 1866
	Sherborne	,, Bradford Abbas	1 August 1861
	Bradford Abbas	,, Yeovil Upper Junction	?
	Yeovil Junction	,, Yeovil Town	April or May 1864
3. Yeovil to Exeter	Bradford Abbas	,, Yeovil Jcn.	3 or 4 Aug. 1861
	Yeovil Junction	,, Sutton Bingham	1 August 1864
	Sutton Bingham	,, Crewkerne	1 June 1866
	Crewkerne	,, Chard Jcn.	1 February 1862
	Chard Junction	,, Axminster	1 October 1861
	Axminster	,, Honiton	*
	Honiton	,, Whimple	1 August 1861
	Whimple	,, Broad Clyst	22 March 1865
	Broad Clyst	,, Exeter	11 April 1864

*This section was ready on 19 July 1860 and may have been opened as a double line, although the Board of Trade letter of authority was dated 31 July 1860.

service. Incidentally, in May 1860, the B & E had objected to LSW engines using its shed and turntable at Hendford, making it necessary to move the Sherborne turntable temporarily to Yeovil for the opening of the line and until a permanent one could be erected there. Table 2 (p 95) shows the dates of doubling between Basingstoke and Exeter, as accurately as they can be established.

The line from Waterloo to Exeter, the 'backbone' of the London & South-Western, was unsatisfactory while a portion remained independently owned. In September 1859, S & Y financial difficulties had tempted the LSW to offer to take and complete that line, giving £66 13s 4d in LSW stock for each paid up £100 of S & Y stock. This was refused, as was an improved offer to guarantee a dividend three-quarters of that of the LSW. S & Y profits rose until, before it finally sold to the LSW in 1878, it was paying twelve-and-a-half per cent per annum. Truly, it was a remarkable railway!

A FEW BRANCHES

The S & Y attributed its success to non-encumbrance with branches, but the other lines dealt with in this chapter produced some, of which a few must now be considered. Firstly, Salisbury citizens, being anxious for their ancient market, sought improved accommodation before local farmers diverted products by rail to other centres. On 14 July 1856, an Act incorporated the Salisbury Railway & Market House Company, with powers to build a short branch from a new Market House to the Basingstoke and Salisbury line. With the gradient increased by elimination of Fisherton Street level-crossing, its construction was undertaken by the LSW, which consented to work it for ten years at an annual rent of £160. The agreement was delayed by the market company demanding also a broad-gauge line to connect with the GWR, but without it trade improved so much that an Act was secured in 1864 for further capital to increase facilities.

On 3 July 1846, the Exeter & Exmouth Company got powers to build from Exeter through Heavitree and Topsham to Exmouth, provided the EY & D Bill succeeded in 1846-7, to which company it could sell. On 22 July 1847, the E & E was authorised to shorten its line by using the EY & D between Heavitree and Queen Street, and lease or sell to the LSW. These powers expired, but with an Act of 2 July 1855 the revived E & E intended going ten-and-a-half miles broad gauge from Exmouth to the South Devon line at

BODMIN & WADEBRIDGE—4

(13) Train of carriages, showing the open third, the severe second class, and the first and second composite. (Is the latter an old L & S coach?)

(14) End of the line at Wenford Bridge in September 1952, where in 1966 china clay is still loaded. The 2—4—0T locomotive dates from the W. G. Beattie era, 1874

STATIONS—4

(15) *Crediton station in 1966, looking east*

Exeter, plus a branch to Exeter canal. On 1 August 1857, the directors jubilantly reported having agreed with the B & E and South Devon companies to lease the line, except the branch, for ten years at £3,000 annually, plus four per cent on capital expenditure on stations and twenty per cent of gross annual receipts exceeding £6,000. Instead of applauding, the proprietors appointed a committee, whose report encouraged their decisive rejection of the agreement. Of course, they watched the approaching and geographically more convenient LSW narrow-gauge line to Exeter and, ordering a start on earthworks between Exmouth and Topsham, they began a courtship with Waterloo.

The negotiations proved mutually fruitful. The LSW would make a branch from Heavitree to Topsham and the E & E would extend it on narrow gauge to Exmouth, the companies obtaining their respective powers on 12 July 1858 and 28 June 1858.

The girders of the viaduct over the river Clyst, the most important work, were severely tested during Colonel Yolland's inspection on 20 April 1861, but deflection was slight. The line opened throughout on 1 May 1861, worked by the LSW for half the gross receipts, the remainder being shared according to mileage. The LSW used earth from the cuttings to construct its new quay alongside the existing one it acquired at the deep-water port of Topsham.

On 16 July 1846, the Chard Canal Company got powers to convert part of its property into a railway from Creech St Michael on the B & E to Ilminster, and in 1847 to extend it to Chard. The EY & D Chard branch was authorised in 1848 subject to agreement with the Chard company, but both companies' powers lapsed.

Interest revived in 1859 when the bypassing of Chard by the LSW Exeter Extension resolved its citizens into promoting the independent Chard Railway, if only to protect their lace and cloth industries. Its Act of 25 May 1860, capital £25,000, for a three-mile line to Chard from the extension at Chard Road (later Chard Junction) included a horse-operated freight tramroad to the canal basin. Built by Taylor, the line opened on 8 May 1863. In December 1859, Loveridge, its chairman, had hinted of extension to Taunton, and the LSW, anxious to prevent another broad-gauge tributary, quickly negotiated to purchase the line. Agreement was reached in April 1861, but its independent existence did not completely cease until 1 January 1863, as provided retrospectively by the Act of 22 June 1863 which authorised the amalgamation.

Broad-gauge interests, not to be outdone, had revived the line from Creech St Michael through Ilminster, this time alongside the canal. This Chard & Taunton Railway got its Act on 6 August 1861, but difficulties in raising capital forced it to sell to the B & E in 1863. The line opened unceremoniously on 11 September 1866 to a joint station at Chard, which LSW trains reached by using the tramroad route, though alterations were necessary before passenger trains began running on 26 November 1866. LSW timetables for December 1866 were the first showing the joint station (New Chard or Chard N.S.), where the gauges met without mingling, each retaining its staff and signal-box. The LSW continued using Chard (or Chard Town) also. The last traffic passed along the canal, bought by the B & E, on 29 September 1866, and it was quickly closed.

An independent Lymington Company led by Mr Hutchins, M.P., was deflected from the 1854 session by the activities of Snell (see page 82), but on 7 July 1856 they got powers, capital £21,000, to go from the LSW at Brockenhurst to Lymington Town Quay which, with Lymington bridge, they could purchase. The four-mile single line, worked by the LSW, opened on 12 July 1858 when a train carrying directors and contractors left Lymington at 7.15 am, returning just after 8.0 am. The *Lymington Chronicle* voiced local anger with the railway for not arranging the public celebration it had promised. There was not even, it said, a balloon ascent. Services began with six trains daily each way, and three on Sundays, connecting with main-line trains.

In 1857 the Lymington Company could not interest the LSW in steamships from there to the Isle of Wight, perhaps because of that Company's agreement with the LBSC not to compete with ships. When the line opened, the Solent Steam Packet Company's *Red Lion* made four return sailings to Yarmouth each weekday, connecting with trains. The *Solent* ran to Yarmouth, Cowes and back on Mondays and Thursdays, and additionally to Ryde and Portsmouth on other weekdays.

Another Act, of 21 July 1859, authorised the purchase of the river ferry to Boldre, the toll being one halfpenny per person or article. It also empowered the company to charge tolls on Lymington bridge, though mentioning the absence of authority for those charged by its previous owners for many years. Royal carriages, mail coaches, and servicemen and police on duty were exempt. The jetty authorised by the 1856 Act probably opened on 1 June 1861, the day the *Red Lion* began using it.

However, more of this line in volume 2.

CHAPTER 4

West of Exeter

CORNWALL SEEKS A RAILWAY

West Cornishmen, alarmed at Falmouth's decline now that steamships using less remote ports had displaced the long jogtrot to and from London, determined to restore its 150 years supremacy by promoting their own railway. Besides the port, the south-west peninsula promised useful traffic, including tin, copper and china clay, though railway-making across the wild moors, deep valleys and rivers would be difficult and costly.

A survey in 1836 came to nothing; then a meeting at Bodmin on 2 October 1839, supported by the Earl of Falmouth, resolved to build a line from Falmouth to Exeter or Plymouth. When, in March 1844, the committee chose the southern route, the subscribers, not being consulted, became bitterly divided, while the local press screamed charges of breach of faith. The committee intended to join the prospective South Devon Railway at Plymouth, build to the same broad gauge, possibly use atmospheric traction, and so woo GWR support.

The Exeter, or central line supporters, however, were convinced that the southern line would benefit Plymouth without restoring Falmouth's glory, and be geographically less suited to serve the peninsula generally. They therefore sought and secured LSW co-operation and its promise to take shares worth £250,000, provided Cornishmen strongly supported the central line. So that when, in October 1844, the prospectus of the broad-gauge 'Cornish Railway from Plymouth to Falmouth' appeared, it was challenged by that of the 'Cornwall & Devon Central Railway, a ninety-eight-mile narrow-gauge and locomotive-worked double line from Falmouth through Truro, Bodmin, Launceston, Okehampton and Crediton, to join the proposed narrow-gauge extension from Salisbury at Exeter. It would save fifty miles to London over its rival.

Unfortunately, although really preferring it, the 'Five Kings' rejected the central line in favour of the southern, or coast line, because the South Devon from Exeter was already authorised and traffic did not justify two lines from that city. This announcement on 31 December 1844 discouraged central-line subscribers from paying deposits, so killing an application in the coming session. Pleading lack of Cornish support, the LSW withdrew and escaped difficulty in keeping its bargain of 16 January 1845 with the GWR not to go beyond Salisbury.

A Lords committee on 19 July 1845 refused the broad-gauge line because the ruling gradient of 1 in 60 was too severe, an opinion Dalhousie's board had shared. Some steeper inclines were suspected to be worse than actually shown and curves were sharp. Locke called it 'the most dangerous line I ever saw', and considered speeds of 20 to 30 mph would have been dangerous. An impracticable steam bridge would have crossed the Hamoaze at Plymouth. No wonder Brunel was called in to remedy Moorson's surveys.

Narrow-gauge spirits were doubtless high at the Bodmin meeting on 28 August 1845 when a new and grandiose 'Cornwall & Devon Central Railway' was launched, care being taken to disown connection with its predecessor. The new company's first step was its agreement with the LS & Y, EY & D and LSW, in preparation for amalgamation after each had secured individual powers (see page 69), to form a united narrow-gauge line from London to Penzance. It also secured the Bodmin & Wadebridge Railway unconditionally for £35,000, forestalling the Cornwall Railway's efforts to negotiate a conditional purchase.

The 1845 prospectus for this £3,000,000 scheme also included branches to Plymouth, Tavistock, Bideford, Barnstaple, St Austell and St Ives, but the Bill failed Standing Orders in the 1846 session. Incidentally, a Padstow branch via the Bodmin & Wadebridge had been omitted because surveys were incomplete. The renewed Cornwall Railway application succeeded on 3 August 1846, its branches including one to Bodmin, but narrow-gauge opposition kept it from Launceston and forced a clause compelling the laying of narrow gauge west of Truro if required. A South Devon project from Plymouth to Tavistock was also defeated.

With Cornish support now wavering, the LSW decided on a solo attempt to secure a central line, and purchased the Bodmin & Wadebridge from the C & DC for the £35,000 the latter had paid for it. On 17 November 1846 LSW proprietors heard:

> Your directors, therefore, propose that the entire lines west of Exeter should be undertaken directly by this proprietary. The whole have been most carefully revised in number and detail; and the directors have much satisfaction in knowing that the central line to

Truro has been considerably shortened, the works much reduced, and the gradients improved, so as to contrast triumphantly in security, inclinations and distance, with the coast line.

The revised scheme included St Austell, St Columb, Padstow and Crediton branches. A line through Tavistock to Plymouth and Sutton Pool Harbour would, with an Okehampton to Chulmleigh branch joining the Taw Vale line, complete the link between Plymouth and Barnstaple.

LSW PAWNS IN DEVON AND CORNWALL

Now we must make proper acquaintance with three companies important to our coming story.

The Bodmin & Wadebridge Railway, built for carrying ore mined near Wenford into Wadebridge for shipment, followed abortive attempts to link the Bristol and English Channels with a Padstow to Fowey canal. Its Act of 23 May 1832 authorised a Wadebridge to Wenford Bridge line and a Bodmin branch, plus two branches across the River Camel as railways or 'common roads' to Ruthern Bridge and Nanstallon. In 1833, by local preference, a railway was chosen for Ruthern Bridge.

Construction began rapidly under Hopkins, the engineer, until bad luck arrived to remain this little railway's constant companion. Mr Parke of Bilston had contracted to supply 900 tons of rails and thirty-six tons of pins and wedges, almost the total requirement. He was killed when only a small quantity had been delivered, and his successors witheld the balance until the company agreed a higher price, so adding £1,000 to construction costs and causing loss of revenue by delaying the opening.

Severe gradients made for difficult working. Leaving Wadebridge, the twelve-mile single line, following the Camel valley, went easily for five miles before climbing at times 1 in 144; but the Bodmin branch, one and three-quarter miles, was 1 in 51 and 1 in 46 at its end. The Ruthern Bridge branch, one mile, was 1 in 158.

The track consisted of 15-ft lengths of 42-lb rail, having 2¼-in tops and 3½ in depth, on 10½-lb chairs secured to 20-in square granite blocks about 12in deep. At the scarfed joints chairs were 12 lb and blocks sometimes 6 ft long to embrace both rails and keep the 4ft 8½ in gauge.

The first locomotive, the *Camel*, was built by Price of Neath Abbey Iron Works and ordered when, following differences among the board, Dr Harry, a director, had examined engines working in South Wales. She is described in Table 3. The *Camel* could haul nine wagons containing fifty tons to Dunmere and take them thence to Bodmin in three trips. She was forbidden to exceed 6 mph ascending and 8 mph descending, which was increased in 1841 to 9 and 12 mph respectively. The engine-house and workshop were at Wadebridge.

The earliest trips are recorded in the day-book:—

	1834	Sand Rec'd	Sand Sent	Mud Sent	Goods Sent
4 July	The engine was tried first time				
15 July	Second trial of the engine	60			
29 July	Third trial ,, ,,				
6 Aug.	First trip to Ruthern, two wagons		5½	5	
	(etc, etc.)				
Total carried and received from the commencement to 25 September 1834		1296	1134½	268½	3
	(etc, etc.)				

2¼ of lime
= 1408¼ tons.

September 1834
Thursday, 30th. According to notice,
the road was this day publicly opened.

The 4 July 1834 entry was only a locomotive trial from Wadebridge towards Bodmin for about four miles and back. The second trip on Wednesday, 16 July, (the day-book said 15 July apparently in error) was marred by the locomotive coming off at a displaced rail, throwing passengers from a 'carriage'. Most seriously injured were two girls, one being dragged along when her clothes became entangled in the wheels.

On 20 August 1834, the *Camel* first tried the Bodmin branch, with six wagons of sand and about forty passengers, approximately 36½ gross tons, and on 15 September, 150 inhabitants of Wadebridge were treated to a return trip to Bodmin, one open wagon containing a band playing 'favourite airs'.

At the public opening on 30 September 1834, 300 ticket-holders travelled in seventeen decorated wagons and the *Omnibus* hauled by the *Camel*, which also propelled a wagon of workmen. The Royal Cornwall Militia band occupied one wagon, while Hopkins, Thomas Woolcombe, the clerk, and other notables were prominently placed. Leaving Wadebridge at noon, the train reached Wenford Bridge, then returned to Dunmere before climbing the branch to Bodmin, arriving there at 5.0 pm. **Twenty** constables, sworn-in to keep order, rode one in each vehicle.

The company received sand from local sea dredgings, stored it at Wadebridge and conveyed it inland as required for use as fertiliser. By March 1836 it supplied 475 customers. Starting work with only two wagons built in Wales meant constant and expensive idleness of locomotive and labour. Subsequent wagons were made at Wadebridge, and when by February 1835 two trains were ready, the *Camel* was giving trouble. The day-book records on 18 February:

> The engine leaking so much and the plate being cracked, it became absolutely necessary to leave part of the train at the junction and return. Gave up attempting to work the engine and proceeded to take it to pieces, by order of the directors.

Horses then worked the line until 21 April 1835, costing 1½d per ton-mile compared with engine costs of ⅞d before repairs and ⅝d after. When in service, the *Camel* was usually idle on Mondays for cleaning.

The day-book records another event on 14 June 1836:—

> The *Elephant* with *Omnibus* cab and seventeen wagons proceeded over the whole line with passengers. The *Camel* followed the *Elephant* with fourteen wagons, supposed to have taken 800 persons. Received on account of passengers (see passenger-book) £35 1s 0d at 1s .... No accident occurred during the day.

This excursion celebrated the arrival of the second locomotive, the *Elephant*, and both are described in Table 3. A more powerful version of the *Camel*, she was unreliable in relieving that hard-pressed engine. She worked first on 6 June, but before 1836 was out she had retired with boiler defects. The manufacturers righted her following lengthy correspondence, but May 1839 saw her back at Neath for repairs.

In 1853, the LSW engine *Atlas* was transferred to the B & W for £525 12s 6d, as the 'engine in use' could not handle the developing granite traffic. It seems that the *Camel* and *Elephant* then retired, though the LSW locomotive committee recommended that one be kept ready lest the *Atlas* failed. The B & W vainly appealed in May 1854 for 'a light engine and a more convenient passenger carriage', and in November it reminded the LSW that if the 'one engine on the road' was disabled, traffic would almost entirely cease. Thus the LSW engine *Pluto* joined B & W strength for £400.

The line had opened with one passenger vehicle (other than wagons), the *Omnibus*, having seats inside and out. Fares were

TABLE 3

	'Camel'	'Elephant'	Remarks
Cost	?	* £820	£40 allowed for *Camel* defects, leaving £780 net
Cylinders (perpendicular)			
Diameter	10½ in	* 12½ in	Parallel motion in the *Camel*; worked by bow rods and bell-cranks in the *Elephant*
Stroke	24 in	* 24 in	
Wheels, diameter	3 ft 10 in	3 ft 10 in	Six-coupled in both
Boiler			
Length	?	* 12 ft	50-lb working pressure in both
Diameter	?	* 4 ft 6 in	
Tubes	* Horizontal fire tubes	* Vertical water tubes, copper, 2½ in dia, 18 in to 20 in long, ⅛ in thick	
Weight	12¼ tons	14½ tons	
Chimney height	7 ft 10 in	9 ft 4 in	
Chimney diam.	?	* 13 in	
Safety valves	* 2	* 2	One controlled by the driver
Water capacity of tender	370 gallons	370 gallons	

* These details are from the agreed specification for the *Elephant*. It also said:

  (a) Cylinder exit pipes to pass through two feed water heaters, being 'so continued that the steam be thrown into the reservoir, so as to prevent the puff, at the option of the engineer,'
  (b) Two feed pumps to be stronger than in the *Camel*. Springs to be stronger by two leaves.
  (c) Slide valves to work by cranks, to which the motion shall be given by tooth wheels underneath the engine.
  (d) Plates 'at the smoke end' to be ⅜ in. Door to have four hinges and five handles.
  (e) Fire bar sleepers to have cooling holes.
  (f) Platform at both ends of engine to be larger, thicker (than that on the *Camel*) and bracketed, with a 2 ft 6 in-high rail at the sides at the fire end.

Exterior dimensions are not available, but the *Elephant* was not to exceed the *Camel*.

1s inside and 8d outside, plus half if returning the same day. Free luggage allowance was 28 lb. By November 1841, when another vehicle, the *Albion*, had arrived, mileage fares introduced were 1½d by the *Omnibus*, minimum 5d, or 1d in other vehicles, minimum 3d, plus half for return trips exceeding three miles. Daily hire of the *Omnibus* cost 21s, and 30s for the *Albion*. Fares were paid to the conductor on entering the carriage, but late passengers would pursue and leap on moving trains, an unwise practice as some found, but understandable when we hear that, for many years, the one train left Wadebridge on Mondays, Wednesdays and Fridays, returning from Bodmin on other weekdays. One person could travel free with goods paying a toll exceeding 3s.

Beattie having said that he had a suitable composite vehicle, the LSW locomotive committee instructed him on 1 March 1855 to ship two carriages with the *Pluto*. Before seeking the significance of that, we must examine B & W carriages preserved by the LSW in 1896 and said to date from 1834. The writer recalls, as a small boy, gazing awesomely at one of these, a closed carriage on a pedestal on Waterloo concourse, where for many years it was publicly exhibited. A composite first and second class, it had in service been painted blue with upper parts white and a red underframe. Its compartments, 4 ft 6 in long, 5 ft 9 in high and 6 ft wide, were upholstered in blue cloth stuffed with hay. The first-class compartment had corner arm rests, while upholstery in the two seconds was only shoulder high. A severe second-class coach, 10 ft long on a 6 ft 4 in wheelbase and having no quarter lights, seated sixteen in semi-darkness. A third-class open blue carriage also took sixteen, or four on each seat. It had solid wooden buffers, while the composite had leather enclosing a material, probably hay.

An article in the *Railway World*, February 1896, called these interesting but unexceptional specimens, equal to those used by much more important lines in the eighteen thirties. If they include either of the two coaches sent by Beattie, they are more than B & W curiosities: they may well contain an important example of the earliest London & Southampton main-line vehicles.

Horse haulage on the B & W was forbidden, except for repairs, but in hard times when available traffic did not justify raising steam, traders were permitted to haul the company's trucks of coal, sand, etc, with their own horses to private sidings. In July 1835, with the *Camel* so hard-pressed, horses were put to work on the Ruthern Bridge branch and the *Omnibus* was adapted for them, its capacity being limited to forty-eight persons.

Financially, the line was a failure. Its Act authorised £22,500 capital, £6,000 of it being either shares or loans, plus £8,000 borrowing powers. Three proprietors loaned the £6,000 in October 1833, but on 29 September 1834, the eve of public opening, the railway and all its property was mortgaged for £8,000 in Exchequer bills, repayable at £400 annually plus five per cent interest. An Act (1 & 2 *Will IV, cap* 24) authorised such loans for 'carrying on public works and fisheries and employment of the poor'. A B & W amendment Act of 30 July 1835 increased borrowing powers by £5,000, yet by that November subscribed capital was only £16,000.

Operating difficulties increased costs and depressed revenue. To extinguish mounting debts, shareholders were asked to take one new share for each two held, but by January 1837, when not one had been taken, a call of £2 10s per share was made, with forfeiture in default.

Prospects in 1837 improved as demand for sand increased, 20,622 tons being carried that year, besides other traffics; yet the working profit of £604 1s 5d was quite inadequate to restore prosperity. Increasing iron ore and china clay traffics would have helped had not floods in November 1838 expensively damaged bridges and culverts, and the failure of the *Elephant* following added loss of revenue to the repair bill.

In November 1843, with revenue falling, the board dismissed staff. Still the decline continued, so in May 1844, when establishment stood at the lowest consistent with safe working, pay was reduced, the company promising to give gratuities when net income exceeded £1,000, until permanent increases could be restored. Here are some examples of annual earnings:

		Present rate			Future rate		
		£	s	d	£	s	d
Mr Pethybridge	Treasurer	10	0	0	2	2	0
Mr Dunston	Superintendent	130	0	0	120	0	0
Mr Jordan	Engineer	104	0	0	94	0	0
M. Rosewear	Engine driver	54	12	0	44	12	0
Joseph Hicks	Conductor and Guard	31	4	0	26	0	0
James Lobb	Labourer	31	4	0	26	0	0
Thos Lobb	Fireman	33	16	0	26	0	0

This was the quaint, picturesque liability the LSW acquired, and to whose board it sent Chaplin, Henderson and other LSW directors.

Second in the trio was the Exeter & Crediton Railway, whose initial Act of 23 June 1832, capital £35,000, authorised a line from the Exeter canal basin at St Thomas through Newton Saint Cyres to Four Mills, Crediton, the gauge being not less than 4 ft 6in. Powers expired after three years, so on 20 March 1844, with the Bristol & Exeter knocking outside Exeter, a meeting launching the scheme afresh was held, presided over by J. W. Buller, with a B & E deputation attending. Though following a similar route, the line's eastern end would now join the B & E near Cowley Bridge, linking Exeter with Crediton, north and north-west Devon and north-east Cornwall.

The promoters' sympathies with the broad-gauge B & E precipitated negotiations during 1844, and a provisional agreement was reached on 13 December for that company to lease the line for £3,000 annually, plus one-third of gross profits exceeding £7,000. Optimism trembled on 31 December when the E & C was among those lines the 'Five Kings' recommended to be postponed. Petitions were considered, but realising that the recommendation was not a veto, the shareholders decided on 18 March 1845 to proceed with the Bill and approved steps for confirming the agreement.

The Act succeeded on 21 July 1845, capital £70,000, including powers for the junction with the B & E, and for lease or sale to that or any other company forming a junction with the E & C.

Procrastination followed, the lease being still unsettled when, on 5 December 1846, the shareholders favoured amalgamation and instructed the directors to negotiate. Accordingly, a deputation visited Bristol, returning with a B & E share-for-share offer, plus £2 10s 0d for each E & C £25 paid-up. When the E & C proprietors were asked on 11 January 1847 to authorise sealing of the lease immediately B & E proprietors had approved the amalgamation terms, a lively opposition erupted, led by Mr Thorn of Barnstaple, a Taw Vale Railway director. Staunch E & C proprietors were aware their shares had lately rocketed in value and shareholders had increased from 100 to 280 in a week. Now seeing the Taw Vale Railway & Dock Company chairman among them, they inevitably and correctly suspected an attempted takeover. A poll was demanded, and the lease was rejected by 1,542 to 561.

The Taw Vale is our third company, whose Act of 11 June 1838, capital £15,000, authorised a scheme for good harbour facilities at Fremington with ready access to the Bristol Channel, instead of the difficult and dangerous navigation of the River Taw. The railway, reaching Barnstaple Bridge from Fremington, was specifically authorised to carry passengers. On 21 July 1845 extensions to quays at Fremington were authorised, and construction powers for the railway extended to 11 July 1850.

To extend from Barnstaple to Crediton, a separate Taw Vale Railway Extension & Dock Company was launched in September 1845, and arrangements concluded for its purchase, on incorporation, of the original company for £15,000, that line being as yet unstarted. The first turf was cut by Thorn on Pentole-Marsh on 5 January 1846.

In the 1846 session, this extension Bill was threatened with opposition from the formidable North Devon Railway, a GWR, B & E and South Devon joint promotion having Earl Fortescue (chairman), Lords Clinton, Poltimore and Palmerston, also chairmen and directors of the sponsors on an enormous, influential committee. It intended linking Bideford and Barnstaple with the B & E at Tiverton, plus a branch from near South Molton towards Taunton. Another line was to go from Bideford to Hatherleigh and then fork for Plymouth and for Exeter via Crediton.

The TV extension surmounted Standing Orders undaunted by its impressive adversary which, itself failing that obstacle, determined on 18 May vigorously to oppose the TV in committee. The B & E promised to help quench this opposition and agreed provisionally on 26 May to take the TV for four per cent of subscribed capital during six months after opening, and thereafter at rates approximately five per cent below B & E dividends. Some B & E directors, led by Earl Fortescue and being devoted to the North Devon, caused opposition to continue until, when North Devon dissolution seemed imminent, an understanding was reached that the TV would adopt the broad gauge. However, it was too late for a confirming clause in the Bill, which succeeded on 7 August 1846, capital £533,000. The thirty-one mile single line, straight through Bishops Tawton to Chapelton, would wind along the Taw Valley, past Eggesford, home of Lord Portsmouth. Before Lapford, the Yeo, with its narrower, steeper, well-wooded valley would succeed, before itself diverging and leaving the railway to continue to the E & C. The line, frequently crossing both rivers, would satisfy anyone seeking picturesque north Devon.

The gauge war had caused a Royal Commission, appointed on 9 July 1845, to examine the desirability of a uniform gauge. Following its report against the broad gauge, which was influenced largely by the greater narrow-gauge mileage existing, the Gauge Act was passed on 18 August 1846, requiring future railway construction in Great Britain to be 4 ft 8½ in, except that 'any railway constructed or to be constructed under the provisions of any present or future Act containing any special enactment defining the gauge or gauges of such railway or any part thereof' was excepted; a nullifying provision if ever there was. The TV extension Act succeeding during the incubation of the Gauge Act, its gauge was prescribed as that which the Board of Trade approved.

When two TV directors signed for their company another agreement on 5 September 1846, the B & E imposed such conditions that it stank in the nostrils of the TV board. One particularly objectionable extortion was the restriction of certain stock issues until B & E dividends reached ten per cent. On 18 September Emmanuel Cooper, TV chairman, and his board, angered by B & E sharp practice and disturbed by the South Devon atmospheric fiasco, took the renegade step in the gauge war of offering their line to the LSW, whose close interest in TV fortunes had included urging the Board of Trade, within days of the Gauge Act passing, to decide the gauge, a matter vitally affecting LSW schemes in the peninsula. Now events played into LSW hands. Was the TV free to negotiate, it asked? Yes, replied the TV deputation, reading its board's resolution of 9 September rejecting the B & E agreement. However, that decision was not confirmed by TV proprietors until 26 September.

The upshot was a 1,000-year agreement in December 1846 for LSW lease of the TV, including branches to Bideford and South Molton which the latter was promoting in the next session. The LSW would nominate three of the twelve directors, subscribe a quarter of the capital and pay rent of five per cent on the amount paid up, plus a further 10s per cent if five-and-a-half per cent net was earned, and half the profit exceeding this. With Locke as engineer, the TV would lay narrow gauge, the LSW supplying locomotives and rolling stock. TV proprietors approved this on 18 January 1847; the LSW on 26 February.

The LSW intention was primarily to control the E & C, and secondly to develop a narrow-gauge link between the north and south Devon coasts, usurping sea-borne traffic round the peninsula. The Dartmoor barrier meant the LSW natural route to Falmouth running parallel to or along the E & C. That company's devotion to the B & E ruled out a direct approach, but its Act, we saw, authorised its lease to any other company joining it, such as the TV! On 4 December 1846, the LSW board authorised Locke to lease or purchase the E & C in conjunction with the TV.

Following its victory at the E & C meeting on 11 January 1847, the TV openly offered to lease the E & C on terms resembling its own to the LSW. Buller chaired the E & C meeting on 17 February when Thorne's supporting motion succeeded by 1,681 to 730 on a poll he demanded after defeat on a show of hands. The readiness of the broad-gauge E & C for opening meant nothing to the TV invaders, even when nearly 1,000 Crediton inhabitants, pleading for it, pointed out that the Act had been passed in the public interest. Their grip on the victim tightened when three of them, Cooper, Thorne and Woolmer, were elected to its board on 24 February.

Buller's interests with the B & E increased with his election on 11 March 1847 as director, and as chairman in succession to James Gibb. Two weeks later that company wrote, holding the E & C to its agreement and demanding that it complete at least a temporary junction, which the E & C board resolved to do, despite Thorne's and Woolmer's opposition. However, when Buller, as E & C chairman, and supporters sealed a contract on 7 April 1847 for Geo Hennett to work the line, they triggered off their final overthrow.

Thorne and numerous supporters immediately requisitioned an extraordinary general meeting, where on 12 April 1847 he moved that the board be reduced to six and that Buller, with three other B & E directors, be dismissed. Buller ruled this resolution illegal but allowed Thorne to speak. The latter mercilessly attacked the unhappy four, challenged a B & E statement that its lease of the E & C was signed by both boards, and finally put his motion amid loud cheering and a forest of supporting hands. None showed dissent, his opponents regarding the voting as invalid.

Thorne's declaration that the resolution was carried unleashed pandemonium, amid which one furious gentleman, shouting 'I protest, sir,' stood shaking his fist in impotent rage, while Buller pretended to ignore the resolution and called for other business. Mr Wilkinson now discredited his chairmanship and proposed Thorne to replace him. During further uproar, Buller 'dissolved' the meeting, and while leaving with his fellow B & E directors one of them grasped the minute book, only to be restrained by Thorne. A scuffle followed; the book fell to the floor; the secretary grabbed it, dodged, and whisked away, neatly covered by the departing directors.

The meeting then approved the lease to the TV, already sealed by the latter and the LSW. Cooper and Thorne sought the fugitives to demand the E & C seal from Buller, but as they were unsuccessful the meeting dispersed after resolving against the line opening on broad gauge or completing Cowley Bridge junction.

The deposed directors, denying defeat, continued attending board meetings, so Thorne, Cooper and Woolmer for the E & C commenced proceedings, to prevent their acting as directors and to recover the common seal. The High Court decision that the resolutions of 12 April were valid was upheld against appeal. Thus Buller surrendered the seal, Thorne was properly elected chairman on 26 August 1847, and this Victorian takeover was complete.

LSW PLANS THWARTED

Its backdoor victory profited the LSW little. The E & C and B & E had complained to the Commissioners of Railways that it had engineered their defeat on 11 January 1847 by distributing E & C shares among nominal holders, a ruse favoured by Captain Huish of the LNW, whose 'Euston Troupe' of mobile voters was recruited from porters upwards. The LSW frankly admitted having advanced £30,000 for the TV to purchase 1,700 E & C shares and, anticipating Parliamentary authority for its lease of the TV, of having subscribed for 6,850 shares in that company. The commissioners reported to Parliament on 14 April 1847 that:

> Both these transactions appear to the Commissioners to involve an illegitimate application of the capital of the South-Western Company, but the proceeding appears to be more particularly objectionable in the case in which the funds have been more particularly misapplied for the purpose of controlling the directors and shareholders of an independent company.

Nevertheless, E & C defeat came partly because its directors and other shareholders, gripped by railway mania fever, could not resist a profit on sale of much of their soaring stock.

The TV Act for branches to Bideford and South Molton was passed on 22 July 1847, capital £180,000, but the Parliamentary committee bided its time over the Bill for lease to the LSW, and this was deferred until 1848. In 1847, the LSW launched its grand Bill 'to make railways from Exeter to Truro and Plymouth, with various branches therefrom, to be called "the Cornwall & Devon Central, and Plymouth Railway" '. While broad-gauge opposition was violent, the Railway Commissioners were also concerned that £3,500,000 was needed, and criticised the proposal to raise it and other capital, £5,980,000 in all, by a special Act, instead of the capital for each work under each authorising Act. The Bill failed

Standing Orders on 4 June 1847, but the LSW augmented successful local opposition to broad-gauge Bills, i.e., Crediton & Launceston; Plymouth, Tavistock & Launceston; Launceston & Liskeard.

A few weeks later, the TV petitioned the Commissioners to fix the narrow gauge for its line. The Commissioners sought B & E comments, which naturally championed broad gauge. The E & C Act of 1845 had not stipulated its gauge, but prevented by injunction from opening on broad gauge, that board on 3 December 1847 ordered the rusting lines to be made narrow. Immediately the B & E protested to the Commissioners, who replied that as the E & C had not yet been used for traffic, they could not prevent it. However, they also made it clear to the E & C that conversion of its line would not influence them when deciding the gauge of the TV.

The Commissioners sent Captain Simmons to inspect the TV, and while there he was pressed to examine the E & C also. He made it clear that his instructions embraced only the former line, but to assist the Commissioners he looked over the E & C. His report, inter alia, said:

> The junction with the Bristol & Exeter was to have been made at a point near Cowley Bridge, and about one and three-quarters of a mile from the city of Exeter, where the Bristol & Exeter Railway is carried on an embankment close to the left bank of the river, and the original intention of the Exeter & Crediton Railway Company is evident from the construction of a timber viaduct, curved to suit the junction and standing partly on the embankment of the Bristol & Exeter Railway. The stations have been entirely completed, and the line ready for inspection previous to being used by the public as a broad-gauge railway for many months, but its opening was prevented by legal proceedings, and the company have lately commenced to narrow the gauge to 4 ft 8½ in, and to construct a temporary station at Cowley Bridge, with an approach to it from the turnpike road; this station and approach have become necessary since the determination to alter the gauge, as by so doing the company can no longer avail themselves of the Exeter station of the Bristol & Exeter Railway, which is adapted to only one, the broad gauge.

After considering Captain Simmons' report, the Commissioners announced on 8 February 1848 that the TV extension should be broad-gauge. The stunned narrow-gauge camp claimed that certain noble Lords with broad-gauge interests had influenced the Commissioners, and pointed out that the Order applied only to the Barnstaple to Crediton line and the Bideford branch, so that with existing narrow-gauge on the E & C and Barnstaple to Fremington lines a passenger from Exeter to Bideford, forty-seven miles, would change

STATIONS—5

(16) *The original stone terminus of the North Devon Railway, in 1966 Barnstaple Junction*

(17) *A view of the first Clapham Junction station showing, from left to right, the* LSW, WE & CP *and* WLE *platforms. Note mixed gauge lines at the latter, and the typical level canopy over the* LSW *platform*

STATIONS—6

(18) Now much overgrown, this impressive colonnaded entrance at Gosport was once familiar to Queen Victoria and her Consort

(19) The shell of the old station

WEST OF EXETER

carriages four times. Gloom descended on the market town of Barnstaple, of whose inhabitants 2,000 had petitioned for the narrow gauge. Incidentally, at that time only the Barnstaple to Fremington single line of the TV was complete, and on 25 April 1848 the directors agreed that Thorne should work this for freight traffic for ¾d per ton mile. He used his own vehicles hauled by horses, and the opening date, now obscure, was probably during late August 1848.

Converted to narrow gauge, the E & C made several attempts to open, but the TV gauge decision proved too serious an impediment and long delay followed.

The Commissioners' Order, bad enough in itself, had come during the post-mania depression, making the TV fearful that the LSW would opportunely renounce its declared intention of November 1847 to try again with the Bill for leasing the line. The LSW, as yet, had no such thought. After losing its Cornwall Bill in June 1847, its board had sought Locke's advice for 1848, and he, confident of narrow-gauge success between Salisbury and Exeter, reported lengthily on 15 July 1847. Space allows but brief extracts:

> When I originally selected an independent line from Exeter towards Cornwall, I had no thought of adopting the Exeter & Crediton line. but having subsequently found that it would be very easy to connect that line with the proposed new station at Exeter, I now think it better to adopt this latter course than to pursue an independent parallel line of railway from Exeter to the Taw Vale near Colbrook. If this course be adopted (with the exception of making a junction at Exeter) a Central Devon & Cornwall Railway may commence by a junction with the Taw Vale at Colbrook, and the large expenditure involved in the former plan entirely avoided. Commercially speaking, this course is so evidently advantageous that I shall not hesitate to recommend it to you for adoption, and as a consequence, that the Taw Vale and Exeter & Crediton lines should be secured to the South-Western and both made on the narrow gauge.
>
> The Taw Vale line and the extension to Plymouth are clearly objects which we are entitled to obtain—and nothing in my opinion should be done by the directors that could either for the next session or for all future time weaken their claim for an entire narrow-gauge line from Plymouth to London, nor to admit the wide-gauge party to intersect that line by any new wide-gauge project whatsoever. No compromise ought to be listened to which weakens the integrity of either of those views.

If financially or otherwise limited, he said, 'you might adopt the line from the Taw Vale to Plymouth with a branch to Launceston, and this line, whilst it would give to Plymouth all that it could

H

desire, would by the branch to Launceston pave the way to that further extension, whenever you might find it convenient to make it'.

The board agreed and prepared a Plymouth Bill, but the depression made it necessary in November 1847 to revise the application to a two-mile junction line between the EY & D Exeter terminus and the E & C at Cowley Bridge, which would permit narrow-gauge working between London and the North Devon coast via the E & C and TV, besides nicely placing the LSW for proceeding to Plymouth and Cornwall in more advantageous times.

It was destruction of this plan by the TV gauge decision which worried the TV deputation at the LSW board on 11 February 1848. However, the latter promised its utmost efforts to persuade the Commissioners to change their decision which, Chaplin said, would be helped 'by the suspension of the works on the Taw Vale Extension line, and by not proceeding more rapidly than need be with the Bills relating to the Exeter & Crediton and Taw Vale railways, now pending in Parliament'.

When, in June, Parliament rejected Bills for the Exeter & Cowley Bridge Junction line, and for effectuating the LSW acquisition of the TV, E & C and B & W, Chaplin blamed it on being heard before the successful Salisbury to Exeter schemes, while the board decided against advancing further monies to the TV or E & C, except calls on shares held.

This attitude was impossible towards the B & W, which the LSW still held without Parliamentary authority. Troubled enough in prosperous times, its difficulties now soared and its scheme for a Boscarne to Lanivet branch and an extension from Ruthern Bridge had been dropped. Few proprietors bothered to attend meetings, with the result that one appointed for 10 May 1847 had to be postponed on four successive weeks, until eventually it was held on 7 June. The minute book shows this was not unusual.

Its employees, too, found things difficult. Following repeal of the Corn Laws in 1846, they received assistance from a fund providing corn for sale to the poor. The B & W conveyed it free, and paid its bargemen one shilling extra weekly during the scarcity.

In the second half of 1847, the fall in traffic following closure of the Lanivet mines was aggravated by flood damage. Traffic stopped on much of the line during repairs costing £1,300 9s 3d, and a deficit accrued. The LSW assisted in February 1848 with a £1,000 loan, but by June 1848 the B & W repayment of its £8,000 exchequer loan was in arrears of £4,400, plus interest. The Loan

Commission threatened to realise its security, so again the LSW paid up, and succeeding months saw it meeting B & W bank overdrafts.

Isolated so far from its foster-parent and relying on local traffic, the line dwindled. The demand for sand diminished; copper and other mines were abandoned, and passengers contributed little, viz:

Year	Passengers	Revenue £ s d
1847	3650	96 3 4
1848	4613	123 12 7
1849	3368	92 15 7
1850	3470	103 16 9
1851	?	79 13 1
1852	?	95 7 2
1853	?	86 18 9

Eventually, in 1861, the LSW placed all its directors on the B & W board, assumed complete control, and appointed Mr Kyd as superintendent. We shall examine the succeeding years in Volume Two, but note here that Parliamentary authority for LSW ownership was not granted until 1886.

THE FIRST OPENINGS IN NORTH DEVON

January 1849 found Chaplin's board wondering how to lease the E & C to the broad-gauge camp without prejudicing future narrow-gauge interests. Dilatory talks with the B & E culminated in February 1851 with that company agreeing to rent the five and three-quarter miles from Crediton to Cowley Bridge for seven years (or until the TV opened throughout) for a third of gross receipts, working it as a broad-gauge single by converting one of the narrow-gauge double lines, and public opening took place on 12 May 1851. (With the TV opening in 1854, the lease was revised to last for one year from that date).

Liabilities having exceeded authorised capital by £18,000, an Act for another £20,000 was obtained on 10 June 1850, which also permitted improvements to Cowley Bridge station. Neglect of the works had not enhanced invested capital. Severe flooding of the river Creedy in November 1849 had damaged embankments, but a year passed before the LSW was asked for the money to repair them. The works suffered under traffic, and when in 1855 renewal of the lease was imminent, the B & E refused to consider it unless the line were made safe. Immediate first-aid remedies preceded extensive treatment under Errington in the summer of 1856. In March 1856, it cost £227 19s 11d to prop collapsing timber bridges, after which Thomas Tate was appointed at £250 per annum to superintend their repair.

The confused TV situation, and opposition by LSW proprietors to activities beyond Exeter, had led to dissolution in September 1848 of the LSW agreement to lease the TV; the LSW keeping its TV shares and leaving the latter free to seek its fortune with the B & E. Work almost ceased; the South Molton branch was never constructed, while the Bideford branch languished, contrasting with earlier enthusiasm when culm deposits were discovered there and 1,000 tons weekly were expected to pass to south Devon.

In those sad, lean years, only Thorne's plodding horses showed activity on the TV; then, having disposed of his lime-kilns and warehouses erected on the company's land, he terminated his lease of the Barnstaple to Fremington line from 18 May 1850. His successor's application to adopt it was rejected, for the horses had badly damaged the track. To locomotives, there was no objection. Despite stoppage of traffic, the board discovered someone was illegally using horses to haul their goods in TV trucks. Efforts to suppress it caused Thorne, insisting on a citizen's right of way, to secure an injunction against interference with his own carriage and horses, but subsequent proceedings ended favourably for the company, which promptly banned horses from the line.

Works completed for nine miles between Barnstaple and Umberleigh, costing £170,000, would remain a white elephant unless extended to the E & C. Accordingly, the board contracted with Brassey to complete a broad-gauge single line from Crediton to Fremington, and to work it for seven years for £12,000 annually. The LSW was consulted, for it would have to pay £30,000 on its shares. Considering the mood of LSW proprietors, it was a delicate task securing their support, but on 25 October 1850 they agreed, perhaps influenced because payment would be in surplus rails instead of cash.

On 24 July 1851 an Act legalising LSW shareholdings and Brassey's lease also authorised deviations at Prestbury, Eggesford and Nymet Rowland, and restyled the company as the North Devon Railway & Dock Company with a reduced capital of £426,000.

Brassey's industrious army worked well, but at Copplestone, where work first resumed with a turf-cutting ceremony on 2 February 1852, slipping of cuttings caused concern; then, when opening in February 1854 was confidently predicted, floods 'such as have not occurred for forty years' badly damaged new bridges, and swollen streams delayed repairs. The reputable Brassey strove so well that on 12 July 1854, by his invitation, North Devon and B & E directors travelled from Crediton to Barnstaple, there being met by joyous citizens who had long planned their celebration holiday, and the North Devon Mounted Rifles headed a procession including many civic dignitaries through streets gay with triumphal arches. That day, 600 poor persons attended a tea provided by local tradesmen, and said the *North Devon Journal* of a banquet for 760 (at 4s 6d each) in the New Corn Market, 'we have never known such a comfortless public dinner, or one which gave such general dissatisfaction'.

The government inspector was less gay and, by insisting on additional signals at sidings and stations, he delayed public opening from Crediton to Fremington until 1 August 1854. Brassey arranged with the B & E to supply locomotives and rolling stock, and the electric telegraph was laid throughout. The biggest work, the bridge crossing the Taw near Barnstaple, had three cast-iron arches, each spanning 83 ft 6 in and resting on masonry-filled iron cylinders.

The line was worked conjointly with the E & C, and after initial nervousness because of rumours that the works were dangerous, passenger traffic grew modestly. By October 1854, local 'watering places' were crowded, while at Ilfracombe beds were unobtainable. Freight traffic, chiefly coal, lime, timber and cattle, increased rapidly.

The E & C opened in 1851 with seven trains daily each way, four on Sundays, all carrying first and second-class passengers. One took third class as well, leaving Exeter at 9.15 pm on weekdays and 10.30 pm on Sundays, and Crediton for Exeter at 6.0 am every day. The ND opening service was four weekday and two Sunday trains each way, most taking 1 hr 50 min between Barnstaple and Exeter.

Reluctance by ND proprietors to invest in reviving the time-expired Bideford line led local residents to form the Bideford Extension Railway and secure powers on 4 August 1853, capital £55,000. Brassey, its main subscriber, agreed to construct the six-and-a-half broad-gauge miles and work them for £2,250 annually for seven years, after which the ND would lease or purchase them. The first sod was cut on 20 August 1853, and on 29 October 1855 opening celebrations were held at Bideford. The *North Devon*

Journal described how about 300 guests from Barnstaple and elsewhere travelled free by train, some returning at 4.0 pm but most staying for a ball, intending to catch the 9.0 pm train. To their surprise, it passed through the station, stopped to entrain some apparently privileged persons and then departed. The 100 or so stranded guests protested, but with no further conveyance forthcoming they dispersed, some hiring road vehicles or walking home, some lodging in Bideford and some camping on the station. The *Journal* said the lesson was never to accept free railway trips, but its issue of Thursday, 8 November 1855 described how still more were caught:

> Since the opening of the rail, there has been a flood of travellers and pleasure-seekers moving over the line; on the evening of Friday last the trip from hence to Barum was as cheap as cheap could be, but many who went down at night were made to "laugh on t'other side" when they came to return. The licence for working the line had arrived meanwhile, and immediately the gratis coloured tickets finished, greatly to the annoyance, it is said, of some light-pursed voyagers who were left, so gossip says, in that most forlorn of mortal conditions in these days, not having a penny to help themselves.

With ND services extended to Bideford, the line thus opened on 2 November 1855 for fare-paying passengers, of whom 13,499 travelled in the first month.

A TRY FOR PLYMOUTH

In south Devon, Chaplin's prime target was the growing, historical port of Plymouth which, with Devonport and Stonehouse, comprised the 'three towns'. A line surveyed by Locke from Exeter to Plymouth through Okehampton and Tavistock would provide a narrow-gauge route to London to oppose the broad-gauge, steeply-graded South Devon atmospheric, besides carrying potential traffic between north and south Devon. Plymouth proudly flew the broad-gauge flag and generally opposed this idea, so Chaplin planned to court Plymothian sympathy with an LSW subscription towards the improvements at Sutton Pool Harbour, made necessary by growing trade. This was a direct challenge to the GWR scheme for docks at Millbay. Sutton Harbour was built on The Sound, near the Plym estuary, on land obtained in February 1812 from the Duchy of Cornwall, and the company, incorporated by an Act of George III, was directly supported by the chamber of commerce.

A party led by Chaplin toured western counties to stir enthusiasm and, reaching Plymouth, made provisional arrangements with the Sutton Harbour directors before attending a public meeting at the Guildhall on 18 December 1846, which voted unanimously for the narrow-gauge line.

The LSW Plymouth line, of course, was part of the ill-fated Cornwall & Devon Central, and Plymouth Bill of 1847, but the harbour improvements Act was passed on 23 July 1847, incorporating a new Sutton Harbour Improvement company, to which the LSW might subscribe £15,200 and appoint two of the board. It did subscribe over £12,000 which, after the mania, was accounted for with 'lines suspended' items.

Our call at Plymouth was brief but we shall return there in Volume Two, as we trace the second, greater, and more successful invasion by the LSW of the broad-gauge west.

CHAPTER 5

Struggles in the East

A PORTSMOUTH LINE THWARTED AND A SUBSTITUTE TO GOSPORT

No sooner was the London to Southampton line begun than its promoters turned to Portsmouth, the greatest English naval port with a fine natural harbour, at which also a substantial passenger traffic existed, 1,000 persons being said to have sailed from there for New York in a month.

The idea of a Portsmouth line was not new. Dr Abraham Rees's *Present State of the Canals of the UK*, 1806 (British Museum, ref 453 K 19, para 1395) tells us that William Jessop was employed in 1803 to survey a line from Portsmouth to the west end of Stamford Street, near Blackfriars Bridge, London, estimated to cost £400,000. If constructed, this would doubtless have been a tramway, and have been linked with the Surrey Iron Railway and the Croydon Merstham & Godstone Railway.

Now a satellite of the London & Southampton Railway was formed—the Portsmouth Junction Railway, capital £300,000, for which Giles surveyed in 1836. Its undated prospectus showed a branch from the L & S at Bishopstoke, through Botley and Fareham to Portsmouth, to be constructed to permit a Gosport branch being added. Needing only about twenty miles of new line for a quarter the cost of any other route, it would increase the port's prosperity by linking it with London, Exeter, Plymouth, Birmingham, etc, through the shaping English railway network, besides annually producing £30,000 net for its promoters.

Unfortunately, Portsmouth citizens would have none of it, and looked for their own direct railway rather than a branch from a main line to Southampton, a town they considered 'very proud and very overbearing'. Their opposition secured defeat of the Portsmouth Junction at its second reading in the Commons. The line was not abandoned, but as a Standing Order required every subscriber to renew his consent, and it was considered many would not, on 20 November 1838 the Portsmouth Junction Railway was dissolved, each subscriber losing 12s 6d of his £3 deposit per share. Further developments were left to the L & S.

On 21 November 1838, Portsmouth citizens gathered at the Sessions House to hear from T. Jackson, their mayor and chairman, of progress with their independent line to London through Chichester, Arundel and Dorking, to promote which a meeting on 21 January 1838 had appointed a committee. The Stephensons viewed this line favourably, and a deputation had therefore sought assistance from 'Stevens line of Railroad', but obtaining no assurance of the latter being built, it turned to the London & Brighton Railway, which had promised every assistance, and to show its desire to unite with the Portsmouth company had lodged plans to reach Horsham where the two lines would join.

The Portsmouth promoters, out for the best bargain, deferred acceptance until they had seen the L & S board, but to approach the latter so soon after opposing its Portsmouth Bill was futile. Easthope thought it was cap-in-hand repentance, and smugly refused their request for the measure they had lately defeated. Now that the L & S had plans to reach Gosport instead, he reminded them of an Act just passed for a floating bridge across Portsmouth Harbour and recommended they 'make the bridge across the water to Gosport as convenient as possible, and use it as often as they can'. They would, he said with more vindictiveness than regret, be sorry they had defeated the branch line by way of Cosham.

Being unable to raise their capital of £1,500,000, Portsmouth promoters got nowhere. They tried Lancashire, 'where cash was made as rapidly as cotton goods', but many people there considered the line would extract a third of L & S traffic, in which they already had an interest. They were unwilling to invest in fifty or sixty new miles when the L & S alternative required only fifteen for £300,000. Besides, critics said potential traffic would not support two Portsmouth lines. Easthope had told L & S proprietors as early as February 1838 of opposition to the Portsmouth people by influential landowners.

> I have a paper signed by His Grace the Duke of Norfolk, the Earl of Surrey, Lord Fitzalan, Colonel Wyndham (the representative of the Egremont property), Mr Pryme, and many other influential and extensive landowners, which is as follows:— "We, whose names are undersigned, hereby express our determination to oppose to the utmost of our power the projected railway from Portsmouth to London, by way of Chichester, Arundel and Horsham, as we consider such a project to be wholly uncalled for, originating in speculation and infringing the rights of private property, without any equivalent public advantage."

By taking their own line just over fifteen miles to Gosport, the L & S directors hoped to save £120,000, land and earthworks being cheaper than on the eighteen-mile route round the harbour to Portsmouth. Their Act succeeded on 4 June 1839, capital £300,000, for the branch from Bishopstoke through Botley and Fareham, to end 'at or near a nursery ground and garden abutting upon the Spring Gardens Road, near the entrance through the fortifications to the town of Gosport'. Because lofty works might interfere with military fortifications, the company was not to build Gosport station higher than the local Commanding Royal Engineer permitted.

Section 2 of the Act made a doubtful concession to Portsmouth, by redeeming Easthope's pledge to 'sink the formidable name of Southampton—formidable only to the good folk of Portsmouth, and to christen their railway by the much more appropriate name of the London & South Western Railway.' By this means they would divest the railway of some of that exceedingly obnoxious quality which the Portsmouth men found so objectionable. This was in return for the Portsmouth people's good sense not to oppose the line, and they 'would be delighted with a railway which, if not exactly what they would prefer, was the best they could have without paying heavily for it. This would relieve them from the danger of laying out their money in a concern which could certainly never pay'.

Work on the line proceeded well under Brassey, who also contracted to build stations at Fareham for £1,391 and Bishopstoke for £1,509, while David Nicholson's tender of £10,980 for Gosport terminus was accepted. The opening was advertised for 26 July 1841, then early in the morning of 15 July disaster struck in Fareham tunnel sufficient to destroy such plans. Locke reported to the directors on 27 August 1841:

> I think you are already aware of the failure which took place a short time since in a portion of the Fareham tunnel, and of the delay in the opening it produced. I beg to lay before you the following explanation, which may enable the proprietors to judge more correctly the extent of the failure, and of the probable time for its reparation.
> The tunnel is upwards of 600 yd in length. It passes on the north side of the hill through beds of yellow and red clay, such as are usually found between the chalk and tertiary formation, and then enters the blue clay (similar to the London clay) through which it continues to the southern side of the hill. The failure occurred on the north side, where the coloured beds of clay exist, just at a period when the last or junction length of earth was being removed for the

brickwork, and such was the weight of the slip and so immediate its effect, that notwithstanding every effort of the miners, the ground fell from the surface and carried with it a portion of the brickwork that had already been built. The thickness of the work was 3 ft.

From subsequent examination, it appeared that the inverted arch and part of the side walls remained good—the arch requiring to be rebuilt for a distance of nearly 40 yd. The most vigorous measures for repairing the work were immediately adopted, and these have been carried on night and day, and will be continued until the whole is completed, which I expect will be accomplished in three weeks.

Locke keenly felt this blow to his personal reputation for punctuality, but worse followed. The original slip extended, and it was decided to make a cutting of the affected portion. Then work was retarded by continuous heavy rain. The Board of Trade chief inspecting officer, Sir Frederick Smith, reported on 28 November 1841 that the ground had become almost semi-fluid, with scarcely any slope in the cutting which would stand, while 'at the north end of the tunnel the slopes have in consequence lost all regularity of form and pour over the retaining walls upon the rails'. Although the Board of Trade suggested waiting, the line was opened on 29 November 1841 with a 20 mph restriction, two days after the directors' trip. Four days later fresh slips appeared, and services were suspended except for freight. After another Board of Trade survey, passenger services recommenced on 7 February 1842. The disaster almost ruined Brassey financially.

The tunnel today has two parts, 56 and 552 yd, separated by the cutting. On 2 October 1904, a deviation up line between Knowle Junction and Fareham East was opened for Eastleigh to Fareham trains, and a down line in September 1906, the tunnel line becoming independent for Meon Valley branch trains on 2 June 1907.

Queen Victoria used Gosport station when visiting Portsmouth or Osborne House, Isle of Wight. An engraving of December 1841 shows the low structure with a long entrance collonade in classic style and rooms abutting on each end. The platform area appears encased by the walls and a ridged roof with glass along the length of its apex. Chimneys do not exceed roof height. doubtless as required by the Commanding Royal Engineer.

After the opening, London passengers could use two fast, four mixed and two goods trains daily; two mixed on Sundays. Through carriages could avoid a change at Bishopstoke. Fares were 22s, fast trains; 21s first and 15s second on mixed trains; 9s, day goods trains.

In June 1842 a train arriving late at Gosport after an engine failure did not stop, but demolished part of the wall and gates. The guard was fined 40s and severely reprimanded, the 'leniency' shown being due to his brake working in a 'contrary direction'.

Intending Isle of Wight passengers in 1839-40 repaired to the Quebec Tavern, Portsmouth, before embarking on the Portsmouth & Ryde Steam Company's vessel, the *Union*, which made five daily return trips to Ryde. The 1841 daily summer service was eight trips by two vessels, but when the Gosport branch opened they used a new pier there for six daily and four Sunday sailings, connecting with trains and crossing within half an hour. Fares were 1s 6d quarter-deck and 1s forecastle.

Though indirect, this London to Portsmouth railway affected coaches, as the following lament from an 1842 Hampshire paper shows:

> The Rail v the Road. A narrative by a Portsmouth coachman, now in good health. "I have lived to see the Portsmouth mail coach put on, and I have lived to see it taken off. Except one coach, I have lived to see all the London coaches put on, and it seems as if I should live to see them all taken off; though at one time there were ten up and ten down every day, and one three times a week. These coaches, if only half filled, must have taken 176 passengers every 24 hours, to and from Portsmouth. One coach, when I was a boy, was two days and one night on the road; it went to Guildford the first day, where the passengers slept for the night and went into London next day. The turnpikes were not then finished. The mail was brought by a man or boy on horseback; I brought it from Petersfield, and got into Portsmouth at two in the afternoon. After that a diligence was put on; that carried three passengers, and sometimes went empty. Then Mr Palmer put the mail coach on, that carried four; prior to which, the way of travelling was on horse with a guide—the guide went to bring the horse back. As for going on foot, 'twas not safe, there were so many footpads about; and there was not a public-house between Halfway House and Mousehill but what had five or six saddle horses ready for passengers to ride on the way to and from London and Portsmouth. After the roads were made good, it was thought a great feat for a man riding with an express to go up to London and back in a long summer day; now it is to be done in nine hours. Oh! These railways! Besides having ruined the road, what will the farmers do with their hay, oats and straw? T.S."

On 13 September 1845, a branch, approximately 600 yd, from Gosport station to the Royal Clarence Victualling Establishment pier, was opened for the Queen at Prince Albert's suggestion. Crossing the moat on piles, it passed through the fortifications without disturbing a public promenade.

EARLY RELATIONS WITH THE LONDON & BRIGHTON RAILWAY

Relations with the London & Brighton Railway over the years fluctuated between hot and cold. That company got its Act on 15 July 1837, finding access to London over the London & Croydon Railway to Corbetts Lane, thence via the Greenwich Railway to London Bridge. It had earlier intended to join the L & S near Wimbledon, at a time when the South-Eastern planned doing likewise at Wandsworth Common, both companies seeking terminal facilities from the L & S at Nine Elms. A report of 7 January 1836 to the L & S board said 'there is every reason to expect that the combined exertion and interest of the three companies will be used to push forward the terminus from Vauxhall Bridge farther into the centre of London, probably to London Bridge'. However, it was not to be!

The story of L & B agreements and disputes with the LSW is complicated and involves Portsmouth, Guildford and London.

In 1842, Locke surveyed two possible LSW branches to Epsom, but the scheme was left until autumn 1843, when he recommended a single line of just over five miles, diverging about eight miles from Nine Elms and touching Ewell. The light works, built to allow doubling, would cost about £51,000, while over £9,000 gross revenue was expected annually, excluding race traffic. The trains would also carry short-distance, main-line passengers, who were too numerous for stopping long-distance trains yet too few to justify their own. The LSW assured the L & B in January 1844 that it had no ambitions beyond Epsom, despite the line Locke had surveyed to Leatherhead in 1842 having only been postponed.

On 29 December 1843, promoters of a Guildford to Woking line successfully sought LSW support, but they intended to build on the wooden principle, which would prevent through working of LSW carriages and cause passengers to change at Woking. This principle, invented by William Prosser, involved flangeless wooden wheels on coaches and engines which were kept on the track by guide wheels pressing at angles to the sides and tops of the wooden rails. It had nowhere previously been tried in service. We shall see how the Guildford Railway escaped it.

At Portsmouth, where discontent with the Gosport line simmered, the Brighton & Chichester Railway, an L & B prodigy, offered to extend into Portsea Island, a facility for which its citizens had agitated.

Thus the stage was set for the 1844 session!

The Guildford Junction Railway got its Act of 347 sections on 10 May 1844, capital £55,000, for a six-mile line from the LSW near Woking station, going through Worplesdon to its Guildford terminus in a field owned by the Earl of Onslow, north of the Guildford to Farnham turnpike road. In 1838, the LSW itself had contemplated making such a line.

Guildford, an ancient market town, had grown at the gap where the river Wey, traversing the North Downs, was itself crossed by travellers between east and west. The centre of local agricultural life, once famous for cloth making, and a stage for Portsmouth coaches, its importance increased when the railway reached it. Today, its growing population already exceeds 51,000, and it supports thriving light industries, brews fine beer, and sends many commuters to London. Had the L & S not looked to Bristol, its main line might well have gone through Guildford.

The LSW Epsom branch Bill was rejected by a Commons committee in favour of a Croydon to Epsom scheme of the Croydon company simultaneously presented, despite the inferior gradients and triple cost of the latter. The LSW opposed the Croydon Bill in the Lords, but their Lordships considered the proposed trial of the Clegg and Samuda atmospheric system of traction on the Croydon company's line so important that they passed the Bill, though convinced that the promoters had exaggerated the traffic prospects. Parliament also feared interference with Southampton and Gosport services should the LSW Bill be passed and its proposed four trains daily to Epsom be exceeded.

The atmospheric system was opposed by Locke but supported by such eminent engineers as Vignoles, Cubitt and Brunel, and it badly burned the fingers of the latter when he introduced it on the South Devon Railway. It required laying a tube between the rails, with a leather-covered slot at the top containing a piston connected to the train by a bar. Strategically placed pumping stations exhausted air from the tube, along which the piston travelled with the leather valve being opened just ahead of it and resealed behind it. The system was in service on the Dublin & Kingstown Railway, where speeds of $57\frac{1}{2}$ mph were achieved, when Cubitt recommended it for the London & Croydon. That company used it from Dartmouth Arms to Croydon, but it never reached Epsom. This first serious method of supplying tractive power from without the vehicle was killed by the ravages of weather on the leather.

The Epsom failure was disappointing, but Chaplin told pro-

STRUGGLES IN THE EAST

prietors a new attempt was being considered. The board, however, still had eyes on Leatherhead, having on 2 August 1844 decided to encourage a line there from Kingston via Epsom. Chaplin warned that the Croydon camp was surveying to extend its Epsom line to Portsmouth, which the LSW would oppose, and said that the LSW proposed making a twenty-two-mile single line to Portsmouth and Chichester from Fareham for about £220,000, to forestall the Brighton & Chichester Company's plans which threatened the £400,000 spent on the Gosport branch.

Chaplin knew he must move quickly to stop the Croydon company's prodigy, the Direct Portsmouth Railway, and how better than to play on the Brighton company's own anger over the scheme, with which, it thought, the Croydon company was invading its territory. It so happened that the LSW was then seeking a new terminus between Waterloo and Hungerford bridges, partly because its facilities at Nine Elms were strained, and also because promoters of a line from Richmond intended going to the bridges after crossing the LSW near Nine Elms. In addition, because it hoped to build a Wandsworth to Croydon branch, the LSW had in August 1844 paid £1,000 deposit on its purchase of the Surrey Iron Railway (the Tramway) for £19,000. These two schemes became its bargaining pawns.

First, it was necessary to make terms with Chadwick and his fellow promoters of the Richmond West End Junction Railway. They agreed their line should be worked by the LSW, join the latter company's line near Falcon Bridge (Clapham Jcn) and use its terminus, and that the LSW should make the extension to the bridges. Now Chaplin could offer the L & B the use of the Tramway for its own intended Croydon to Wandsworth branch with participation in the extension and room at the new terminus, and so woo it away from the Croydon company and from Portsmouth. If the South-Eastern company (also relying on the Croydon company for access to London) would likewise co-operate, LSW expenditure would be reduced, and the three united companies would neutralise the Direct Portsmouth and stifle attempts by the Croydon and Greenwich companies to promote a West End extension.

On 13 September 1844 Captain Kelly led a Brighton deputation to Chaplin's board and reached a provisional agreement (we will call it Agreement A) jointly to make and finance the extension and the Wandsworth branch, with immediate L & B participation in the purchase of the Tramway, whether the branch be authorised or not. Four LSW and three L & B directors would form a joint committee, but, the L & B reluctantly agreed, should the SER participate, LSW control would be preserved because of its larger traffic, and each would subscribe a third of the capital. The Waterloo (or Metropolitan) extension would fall entirely to the LSW if the Wandsworth branch failed.

The Surrey Iron Railway, which the LSW had intended converting for locomotive traction, was the first public railway to obtain an Act, granted on 21 May 1801. Its nine and a half miles of double line left the Thames at Wandsworth, just east of the river Wandle, where its authorised basin, now South-Eastern Gas Board property, can still be seen. It passed through Mitcham to Croydon, with a one-and-a-half-mile Carshalton branch diverging near the present Mitcham Junction station. The track was laid on stone blocks, the plate rails having a flat surface for the passage of the wheel and a flange to guide its inner side. The line, engineered by William Jessop, exceeded in construction costs its original authorised capital of £50,000, and suffered severe rivalry from the Croydon canal from Rotherhithe. Its last dividend, 10s a share, was paid in 1825. The horse-drawn wagons carried mostly their owners' lime, chalk and agricultural produce to London, returning with manure and coals.

When the highly indignant Croydon company heard of the negotiations between the LSW and the L & B, it pointed to its own agreement with the latter which prevented the L & B making a line from Croydon or its London side without inviting the Croydon company to participate. The LSW, considering the Croydon company hopeless to deal with, decided to leave it and the L & B to settle their own differences.

In September 1844, Frederick Mangles of the Guildford Junction suggested to Chaplin that that line be extended to Chichester. The LSW welcomed it, provided the wooden principle were abandoned, because changing carriages would discourage passengers, and freight transhipment would be costly and time-consuming. The Guildford Junction, insisting that its wheels could be adapted for LSW track, argued that the experiment on that line would decide whether the wooden system should be introduced on Scottish lines. Mangles wanted £10,000 to abandon it, but Chaplin refused. The LSW board resolved on 25 September 1844:

> The question considered was whether this company should undertake the line from Guildford to Chichester with a purchase of the present branch. That a set of wooden and iron rails should be laid

STATIONS—7

(20) View of Guildford, looking south, in the 1860s. These platforms were approximately where platforms 2 and 3 now stand. Note the station sign Guildford Junction!

STATIONS—8

(21) *A contrast in styles. (1) The 'old' Godalming station, once an LSW terminus, now in 1966 a goods depot. The original low platform survives (compare with the Guildford plate) and the style closely resembles Micheldever*

(22) *A contrast in styles. (2) The 'new' station, still in 1966 the town's passenger depot, on the Portsmouth Direct line*

down, the latter being provided by this company. That, at the expiration of an agreed period when the wooden rails have been fairly tried, they can be exchanged for iron, and that the branch be purchased at par whether the principle succeeds or fails.

This extension to Chichester linking with the planned line from Fareham offered the best chance of defeating the Direct Portsmouth and occupying territory between the LSW and the coast, but it rocked the new relationship with the L & B. Kelly promised that the L & B and the Brighton & Chichester would oppose this threat to their traffic at Chichester, but Chaplin said the LSW was acting in self-defence, and though engineering difficulties forced this route on them some arrangement could be reached over the coast line.

On 27 September 1844 the Guildford Junction agreed to sell to the LSW for £75,000 in cash or in shares of the proposed Chichester extension. The LSW decided to pay cash, but at its own expense the Guildford Junction was to complete its single line by 1 May 1845 in iron instead of wood, with earthworks and bridges for doubling. Though the LSW recognised the Guildford Junction's obligation to compensate Prosser, no separate sum was included in that agreement.

Prosser took his wooden system to a circular test track of ten chains radius on Wimbledon Common, there demonstrating its capabilities on gradients up to 1 in 50. An *Illustrated London News* engraving of 8 November 1845 shows it near the windmill there, while an article mentions another trial line of 174 yd near Vauxhall Bridge, where several engineers watched experiments meant to prove the impossibility of derailing wooden-wheeled trains.

On 28 September 1844, the now disquieted L & B demanded that the LSW should surrender any advantage from Chichester traffic, in return for its like undertaking concerning Portsmouth traffic. Chaplin thought this would be making the line and giving away the profit, but if he made no concession the L & B might fly to the Croydon company or to the promoters of Stephenson's Direct Portsmouth Railway, and the object of the deal over the Tramway would be lost. The problem then was how much to offer, having rejected the idea of inviting the L & B to make the Guildford to Chichester line as equal partners.

New negotiations with the L & B, which began in October 1844, ended with an agreement (to us, Agreement B) signed on 7 January 1845 after proprietors approved it on 7 December 1844, when

J

Chaplin buoyantly announced:

> I am most happy to say that it is a reciprocal guarantee between this company and the Brighton company, for the protection of the coast line, an arrangement which has obviated all collision, and removed all the angry feelings which otherwise might have arisen.

By this agreement, the LSW would construct the Metropolitan extension, the Guildford to Chichester, and the Chichester to Portsmouth and Fareham lines at its own cost. It would bear fifty per cent of an L & B guarantee to the Brighton & Chichester Company for fifteen years, receiving half the L & B share of surplus profits. The L & B, which could lease the Brighton & Chichester, would construct the Croydon to Wandsworth branch provided the Metropolitan extension were made, paying the LSW for use of that extension seventy per cent of its gross earnings over it in perpetuity, subject to an annual minimum of £7,000 for twenty-one years. Sections 11 and 12 of the agreement were particularly important:

> 11. The South-Western Company not to construct or in any way promote or be concerned in any branch from the present South-Western line or from the proposed extension thereto to Waterloo Bridge and Chichester to the south or east of the intended continuous line from Waterloo Bridge to Chichester, except any line which shall not proceed south of Epsom. If they make any line to Epsom and the same shall be extended southward by any other party, the Brighton company are to have the option of purchasing half the ownership of the Epsom branch at half its cost of construction within one year after such southward extension shall be sanctioned by Parliament, paying such interest on such half cost as will make up the profits upon such half cost five per cent per annum thereon.
>
> 12. The Brighton company not to construct or in any wise promote or be concerned in any extension of the branches to Horsham and Dorking for which they intend to apply to Parliament in the next session, or any other line extending more than ten miles to the westwards of the main Brighton line.

The companies agreed to oppose the Direct Portsmouth together. Section 4 provided:

> That the Surrey Iron Railway which the South-Western Company have agreed to purchase shall be resold under the direction of a joint committee of six, viz, three Brighton directors and three South-Western directors, and the loss (if any) upon the resale with all costs attending the purchase and sale to be borne by the two companies in equal shares.

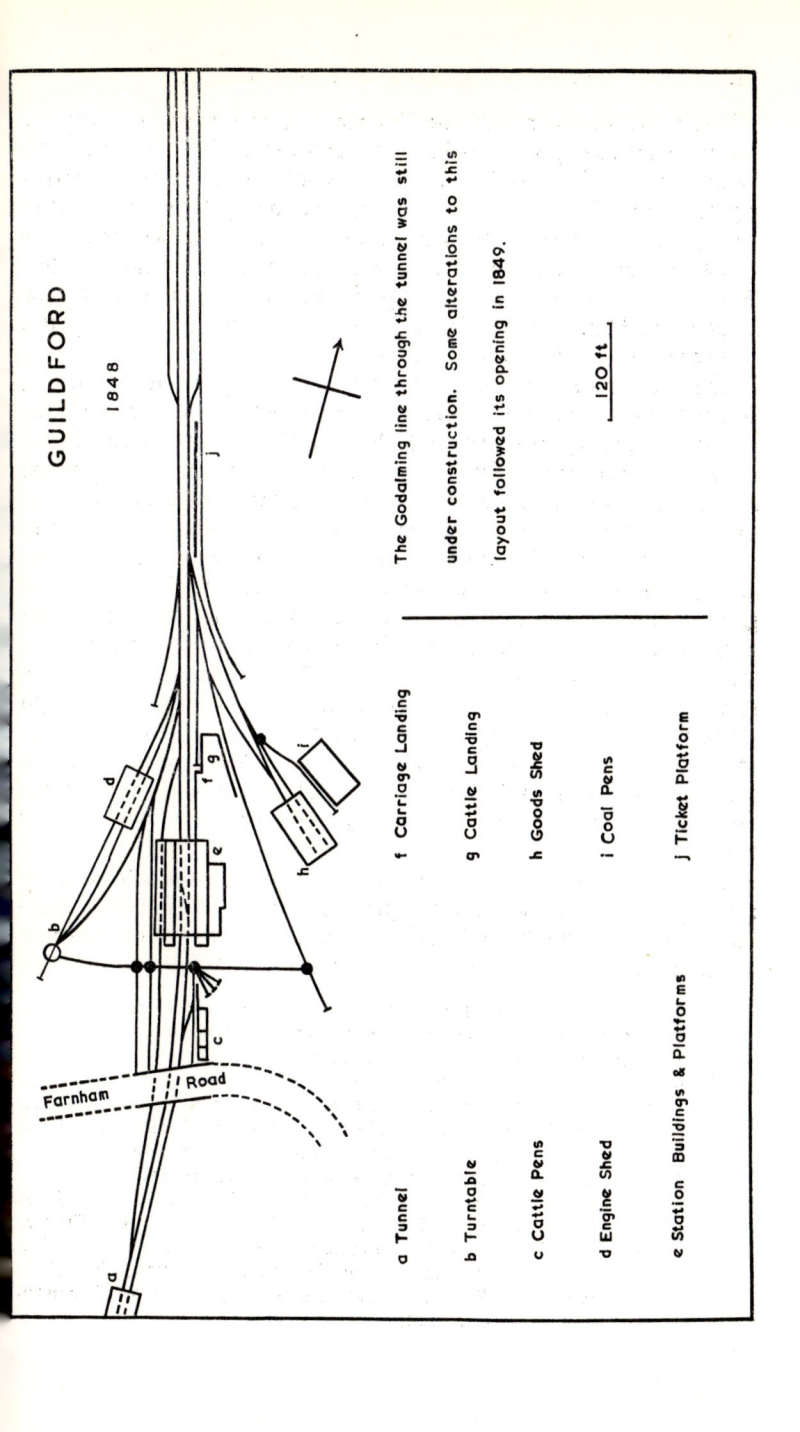

GUILDFORD
1848

The Godalming line through the tunnel was still under construction. Some alterations to this layout followed its opening in 1849.

120 ft

a Tunnel
b Turntable
c Cattle Pens
d Engine Shed
e Station Buildings & Platforms
f Carriage Landing
g Cattle Landing
h Goods Shed
i Coal Pens
j Ticket Platform

Farnham Road

The LSW, however, sold the Tramway to the Brighton company for its purchase price. Locke had surveyed it for conversion to locomotive working and found there would be difficulties in crossing two turnpike roads. The Brighton company found it of little value, and in 1846 Parliament authorised its abandonment, the *Railway Times* baldly announcing on Saturday 29 August 1846: 'Surrey Iron Railway. The passage of wagons on this line will be stopped on Monday. The line has been purchased by the Brighton company. It is a common tramroad.'

The Brighton & Chichester, strongly objecting to the agreement, demanded that the LSW abandon its proposed Chichester line. This Chaplin cursorily rejected and the Guildford, Chichester, Portsmouth & Fareham Railway was formed to promote it, capital £1,000,000, with Chaplin, Henderson and other LSW directors on the committee. Its prospectus, showing G. W. Horn, secretary, and Locke, engineer, said one-third of the shares were reserved for LSW proprietors, whose company would lease the line on terms giving four per cent to those subscribers and equal division of surplus profits. Paid-up capital would receive four per cent interest until the Act was obtained or, if it failed, deposits would be returned without deduction. The double line would go through Godalming, Witley, Lurgershall, south-west near Heyshott, north of Singleton, south again to Chichester via Mid-Lavant, then by the coast to Portsmouth. The Fareham portion would carry northwest beyond that town to an easy junction with the Gosport branch.

The Guildford Junction, opening four days late on 5 May 1845, passed into LSW possession, but plans generally for 1845 were unsuccessful. First, the 'Five Kings' examined in January the multitude of schemes offered for the area including those listed below:

1. Guildford, Chichester, Portsmouth & Fareham Branch
2. London & South-Western Metropolitan Extension
3. Brighton & Chichester (Portsmouth Extension)
4. Direct London & Portsmouth Atmospheric
   (Engineers: William and Joseph Cubitt. From Epsom through Ashtead, Leatherhead, Mickleham, Dorking, Godalming, Haslemere, Liphook, Petersfield and Havant to Portsmouth).
5. London & Portsmouth, with a branch to Shoreham
   ('Stephenson's line'. Engineers: Robert Stephenson and G. P. Bidder. From Hungerford Bridge, London, through Epsom, Leatherhead, Dorking and Horsham to Arundel. Then a junction with the Chichester line, along the coast to Portsmouth and to be extended to Fareham. Branches were planned to Shoreham and to the SER at Reigate.)

6 London & Brighton Wandsworth Branch
    7 London & South-Western Epsom Branch
    8 Epsom & Dorking
    9 London & Croydon Dorking Branch
    10 London & Brighton Dorking Branch
    11 South-Eastern Branch to Reigate and Dorking

The 'Five Kings' reported in favour of Nos 1 and 2, against Nos 3 to 7, and recommended postponement of Nos 8 to 11.

Examining those of these schemes whose Bills came before Parliament in 1845 we find, in order from London, that the LSW Metropolitan Extension Act was passed on 31 July, but that the Commons threw out the L & B Wandsworth branch. The LSW Epsom branch and the L & B Dorking branch failed Standing Orders, while the Epsom & Dorking was withdrawn. The Commons passed the Direct Portsmouth (Stephenson's Line was not proceeded with) with freedom to choose or reject atmospheric traction, though the committee felt the line into Portsmouth should be steam-worked to avoid the tube interfering with steam trains. The Guildford, Chichester, Portsmouth & Fareham branch, for which the LSW had L & B support, was badly mauled, the Commons committee by one vote approving only the Guildford to Godalming and Fareham to Portsea portions, with junctions at Godalming with the Direct Portsmouth and at Cosham with the Brighton & Chichester Portsmouth extension which it also passed. The committee approved the three lines converging on Portsmouth, subject to a joint station being built there, but of these only the Brighton & Chichester extension with a Fareham branch got its Act that session, on 8 August, and the Lords ordered another committee enquiry in the next session into the Guildford, Chichester, Portsmouth & Fareham. Likewise, the Direct Portsmouth was postponed.

Chaplin blamed their failures on 'the adventurous spirit of the times, the abundance of unemployed capital, and a variety of other causes'. Clearly, he said, Parliament encouraged competition by every means. Dalhousie's board had helped railways in a few inferior points, injuring them in more important matters, but 'I do feel that some controlling interest is necessary for the salvation of railway interests, and to obviate that competition which, in the present state of things, must otherwise continue to exist' He criticised Parliamentary committees. Five members would do better than fifteen, and they should know about the areas they were considering, whereas 'in fact, gentlemen, it is a perfect lottery, and if an active, intelligent man, with a bias either way,

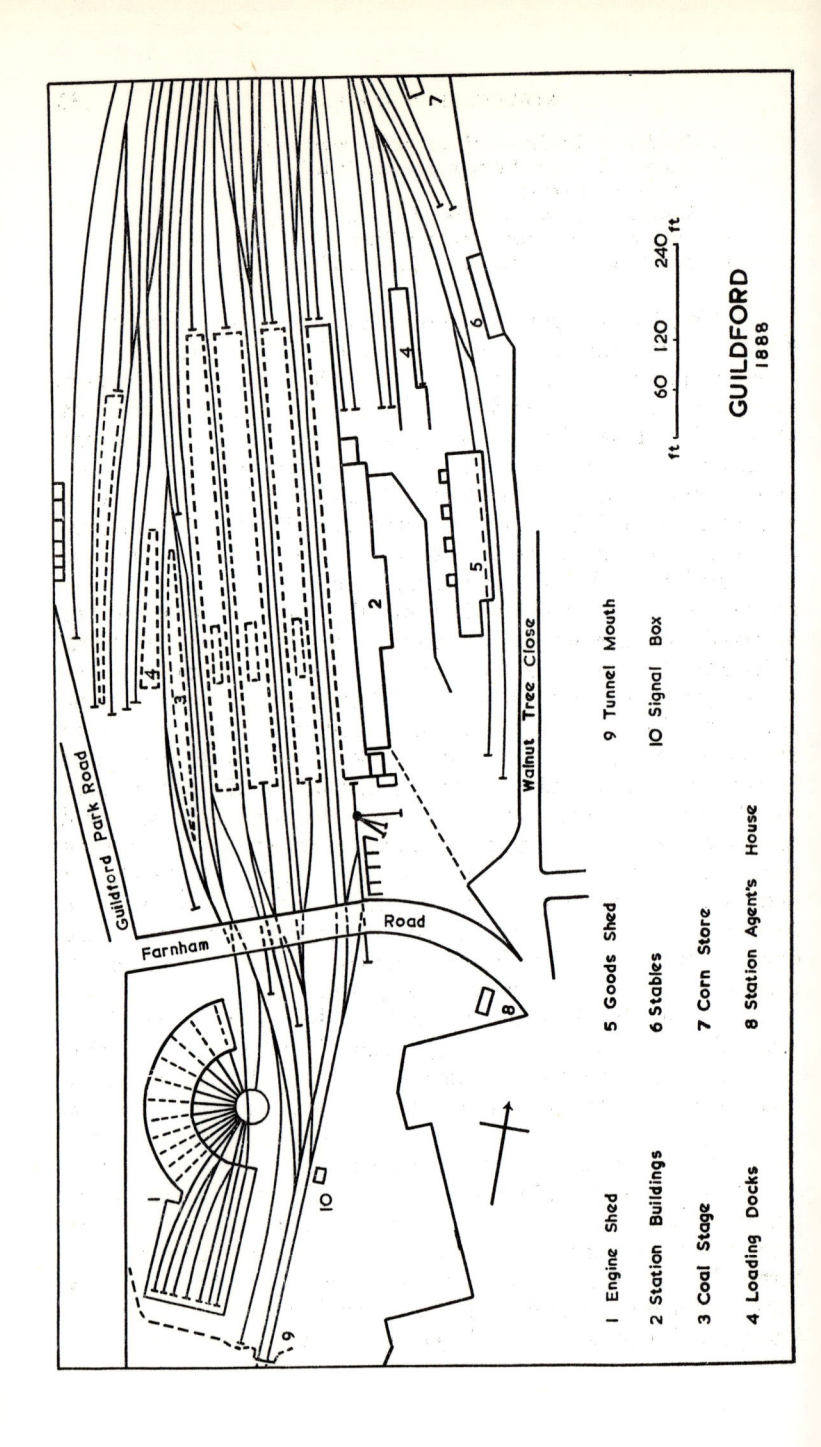

1 Engine Shed
2 Station Buildings
3 Coal Stage
4 Loading Docks
5 Goods Shed
6 Stables
7 Corn Store
8 Station Agent's House
9 Tunnel Mouth
10 Signal Box

GUILDFORD
1888

should get into the chair, the question is, in point of fact, almost decided by him'.

During 1845, amalgamation of Portsmouth projects was frequently suggested; a move the L & B clearly favoured. On 24 January 1845 it supported suggestions by Stephenson's Line that great advantages would come from a union of that, the L & B and LSW, but the idea petered out. Six weeks later the LSW proposed to the Brighton & Chichester an amalgamation of all lines from Shoreham to Portsmouth and Woking to Chichester, on similar terms to those between the LSW and the Guildford, Chichester, Portsmouth & Fareham. The Brighton & Chichester counter-suggested that it and the LSW should jointly finance, construct and manage the Chichester to Portsmouth line. Both suggestions were declined, and the L & B was angered to discover these negotiations. In September 1845, the L & B suggested that the LSW, L & B and L & C should amalgamate, an approach which the LSW also rebuffed.

Another agreement did materialise. The L & B having contracted to purchase the Brighton & Chichester immediately after that company's Portsmouth Extension Act was passed, the LSW accepted half ownership with the L & B of the Chichester to Portsmouth line, both companies jointly to finance and construct it. The LSW shareholders approving this on 26 January 1846 (say, Agreement C), the necessary Bill reached Parliament and a joint committee of three LSW and three L & B directors put the line under contract. Then the L & B patched up its quarrel and agreed to amalgamate with the L & C. Perhaps retrospectively it judged Agreement C a bad bargain by yielding to the LSW a Portsmouth monopoly with power to make an Epsom line in exchange for less valuable alternative London terminal facilities for the L & B. The Act authorising the amalgamation to form the London, Brighton & South Coast Railway was not passed until 27 July 1846, but meanwhile the L & B could not continue supporting the Guildford, Chichester, Portsmouth & Fareham, and its desire for an alternative London station receded.

In discarding Agreement C and assuming support for the Direct Portsmouth, the L & B needed to save face by blaming the LSW. It therefore unreasonably demanded that the latter should insert in its current Bill a clause fixing the toll payable by the L & B between Wandsworth and Waterloo, and giving it legal rights at the terminus. Chaplin refused pending an Act legalising Agreement B, whereupon the L & B alleged that the LSW intention to take the Metropolitan extension to London Bridge infringed the agreement, an untenable argument as that line was north of Epsom. On 22 April 1846 the L & B directors resolved:

> That referring to the conduct of the South-Western Company in refusing to arbitrate as provided by the agreement on disputed points, in entering into arrangements with the Reading, Guildford & Reigate Company, without the concurrence of this company, and thus promoting the line, and in refusing to admit the toll clauses into the Wandsworth Branch Bill, this committee are of opinion that unless the South-Western Company consent to the insertion of such clauses before the day appointed for the reassembly of Parliament, it will be the duty of the board to oppose the progress of the Guildford and Chichester line, and to suspend the Bill for affecting a transfer of half the Portsmouth Extension line to the South-Western Company.

Chaplin's board, maintaining its position, insisted that disputes concerning Agreement B did not justify terminating Agreement C, and Agreement B should be legally authorised as a whole and not clause by clause. By giving the Reading, Guildford & Reigate use of part of its Alton branch, the LSW denied it was promoting that company, and what it refused the L & B in negotiation it would not concede under threat.

Chaplin then met the L & B, suggesting joint purchase of the Direct Portsmouth with joint interest between Godalming and Epsom, the LSW taking five-eighths profits and the L & B three-eighths. The L & B declined, refused arbitration and declared the agreement ended. Chaplin refused to recognise this declaration and on 20 May 1846, the date for the next joint committee meeting, accompanied by Smith and Uzielli, directors, and Campbell, secretary, he attended London Bridge station and asked for Williams, joint committee secretary. The latter insisted that the committee was dissolved and declined to conduct its business or surrender copies of past proceedings. All records, he said, were with Captain Hotham, the Chichester chairman. He refused to record this discussion, but Campbell did, his memorandum concluding:

> At this point Mr Clarke came into the room, and after the usual complimentary salutations, Mr Smith said. "Well, Mr Clarke, have you any business for us this morning?", and Mr Clarke replied laughingly, "Why, no, no, there is no business to be done". Mr Uzielli, at the same moment interposing, "Well, we've done all we can and all we have got to do here, so we had better go". Having said "good morning", the South-Western party retired and left the station. This memorandum was written by me within one hour after.

Chaplin blamed Wilkinson, L & C chairman who became deputy-chairman of the LBSC, for urging the L & B to oppose them (a charge Wilkinson strongly denied), but he considered Grenfell, the new L & B chairman, could from his ignorance of the agreement be excused for charging the LSW with breaking it.

The 1846 session brought little comfort to the LSW. With the truncated Bill of 1845 pending in the Lords, the Guildford, Chichester, Portsmouth & Fareham introduced another for the remainder of its line, adding branches to Petersfield, Chichester Harbour and Portsmouth Dockyard, but the Act passed on 27 July 1845 styled the company as the Guildford Extension and Portsmouth & Fareham, reduced its capital to £500,000, and authorised only the Fareham to Portsmouth and Guildford to Godalming portions. The first, through Portchester, Cosham and the northern fortifications of Portsea Island, would terminate near Unicorn Gate, with a junction at Cosham with the Brighton & Chichester extension. At Godalming, the second portion would join the Direct Portsmouth, successful with its Act on 26 June 1846 despite the lighter works, better gradients, shorter mileage and superior local service of its rejected rival. Still confident of success, Chaplin predicted that the intended renewed application for the middle portion would be supported by the great landowners lately opposing it.

The Guildford extension proprietors, bitterly disappointed at their failure, met at Nine Elms on 26 August 1846 and accepted their board's recommendation to sell immediately to the LSW, which would return their deposits with five per cent interest from time of payment, meet all expenses and accept every liability. They rejected the alternative of building their authorised fragments for lease to the LSW. Three days later, LSW proprietors approved the purchase.

The LSW Epsom branch failed again in 1846, being thrown out by the Commons committee, while the L & B, successful with its Wandsworth branch, suspended further proceedings on the Bill for the joint extension from Chichester to Portsmouth.

In October 1846, Chaplin led a deputation seeking settlement with the LBSC of outstanding differences. Parliamentary powers obtained at great cost could not be nullified by disputes, and senseless competition was to be avoided in the country separating them. The result was an agreement, provisionally signed on 24 October 1846 (Agreement D), for seeking joint ownership of the Direct between Dorking and Portsmouth, the LBSC to have the Epsom to Dorking portion. The Bill to sanction this would include a clause legalising LBSC use of Waterloo. The Cosham to Portsmouth branch would be made and managed jointly, traffic involving the Brighton direction providing two-thirds of receipts to the LBSC, one-third to the LSW; and vice versa for traffic involving the Fareham direction. Neither company would promote any scheme in the district without mutual consent, and each would bear its mileage proportion of LBSC expenses in securing the Direct.

LSW proprietors approved this on 17 November 1846, giving their board a free hand. Three days later, the LSW told the LBSC 'that all proceedings with reference to the further promotion of the Godalming and Portsmouth, Wimbledon and Shoreham lines be abandoned', and in return was assured that the LBSC had dropped its own schemes in those areas. For the time being, therefore, all was sunshine again.

Projects the LSW abandoned included a line Locke was going to survey from Wimbledon to Brighton through Dorking and Shoreham, with a Dorking to Petworth branch. It had been instigated by a deputation, headed by Sir John Duke, from the 'Dorking, Brighton & Arundel Company', which sought terms with Chaplin. Bognor had been another LSW target. In July 1846, Lord George Lennox enquired whether the directors would adopt a line to there from Chichester which had failed Standing Orders that session. The LSW board had agreed, subject to its own Chichester line being successful, and had offered £3,000 towards expenses. Locke was instructed to survey, and in anticipation a house of Lord Lennox at Bognor (Lennox Lodge) was purchased by the LSW for £1,007 19s and a caretaker staff installed. When it was publicly auctioned in 1848, the company placed on it a reserve of £3,000.

The Act sanctioning LBSC use of Waterloo was passed on 22 July 1847—a barren power as the Wandsworth branch was never built. It also authorised LSW and LBSC joint ownership of such part of the Brighton & Chichester extension west of the latter's intended junction with the Direct at Havant 'as may be agreed upon', to be known as the Joint Line. Meanwhile, work on the authorised portions of the Guildford extension proceeded, Brassey having contracted for the Guildford to Godalming portion for £66,679 14s and £53,009 between Fareham and Portsmouth. By 30 July 1847, he had also doubled the Woking to Guildford line, which he contracted to maintain for £175 per mile per annum.

Despite the agreements, Parliamentary powers existed for three lines into Portsmouth, i.e., the Direct and the Brighton & Chichester extension running parallel to a common terminus, while the LSW got powers on 9 July 1847 to extend its independent and more westerly though parallel line from Cosham to a separate terminus where Lion Gate Road (now Edinburgh Road) joined Union Road (now Commercial Road), and abandoned the Unicorn Gate portion authorised by the Guildford Extension & Portsmouth & Fareham Act. A branch would now diverge near the present Prospect Road, following a course into the dockyard along the shore.

The Brighton & Chichester extension opened to Havant on 15 March 1847 and to Portsmouth on 14 June 1847. Notwithstanding arrangements for the Joint Line, the LSW haughtily told the LBSC on 2 August 1848 that, while refusing any proposal which meant abandoning its own line, it would consider traffic and other arrangements if a deputation attended York Road on 4 August. The LBSC declined this virtual summons. However, both companies met in September 1848, reaching yet another agreement (say Agreement E), this time for their purchase from the Brighton & Chichester of the Joint Line which would be from Cosham to Portsmouth. Because, as we saw, the LBSC had itself already contracted to purchase the Brighton & Chichester, it would pay the latter a nominal 5s and take £60,000 from the LSW for that company's share. A joint committee of three LSW and three LBSC members would provide a 5½-acre station at Portsmouth, with a platform each side of a shed, and each company could lay the electric telegraph. After deducting thirty per cent for expenses, both companies would pool the balance of their respective receipts from London and Portsmouth traffic, five-eighths going to the LSW, three-eighths to the LBSC. London traffic was defined as that which came from or went north of points two miles south of New Cross or Wandsworth stations. This agreement, operative from 1 October 1848, was signed on 9 October 1848, while another next day (say Agreement F) fixed rates, fares and services, of which the principal are shown in Table 4. The LSW agreed not to deviate legitimate Portsmouth traffic via Gosport, and neither company would use steamboats to secure an advantage.

The LSW now abandoned its independent Portsmouth line. The Joint Line ran almost centrally down Portsea Island, then west at Fratton along the disused bed of the Portsea canal until the latter turned into its Landport basin. The line terminated at Union Road.

Portsmouth's population in 1841 was 53,941, the inhabitants gathering chiefly in the south-west round the dockyard and Navy, from which the town drew life. Trade with surrounding areas was hampered by the natural barrier of Portsdown Hill, across which had come the coaches, but through or over which no railway engineer ventured. Three lines were financially unworkable, so the Joint Line was a marriage of convenience in the wake of the mania. Chaplin's board was also influenced by the Board of Ordnance demand for £12,000 to restore the 'equilibrium of defence' after the LSW line had passed through Hilsea fortifications.

TABLE 4

Fares LSW
Waterloo to:

	Exp. Single		Exp. return		Ordinary single			Ord. return		Mile
	1st	2nd	1st	2nd	1st	2nd	3rd	1st	2nd	
	s d	s d	s d	s d	s d	s d	s d	s d	s d	
Fareham	20 6	18 0	34 6	30 0	18 0	12 6	7 1	30 0	22 0	85
Cosham	21 0	18 0	36 9	31 6	18 0	13 6	7 6	31 6	23 8	90
Portsmouth	21 0	18 0	36 9	31 6	18 0	13 6	7 6	31 6	23 8	94

Fares LBSC
London to:

		1st	2nd	1st	2nd	3rd	1st	2nd	
Havant	No trains run at present between London and Portsmouth at a higher rate of speed than 25 miles an hour	17 6	13 0	7 6	30 0	22 6	88		
Cosham		18 0	13 6	7 6	31 6	23 8	91		
Portsmouth		18 0	13 6	7 6	31 6	23 8	95		

LSW *Trains*   LBSC *Trains*

Up weekdays	Down weekdays	Up Sundays	Up weekdays	Down weekdays	Up Sundays
8.20 am	7.30 am	8.40 am	6.30 am	6.00 am	4.00 pm
10.10 am	8.20 am	5.10 pm	8.50 am	9.00 am ⎱*	Down
12.10 pm	10.30 am ⎱*	Down	11.30 am	10.00 am ⎰	Sundays
2.00 pm	11.30 am ⎰	Sundays	3.30 pm	12.00 noon	7.00 am
5.11 pm	1.00 pm	8.20 am ⎱*	6.40 pm	2.00 pm	10.45 am
	3.45 pm ⎱*	10.00 am ⎰		4.00 pm ⎱*	
	5.00 pm ⎰	5.00 pm		5.00 pm ⎰	

* Arriving at the same time at Portsmouth

The LBSC had opened the Portcreek Junction and Farlington Junction lines to Cosham Junction on 26 July 1848, though LSW passenger trains did not run until 1 October 1848. The LBSC dropped its Fareham to Cosham branch in favour of the LSW line, which opened between those points on 1 September 1848

Reverting to Guildford, immediately south of that station the line pierced the North Downs by a 938-yd tunnel through chalk, then a short open section and a 132-yd tunnel through sand.

Hopes of opening between Guildford and Godalming in August 1849 fell with the sand tunnel roof during May. The quality of the bricks was suspect and, despite Locke's efforts, Captain Laffan reported to the Board of Trade on 17 August that the line was unsafe. It opened on 15 October 1849, with a further closure from 22 to 24 October 1849. The chalk tunnel today is 845 yd, the engine shed standing where its northern end has been opened out.

The LBSC soon grew restless over the 1848 agreement and, to maintain peace, the LSW in 1852 admitted the Fareham to Gosport line into the joint purse, amended expenses to fifteen per cent and division of receipts to give the LBSC one-third and the LSW two-thirds. The revised agreement (say Agreement G), now limited to twenty-one years, also prevented both companies promoting new lines in their intervening country except by mutual consent, and required their co-operation in repelling invaders.

This appeasement proving insufficient, the LSW conceded in January 1858 (say Agreement H) division of receipts according to each company's actual carryings from 1854 to 1856, but insisted the agreement must now expire in December 1862 or, by mutual consent, 1866.

On 15 November 1852, both companies announced that, growing traffic making further London terminal facilities necessary, a Bill for amalgamation would be presented next session. London Bridge, Waterloo and Vauxhall would be reciprocally used for passengers; Bricklayers Arms, Deptford and Nine Elms for goods. Other large companies were also seeking amalgamation, but Parliament feared giant monopolies and witheld consent. A Southern Railway was not yet to be!

DIFFICULTIES OVER THE PORTSMOUTH RAILWAY

Direct Portsmouth hopes ended when a Commons committee, doubting the promoters' intentions to build, rejected in 1847 a Bill for its amalgamation with the LBSC, which the LSW opposed as contrary to the spirit of Agreement D. LBSC and LSW-intended joint ownership of the Direct did not materialise, neither did Chaplin's attempt in March 1848 to get running powers between Godalming and Cosham. Post-mania depression delayed construction, and in 1852 the Portsmouth Railway appeared with a similar route, by agreement adopting and realising the assets of the Direct, which obtained a winding-up Act on 31 July 1854.

Influential Portsmouth Railway promoters, led by John Bonham Carter, M.P. for Winchester, and strongly supported in Parliament and Portsmouth, secured their Act on 8 July 1853 against determined LSW and LBSC opposition. Capital was £400,000 for the thirty-two mile line from the Chichester extension at Havant, through Petersfield, Haslemere and Witley to the LSW at Godalming. Brassey contracted to purchase the land, build and hand it over complete for £350,000, single but with bridges and earthworks for doubling. Locke and Errington were the engineers.

Bonham Carter cut the first turf on 6 August 1853 on his own hillside overlooking his home, Buriton Manor House, from which the Portsmouth Royal Marines band had led the procession of guests. His coat thrown off and wielding a silver spade, he filled a mahogany barrow with turf mingled with flowers thrown by the ladies. Before subsequent refreshments were finished, Brassey's men had cut deeply into the hillside near the north portal site of Buriton tunnel, beginning the short route to Portsmouth which was to disturb the uneasy equilibrium between the LSW and LBSC.

The picturesque wealden scene typified the route, undoubtedly the most attractive to Portsmouth. To enginemen, however, it could be a nightmare, being built on the follow-the-contour principle then advocated by some engineers and Dr Dionysius Lardner, the author of many fallacious theories on practical railway matters. Leaving Godalming, the first gradient between Milford and Witley is small compared with the following climb, first on an enormously curved embankment leading to a 1 in 80 cutting edged by woods which in season shimmer with bluebell hue. or momentarily reveal the startled scamper of deer with which they abound. Over the summit at Haslemere, the home of many London commuters, then a twisting descent of 1 in 100 by the edge of Woolmer Forest and down Liphook bank of 1 in 80 to maximum speed through Liss. Another climb from Petersfield at 1 in 100 passes Buriton Manor and enters the 485-yd tunnel through the South Downs, emerging to a wildly meandering descent of 1 in 80 (to aid trains making the difficult northbound climb) before flattening out towards Havant.

Despite a two-year estimate, work continued until May 1858, heavy cuttings at Haslemere, Witley and Liss being the last tasks on which 1,100 men and 150 horses toiled.

The company got powers on 24 July 1854 to extend northwards from Godalming, at first alongside and then over the LSW by a bridge, to join the SER near Shalford and reach London Bridge, by an eighty-two-mile route. Its negotiations in December 1857 with the SER and the LBSC, for traffic arrangements from Godalming to London Bridge and Havant to Portsmouth respectively, were unsuccessful. Earlier that year, by agreement with the LSW, it had abandoned the bridge and extension, except a short curve with flat junctions to link the SER with the LSW, and had secured use of the LSW line between Godalming and the junction, each company having access to the other's Godalming station. The embankment for the curve was built but apparently never carried metals, the LSW relieving the Portsmouth company on 26 January 1860 of liability for completing it. Its grass-covered form still remains, partly veiled by trees.

Portsmouth Railway and LSW negotiations began in 1856 when the former offered to lease its line for forty-five per cent of gross receipts. Chaplin insisted that any agreement must have LBSC approval, and talks petered out. Despite considering the LSW its natural ally, the Portsmouth company offered its line to the SER, which refused it on 5 August 1858 because of agreements with the LBSC. Seven days later, Brassey was offered and refused a ten-year lease. The LSW could not now hesitate. Epsom to Leatherhead line promoters of 1856, who also sought extension to Wimbledon in 1857, were Portsmouth Railway proprietors apparently forging links in a railway chain towards London independent of the LSW, in case no purchaser or lessee for the Portsmouth line were found. The LBSC could snap up the line, or the SER conscience might even be overcome; so on 24 August 1858 the LSW agreed to lease it for £18,000 annually.

The LBSC were immediately told and offered participation in the profit and loss, but Schuster, its chairman, wanted a joint lease, doubtless recalling this mutual resolution in Agreement H of January 1858:

> ..... the South-Western Company would make no arrangement of a permanent guarantee with the Portsmouth line, nor acquire any interest in it, but might work it as far as Petersfield without accounting to the Brighton company, or might work the whole line at cost price for ten years, on bringing the revenue they might derive from the through London and Portsmouth traffic to the joint Brighton and South-Western account for division.

These developments sparked off hostilities between the LSW and LBSC that had been brewing since their amalgamation failure. Despite territorial agreements, the LBSC had, as we shall later see, dabbled in schemes more than ten miles west of its main line, so how could it complain, asked Captain Mangles, if the LSW broke its own promises? The LSW counter-proposed bringing London and Portsmouth through traffic via the new Portsmouth line into the joint purse, giving the LBSC one-third of net receipts by all routes, less £5,000 towards the £18,000 rental. Such traffic over that route would be toll-free between Havant and Hilsea, with other new-line traffic paying sixty per cent of gross receipts over that portion.

Meanwhile, anticipating Schuster's further refusal, counsel's opinion was sought concerning LSW rights to take Portsmouth Railway traffic over the Joint Line, and preliminary moves were begun towards making the independent Portsmouth Railway lines authorised on 12 July 1858 from Havant to Hilsea and Cosham. The same Act granted the Portsmouth company running powers over the parallel Chichester extension and the Joint Line, but not into the joint station unless by agreement made before 12 July 1859, failing which the Portsmouth company could build its own more southerly terminus on land including parts of Blackfriars Road, Greetham Street and Telegraph Street.

Pending an Act authorising the LSW to lease the Portsmouth Railway, these companies reached a provisional agreement in August 1858 (which was formally signed on 24 December 1858) to take effect from 1 January 1859. However, in November 1858, the furious Schuster, seeing the LSW with a 73-mile route compared with 94¾ via Bishopstoke or 95¼ via Brighton, demanded that his company's position concerning joint traffic should be quite unaltered by these arrangements. The LSW suggested modifications to its previous offer, the main being that the LSW should bear all the new line rent, but requiring use of Havant station and the Joint Line and station for Portsmouth Railway traffic on terms like those for joint traffic. Additionally, the LBSC was to disavow connection with advertised new schemes from which Agreement H restricted it. These proposals of 7 December 1858 preceded by two days a letter from Crombie, LSW secretary, suggesting that both companies' solicitors should agree clauses for insertion in an imminent LSW Bill, to allow both companies to make arrangements from time to time concerning joint traffic receipts. Schuster did not reply, so the LSW inserted such clauses in LBSC interests.

On 16 December 1858, the LBSC sent and also published lengthy and revolutionary counter-proposals, so framed as to free the companies from Agreements G and H. The accompanying letter clearly showed that the LBSC regarded territorial arrangements as

STATIONS—9

(23) *Exterior of Windsor station, with doors for cavalry horses and with monograms and date picked out in darker bricks*

(24) *Royal waiting room, which faces a private road from Windsor Castle. Observers in the tower could warn those below of the Sovereign's approach*

BRIDGES

(25) At Staines, carrying the line to Egham, Weybridge and Reading. It has been strengthened since its opening in 1856

(26) At Black Potts, Windsor, looking towards Datchet. This bridge replaced the original about 1892

ended. The LSW board, on slender majority and for the sake of peace, adopted those counter-proposals as a basis, returning a copy with only essential alterations. The LBSC immediately refused any modification whatever and withdrew the counter-proposals, making rupture inevitable.

1 January 1859 being fixed as opening day of the Portsmouth Railway, Slight, LBSC secretary, wrote indicating his company's opposition to Portsmouth Railway traffic using the joint station. The LSW reply that it would do just that was a virtual declaration of war. The LBSC stiffened and declared that, pending proper arrangements, no Portsmouth Railway train would be allowed over the Chichester extension.

The LSW decided on a trial of strength by announcing that a goods train would run to Portsmouth over the new line on 28 December 1858 and daily thereafter, arriving at Havant at 9.58 am. Hawkins, LBSC traffic manager, having failed on 27 December to dissuade Scott, his LSW counterpart, organised battle stations at Havant Junction, where the defenders removed a tongue of the points and a rail from the Portsmouth Railway down line. The invading army of about eighty navvies set out under cover of darkness, led by Scott and with 'a supply of provisions and a barrel of beer'. The early arrival of their train, powered by 'two rusty-looking engines, *Minos* and *Windsor*', one hauling and one propelling, failed to surprise the defenders. The LSW men replaced the Portsmouth line rails as fast as possible.

The Battle of Havant that followed was described by Hawkins in a report to his board the same day:

> About 7.0 am this morning, the Direct Portsmouth people, with Mr Scott, Mr Godson, Horne, Ray, etc, arrived at Havant junction with a goods train, two engines and about eighty men, and demanded passage along the line, threatening the switchman with immediate imprisonment unless he gave up the tongue of the points. He, however, refused and they then placed eight or ten men on our engine, who put the driver and guard forcibly off, and shunted the engine aside. They then drew their own train along our up road through the station, crossing on to the down line, blocking both up and down roads.
>
> In the meantime, we had removed a piece of rail from our own down line to the west of the crossing, effectually preventing them from proceeding. I suggested to Mr Scott that, having now endeavoured to force their way through and being resisted also by force, whether he had not done enough to enable them to try their right before a proper tribunal, and requested him to withdraw. This he refused, and as I refused to replace the rails or allow them

K

to proceed, matters remained in this condition until about 1.0 pm.

I worked the traffic over the line between Havant and Portsmouth on the one side and Havant and Emsworth on the other, by bringing empty trains and engines on both sides of the obstruction and getting the passengers across on foot. You will see by the returns this operation was necessarily attended with considerable delay, but I did all I could to lessen it.

At 1.0 pm Mr Scott made up his mind to withdraw under protest, and fortunately our mail train was allowed to proceed without molestation. They further refused to pledge themselves not to make a similar attempt at any time, and I have accordingly been obliged to remain at Havant with two engines and men to watch their proceedings.

Not surprisingly, the story of the 'battle' has grown with the telling, whereas the preliminary skirmish comprised the only violence of the event. It was really a display of tactical obstruction by both sides. By 1.0 pm, when 250 extra Brighton men had arrived and two LBSC engines neatly blocked the LSW train, half the local inhabitants were there, with several young ladies in 'linsey woolseys and crinoline', and 'spicily dressed young gentlemen'. Arriving passengers viewed with astonishment a scene resembling an election with the signal-box as the hustings, while an enterprising trader stood on the line serving biscuits, oranges, etc, from two baskets.

Of course, the affair smeared the public image of both contestants. Strangely, or not so, LSW records do not describe it, save for minor references in words of unusual Victorian brevity. T. E. Harrison, Chief Engineer of the North-Eastern Railway, had arbitrated, but his award of 10 January 1859 was rejected. The LBSC commenced legal proceedings, and the LSW received an injunction on 31 December 1858 restraining it from using the line from Havant to Hilsea meanwhile. Nevertheless, the Portsmouth Railway opened to Havant on 1 January 1859.

Vice-Chancellor Wood heard the case on 19 January 1859, deciding that London to Portsmouth traffic over the new line was bona-fide LSW traffic, and refused the order the LBSC sought. The first train over the Portsmouth Railway to Portsmouth ran on 24 January 1859, being permitted by the LBSC without prejudice to its rights. Peace being essential, both companies met on 21 February 1859, but the vague discussions were fruitless. Four days later Captain Mangles sent Schuster proposals for eliminating competition by applying equal rates between all competing points. London to Portsmouth traffic by any route and Joint Line traffic should be joint, the LSW taking two-thirds and the LBSC one-third of ne

STRUGGLES IN THE EAST

receipts. He required the Havant to Hilsea line to be added to the Joint Line, both companies to use the whole toll free. Negotiations broke down and Captain Mangles, refusing arbitration, prepared to build the parallel Havant to Hilsea line at an expected cost of £40,000.

Schuster then embarked in early March 1859 on a foolish war, introducing two new London to Portsmouth trains and another between Brighton and Portsmouth connecting with a London express, through fares being:

	1st	2nd	3rd
Return	10s	8s	5s
Single	8s	6s	4s

(Including pier dues and boat between Portsmouth and Ryde or Cowes)

The LSW retaliated on 28 March 1859 with two Portsmouth express excursion trains, taking 1¾ hr to or from Waterloo via the Portsmouth Railway, with fares:

	1st	2nd	3rd
Return	8s	5s	3s 6d
Single	7s	4s	3s

Fares on other trains and via Bishopstoke were unaltered.

The LBSC then introduced a boat extension from Portsmouth to Southampton, including the charge in the competitive fare to Portsmouth. Its appeal against Vice-Chancellor Wood's decision was heard in April 1859, reserved judgement being given in its favour in June. Restrained by injunction, the LSW was now forced to wage the fares war by stopping its trains before Havant and conveying passengers the last nine miles by road, thus losing much of the advantage of its shorter route, while LBSC trains steamed triumphantly to the terminus. All this occurring in a glorious summer when passenger demand soared, the contestants are said to have lost £80,000, an amused public being the only winners.

The Joint Line, insufficiently maintained, became dangerous. It was reported on 7 July 1859 as 'much overrun with grass and weeds, frequently causing the engine wheels to cut the weeds off on the metals, and that some of the bearings of the rails are 5 ft 5 in from chair to chair'.

An appeal for reason was rejected by Schuster as an LSW wince under LBSC power, but Captain Mangles rightly said that the affair proved the inability of the LBSC to hurt them. Eventually, on 29 July 1859, the companies agreed to eliminate competition

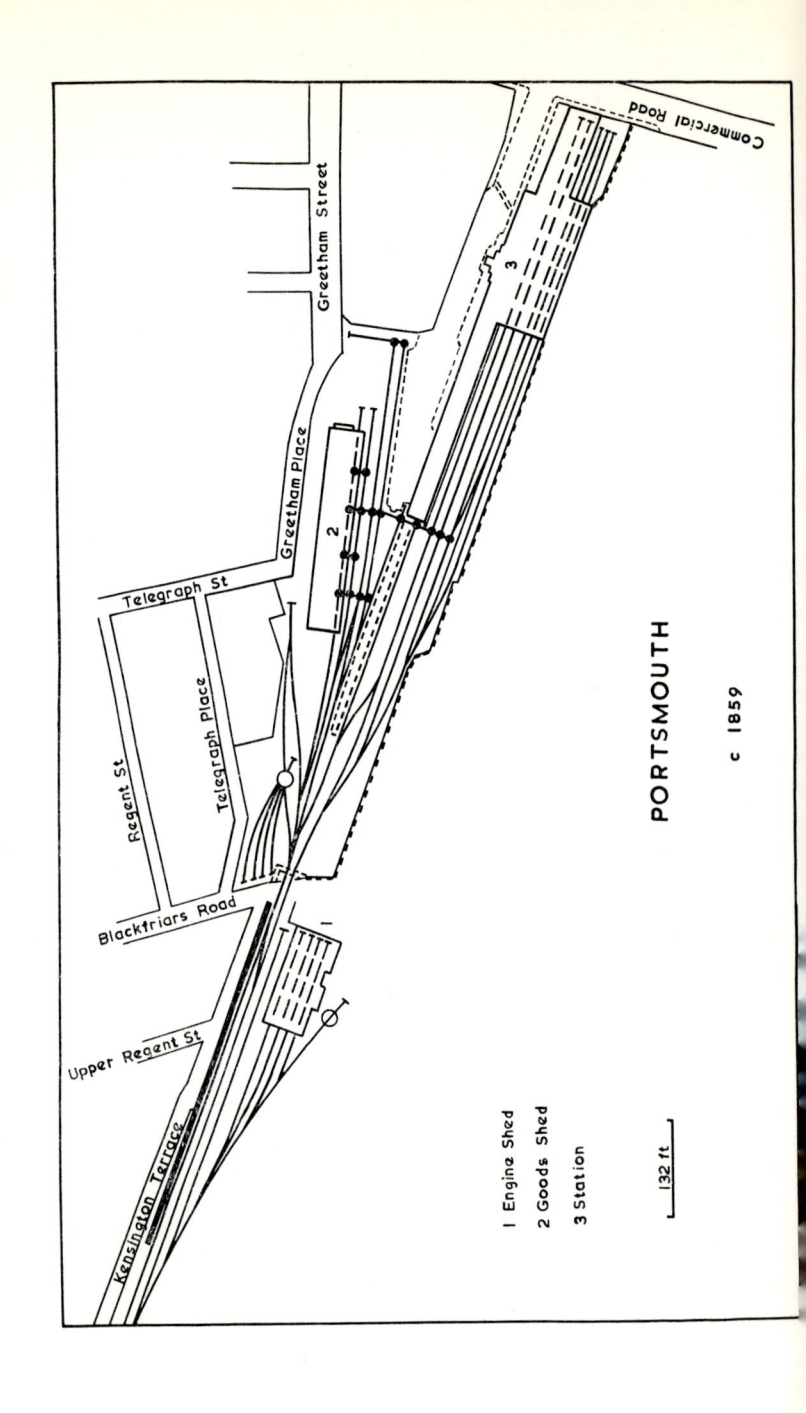

PORTSMOUTH

c 1859

1 Engine Shed
2 Goods Shed
3 Station

132 ft

from 8 August 1859 (say Agreement J), to charge equal fares and rates and distribute net receipts as before, the LBSC paying £15,000 annually towards the Portsmouth Railway rent between Goldalming and Havant. Through trains over that line resumed on 8 August 1859, all excursion trains being concurrently withdrawn. The injunction dissolved, the LSW would pay the LBSC £2,500 annually to use the Havant to Hilsea line, instead of the toll payable by the Portsmouth company under its Act of 1858. This included the Farlington Junction to Cosham Junction line, which track the LBSC had uplifted as useless. It now undertook to relay it, and the line re-opened on 2 January 1860 with a weekday service of one train each way between Cosham and Havant, and two trains (increased to three in February) each way between Portsmouth and Havant via Cosham. The LSW forewent, and obtained powers on 6 August 1860 to abandon, the proposed parallel Havant to Hilsea and Cosham lines and an independent Portsmouth station.

During the turbulent events described, a group of Portsmouth Railway shareholders led by Locke urged the proprietary to reject the terms of lease agreed with the LSW, and to seek £20,000 rental instead of the £18,000. The LSW refused, the rebels withdrew, amalgamation was agreed upon, and an Act authorising it was obtained on 21 July 1859. The Portsmouth proprietors would receive five LSW 2s 6d annuities for each £20 share surrendered. The Portsmouth company's accounts closed on 15 July 1861.

Determined on getting good service, Portsmouth citizens had won clauses during the passage of the amalgamation Bill requiring the LSW to run over the new line, Sundays excepted, six trains daily each way during every six months ended 31 October and four during the other six months; otherwise five daily throughout the year. These included two third class and one express, with speeds at least equal to like trains between London and Southampton. Maximum fares fixed were, 1st class, 15s 6d; 2nd class, 10s 6d, and 3rd class, 6s 2d, while 'the South-Western Company shall at all times work the line of railway between London and Portsmouth, through Godalming, fairly, as being a through line, and as being the shortest route by railway between London and Portsmouth'. Despite this, the LSW seemed determined that the line's advantages should not overshadow the original routes, and apparently only the minimum services were provided.

The Portsmouth Railway Amendment Act, 1858, required its doubling when receipts averaged £45,000 annually, and this work was completed as follows:

Godalming	to	Witley	1 June 1875
Witley	to	Haslemere	2 October 1876
Haslemere	to	Liphook	1 January 1877
Liphook	to	Liss	9 July 1877
Liss	to	Rowlands Castle	1 April 1878
Rowlands Castle	to	Havant	4 June 1877

The Portsmouth Railway possessed a more central Godalming station, sixty chains south of the junction with the original line, but passenger services to the old Godalming, a terminus, continued until Farncombe station opened on 1 May 1897. Today the old station exclusively handles freight.

Electrification in 1937 sparked new life into the Portsmouth line, with regular and more frequent stopping and fast trains at higher average speeds. Local passengers and season holders for London, etc, increased, while the war soon following saw thousands of Servicemen using the stations, especially Liss, where Longmoor Military Railway trains terminated (and still do) at a private platform parallel to the up main line. Other indigenous traffic is predominantly agricultural, but undoubtedly the line's importance remains as a short route between London and Portsmouth. Holiday-makers for Southsea and the Isle of Wight have year after year packed the intensive Saturday service, though queues at Waterloo have lately diminished as private car numbers have increased.

Portsmouth has long overspilled its population to the slopes and footings of Portsdown Hill. Though the dockyard has lost much importance, many light industries have sprung up, while Southsea remains an attractive resort. Isle of Wight passengers have passed through to Portsmouth Harbour since 1876, and the story of that extension, the tramway to Clarence Pier preceding it, and other local railway developments, will be considered in Volume Two.

INTERMEDIATE LINES

In 1845, Mitcham citizens, dissatisfied with the Surrey Iron Railway, launched a three-and-a-half mile Mitcham & South-Western Railway from Mitcham to the LSW near Garret Green (Earlsfield). The LSW opposed it in favour of the L & B Wandsworth branch, and the Bill foundered in 1846.

The LSW and LBSC both objected to a Wandsworth & Croydon Bill before Parliament in 1852, and negotiations secured its withdrawal, the promoters agreeing to construct a line from Wimbledon to Mitcham and thence to the Epsom to Croydon line near Croydon. The prospectus that September showed Henry Tootal as chairman, G. Berkley the engineer, and William Reed among the directors. The LBSC would take the Mitcham/Croydon for a minimum rental of £820 annually, and the LSW board provisionally agreed £1,500 for the Wimbledon/Mitcham section, considering it a useful main-line feeder.

However, in August 1852, LSW proprietors rejected it until their engineer had checked G. P. Bidder's estimates for making it. Six months later, with the guaranteed rent now £1,000, they spurned it as of little use except for improving certain landowners' properties.

The Wimbledon & Croydon Act succeeded on 8 July 1853, capital £45,500 and Peto & Betts built the line. In 1855, G. P. Bidder leased it for a rent, excluding office expenses, equalling four-and-a-half per cent of its capital, and it opened on 22 October 1855 after two Board of Trade postponements because of insufficient junction signals. Disaster immediately struck! After several trains had passed, carriages began swaying alarmingly until navvies restored the sinking track. On 24 October 1855 a train was completely derailed near Mitcham, killing the driver, and a 20-mph limit was imposed until the track consolidated.

LBSC objections forced the W & C to terminate Bidder's lease in favour of a Brighton company rental for twenty years at four per cent, including expenses. An authorising Act was obtained on 21 July 1856, and the LSW board provisionally negotiated equal participation with the LBSC, Parliament approving that on 10 August 1857.

The restless, suspicious LBSC was always a difficult neighbour, but more so when the Portsmouth Railway camp, searching for access to London, entered the intermediate district with Epsom & Leatherhead and Wimbledon & Dorking schemes. Matters worsened when promoters of a Horsham to Shoreham scheme instigated by Locke unsuccessfully sought LSW assistance. Although the latter pleaded its neutrality, Schuster raged with delusions of an imminent LSW march on Brighton and would not be pacified. In this and concerning the Portsmouth Railway he had fixations about Locke, still calling him the LSW engineer and holding that company responsible for his actions, although he had been independent for ten years. Schuster now delayed ratifying their agreement by reviving negotiations on terms which the LSW had previously rejected, while from Horsham, already reached by the LBSC from

Three Bridges, he launched a defensive line to Shoreham which Parliament approved on 12 July 1858. Locke's line foundered in the same session. For three miles south of Horsham, Schuster's line would share metals with the single Mid-Sussex, authorised on 10 August 1857 from Horsham to Coultershaw, near Petworth, which took the Brighton camp seventeen and a half miles nearer Portsmouth and opened on 10 October 1859.

We must now more closely examine the newcomers: the Epsom & Leatherhead (E & L) and Wimbledon & Dorking (W & D).

Herapath's Journal reported that lack of LBSC support had defeated attempts in 1855 to extend the LBSC Epsom branch to Leatherhead, but on 14 July 1856, after quelling LBSC opposition with protective clauses, the E & L was authorised. capital £30,000. Parliamentary difficulties prevented it extending each end, so the W & D was formed to sandwich it with Wimbledon to Epsom and Leatherhead to Dorking lines, the prospectus showing a junction with the SER at Dorking. The E & L and W & D had many mutual subscribers. The W & D 1857 Bill sought only the northern section and succeeded on 27 July, capital £70,000, after LSW opposition ceased following agreement that it should work and maintain the line for forty-five per cent of gross receipts, taking £30,000 in shares and appointing two directors. Its Agreement B of 1845 with the LBSC allowed this.

The W & D double line, surveyed by Crosse, was, like the E & L single line, built by Brassey, though bad weather and scarcity of men and materials made him late with both.

Under Agreement H of 1858, the LSW and LBSC had made a territorial truce. The latter would not dabble in extensions of the Mid-Sussex towards Petersfield or Arundel, nor of the Croydon & Epsom or Epsom & Leatherhead towards Dorking or Portsmouth. The LSW had undertaken not to extend its newly-acquired Wimbledon to Epsom line, and to disown publicly connection with Locke's Shoreham scheme. Thus committed, the LSW rejected on 11 February 1858 an E & L attempt to persuade it to work that line, and also opposed a W & D and E & L amalgamation Bill in 1858 lest such, by succeeding, should enmesh it with a line south of Epsom. That Bill was withdrawn.

Sorely snubbed, the E & L in May 1858 accepted Brassey's offer to work its line; then, overcome by longings to reach Waterloo, it again tried the LSW. The latter, having just taken the Portsmouth Railway, now agreed, subject to LBSC approval. Its charge and the service provided would depend on available traffic. The dissatisfied

E & L board tried Schuster, who gleefully and quickly took a lease in perpetuity for £2,000 annually, with a three-year option to purchase the line for £40,000, a victory which led to his breaking territorial agreements with the LSW in December 1858.

Meanwhile, certain subscribers, led by Sir Walter Rockcliffe Farquhar, were dissatified, for the shorter route to Waterloo had advantages over that to London Bridge. The E & L board, uneasy at this opposition, delayed opening the line and called a general meeting on 29 January 1859, when the chairman, Thomas Grissell, moved approval of the LBSC lease. Sir Farquhar now disclosed his talks with LSW directors and, producing that company's written offer to rent the line for £2,000 annually, he moved that the directors should negotiate with the LSW. This amendment succeeding, Grissell immediately announced the board's resignation, but Sir Farquhar and his supporters, with refreshing courtesy, urged it to stay, for the amendment carried no criticism of its actions. Five days later, Grissell left the E & L and W & D boards, and other directors also resigned, but Sir Farquhar, recently appointed High Sheriff of Surrey, declined a directorship. However, he undertook the further negotiations with the LSW, which quickly succeeded.

Schuster's anger was natural, but his own action had enabled the LSW to snap up the E & L conscience-free. In fact, it was acting defensively, for it found that not only was the Portsmouth camp seeking to extend the E & L to Guildford, but that the LBSC, earlier covertly and now openly, was promoting its own line from Leatherhead to Dorking. The latter town, on the north edge of the Weald, commanded the southern end of the narrow, steep-sided gap which allowed the river Mole through the North Downs barrier. That gap had, for centuries, provided the natural road route from north to south. The Portsmouth, E & L and W & D companies had jointly formed an independent Leatherhead & Dorking (L & D) Company to make this the southern portion of the original W & D scheme, and again loyalty to the agreement had so far prevented the LSW from participating. Now, on 17 February 1859, it agreed to subscribe two-thirds of the proposed L & D £75,000 capital. Alas, Parliament rejected it and the LBSC line in 1859.

The LSW leased and opened the E & L on 1 February 1859, providing stock for the seven daily trains each way over the 3 miles 33 chains and connecting as far as possible with London Bridge trains. The LSW and E & L agreement that month required the former to purchase, within six months of an authorising Act, the E & L for £50,000 cash, or for LSW shares, but meanwhile the lease would continue and traffic be so worked that passengers might choose between proceeding to Waterloo or London Bridge. On 8 April 1859 Parliament authorised the E & L and W & D to make a joint Epsom station independent of the LBSC, and on 4 April 1859 the LSW opened the Wimbledon to Epsom line. With W & D consent, the LBSC was offered use of the independent station, except on race days, for interchange of traffic. The Spring Meeting on 15 April that year, with its rich racing traffic, fulfilled a long cherished LSW dream, its delight being matched only by the glumness with which the LBSC counted its diminished receipts.

On 29 July 1859, the LBSC and LSW reached Agreement J, as important for this area as it was for Portsmouth. By it, the E & L would become their joint property, to be doubled at the request of either, and the LSW might extend it to Guildford, the LBSC to Dorking. On 8 August 1859, LBSC trains began running from Epsom to Leatherhead. Three months later, the working of the line was controlled by a joint committee which, in 1861, appointed an independent agent at Leatherhead, each company appointing half the porters. Parliament approved the joint ownership by the Epsom & Leatherhead Railway (South-Western & Brighton) Act, 23 July 1860, and terms of purchase finally approved by E & L shareholders on 30 September 1861 were £44,444 8s 11d in four-and-a-half per cent LSW stock, the LSW taking the £10,000 debenture debt.

A page from the LSW service timetable for January 1860 is reproduced, showing services between Waterloo and Leatherhead. Between Epsom and Leatherhead, the single line was worked by staff and ticket. Note, too, the instruction to take an extra five minutes on the journey! Such restrictions were common on newly-built lines.

Life with the W & D ran less smoothly. Interchange with Brighton trains at Epsom was one thing, but it considered the LBSC joint ownership of the E & L objectionable and illegal, especially as W & D metals at Epsom were involved without its consent. Over Epsom station it became blindly awkward. When called in 1859 to provide shelter there, it agreed only if the LSW paid nine-fourteenths of the cost. Summer and winter passed, and complaining passengers continued bracing themselves against wind and rain. By December 1860, loss of traffic was so great that the LSW threatened to erect a shed and debit the W & D. Horn replied that his board considered no shed on the up platform was necessary, but it seems the LSW ultimatum had the desired effect.

In February 1860, Remington, the W & D chairman, claimed the

LSW service timetable, Epsom line, January 1860

£3 7s per cent dividend was small because of diversion of traffic by the LBSC. The LSW, then bent on purchasing the W & D, had offered it £40,000 in LSW shares for equal W & D shares independently held, £20,000 towards its debts, and to shoulder its debenture debt of £23,000. Locke was prominent among shareholders who rejected it, causing the LSW on 1 March 1860 to resolve on 'all measures offensive and defensive against the Wimbledon & Dorking Company'. Now began a mutual display of tantrums. Mangles sent Gaselee (a veritable thorn in the flesh) to replace Uzielli on the W & D board, but the W & D refused to recognise him. The W & D commenced High Court proceedings to restrain the LBSC using its portion of line at Epsom, whereupon the LSW withdrew a free pass granted to Remington.

In 1860, the W & D obtained powers to increase its capital by £24,500, a move the LSW had opposed, being neither anxious to subscribe more capital nor to weaken its voting power in default. In August 1860, therefore, it secured an injunction restraining the W & D from issuing its new shares. Three months later came a W & D offer to issue them without voting rights, and to hold peace talks. Mangles accepted this olive branch, and agreed that the LSW would subscribe its portion. The talks succeeded, and the LSW acquired the W & D for four-and-a-half per cent preferential LSW stock yielding W & D shareholders three-and-a-half for four years from 3 April 1861, and thereafter four per cent in perpetuity. The LSW also adopted the debenture debt of £23,000 and provided £25,000 towards other debts.

We have not quite finished with the LSW and LBSC reunion of 29 July 1859. During the preceding free-for-all, the LBSC had supported an extension of the Mid-Sussex to Midhurst, which Parliament approved in August 1859, and it would likewise have assisted an extension to Arundel had that not failed Standing Orders. In addition, it had made open threats of a line connecting Guildford with the Mid-Sussex. Under the agreement, the LSW withdrew objections to the Mid-Sussex extensions and agreed that the LBSC might construct or work a line to Guildford. The LBSC reciprocally agreed to the LSW making or working a line to Midhurst from the Portsmouth Railway at Petersfield. Of the Wimbledon and Croydon, it assigned to the LSW that portion between Wimbledon and Mitcham for the remainder of the lease, the LBSC working it throughout but expenses and net earnings being equally shared.

Finally, the agreement killed exploratory talks with Bognor

residents who in June 1859 had sought LSW help with a line to Chichester from the Portsmouth Railway, and likewise died a LSW-proposed line from Leatherhead to Brighton, hatched early in July 1859 in retaliation for LBSC aggressions around Southampton.

CHAPTER 6

London, Windsor and Connected Lines

NINE ELMS AND THE METROPOLITAN EXTENSION

Nine Elms distinguished itself when, on 16 March 1841 in the locomotive storehouse, the storekeeper's naked light ignited turpentine from a leaking carboy. Within half an hour the building was completely ablaze, and five fire-engines joined three already there. Though ample water was available from the road, the railway authorities, led by Stovin, insisted that the engines be driven into the waterless station. Braidwood, the fire chief, was hustled and assaulted, one of his drivers torn from his seat, the engines forcibly possessed, and the firemen frustrated. The railway officials behaved disgracefully, creating hopeless confusion, while onlookers witnessed 'conduct and language used by men professing to be gentlemen, that would be a disgrace to persons in any rank of society'. Evenutally they restored control to the firemen. The blaze destroyed three locomotives and tenders, the store and workshops, but the 'inferior servants' were praised for preventing its spread and saving property. Next day, Braidwood, who had 'never before experienced such ruffianly treatment, even in the worst neighbourhoods of the metropolis', attended an enquiry with insurance officials and complained bitterly. Insurance companies paid £4,142 13s 0d while the LSW purchased its own fire-engine for £92.

Nine Elms had riverside wharf advantages but was never permanently intended for passengers: an extension into London was forecast in 1836. The London passenger found it more inconvenient than other companies' stations. He might leave it by road and frequently dip his hand for turnpike tolls, or for 3d choose the steamer *Citizen*, or the opposing *Bridegroom*, to reach the capital by river, cursing his choice when the rival vessel arrived and cleared the other queue while his own waited half an hour. By 1848 about 1,250,000 used Nine Elms annually, including 300,000 from the Richmond line, among whom lawyers and others daily suffered the rail and river trip between that town and Hungerford and Temple piers. Things improved slightly when the two steamer services combined shortly before the line opened to Waterloo.

That move nearer London had been decided on in 1844, and a ten-acre site near Waterloo Bridge was purchased, bounded by York Road, Cross Street, Griffin Street and Harlington Street, described as 'vacant ground, to a great extent occupied as haystalls and cowyards, and by dung heaps, and similar nuisances'. Parliament authorised the two-mile extension on 31 July 1845, capital £800,000, and anticipating the developing future, further powers were secured on 2 July 1847, capital £150,000, for four tracks and a wider station. The line crossed a 235-arch viaduct from Wandsworth Road (see Appendix 1), preceded by an embankment from Nine Elms junction, about 415 yd south of Nine Elms. The viaduct and station took over 80 million bricks and disturbed 2,367 properties, including about 700 houses demolished. Rents locally rose by up to forty per cent.

Deposited plans had included two short branches diverging north of the new station; one to Waterloo Bridge Road, the other towards Hungerford suspension bridge for possibly extending the Richmond line across the river. That bridge was inadequate for trains and a new one was financially impossible, but perhaps because the company supported the proposed multi-railway Central Terminus scheme (see below) a part of the short spur was built, serving many years with a turntable for locomotives.

The extension was built by Lee for £135,750, plus £39,000 for providing four tracks. The arches were waterproofed with asphalte, in preparation for letting them, and Tite's design for the intermediate Vauxhall station near the fashionable Vauxhall Gardens included a third-class booking office, waiting room and stairs separate from the other classes.

30 June 1848 was notified to the Railway Commissioners and advertised as the opening day, but when Captain Laffan examined the works he considered the tracks badly laid and ballasted, and suspected the strength of the bridge crossing Westminster Bridge Road. He refused to pass the line. The viaduct embodied six bridges over public roads, and local inhabitants had defended free movement by forcing clauses requiring four to be single span. The structure worrying Laffan spanned 90 ft on the skew to clear, as required, the road and footpaths, and was reputed to be the largest at such an angle.

The decision confounded the board, for the extension Act prohibited calculation of dividend on its capital for any period preceding 1 January or 1 July, whichever first followed public opening.

Taunton, the assistant secretary, wrote to the Commissioners on 29 June, pleading 'the rights of proprietors holding shares to the extent of 2½ millions will be affected' and that it would be 'quite out of the power of the directors or of the company to remedy the injury or injustice which will arise if the extension shall not be opened tomorrow, viz, before the 1st of July'. Naturally, he put greater emphasis on the public inconvenience the delay would cause, and explained how the works were 'being subjected to the running of engines and heavy trains of ballast over them, which had exposed them to a greater test than the running of passenger trains would do'.

Bircham and Martin visited the Commissioners that day to augment the appeal, but in vain; the opening was delayed for one month, unless the inspector be previously satisfied.

On 7 July, the senior inspector, Captain Simmons, made practical tests with upright rods at the centre and sides of the arch and touching the girders. A groove in each rod contained a sliding staff to indicate accurately the deflection of each girder as three of the company's heaviest engines, closely coupled, ran across. The deflection never exceeded 3/16 in. After testing the four tracks with engines at speed, the inspector passed the line and opening was accomplished on 11 July 1848, when Nine Elms closed for passenger trains. The first train, an up mail of seven carriages, arrived at 4.30 am with about forty passengers, who struggled out to Waterloo Road past still active workmen.

Designed by Tite, Waterloo occupied three-quarters of an acre, being about 260 ft wide and 22 ft above road level, reached by inclines of 1 in 25, plus pedestrian access by staircases There were two centre lines, and four other lines serving roofed platforms 300 ft long, subsequently extended to 600 ft. Ticket platforms existed at Westminster Bridge Road, trains being roped into the station, which lacked buffers until 1849 after a train nearly overshot the parapet into Waterloo Road. Permanent station buildings opened in 1853, until when temporary wooden booking offices, etc, sufficed, and the general offices occupied inconvenient and insalubrious accommodation in Vine Street.

Except for five extra minutes, train services remained unaltered, but main-line fares were increased by 6d first, 4d second and 2d third class. Portsmouth fares were untouched, because the LBSC refused to increase its own fares to that town. Tickets were printed in the basement at Waterloo, on presses purchased from the Clerkenwell Railway. About 100 specifically-registered cabs plied for hire at the station. Chaplin proudly said:

> We have placed on the railway from here (Nine Elms) to Waterloo Bridge station four distinct lines of rails, in order that we may have no trouble or inconvenience in future in the traffic; and also, that whatever may be the adventurous schemes of the age in future, whatever may be the probability of introducing lines south of London, we may not only have ample means of conducting our traffic, be it what it may, but all ability to let others come and hire, that we may benefit by their enterprise and industry on our property.

In Volume Three we shall trace development to the present fine Waterloo of twenty-one platforms serving eight running lines. All are electrified, and trains almost entirely limited to services over the former LSW network, yet times occur when further accommodation would be welcome. Electrification creates its own traffic and hence its own problems.

Waterloo, we saw, escaped accommodating LBSC trains when that company's Wandsworth branch Bill failed, and by chance also it became a terminus instead of the roadside station intended. In August 1845, Chaplin had suggested to an enthusiastic board that the Metropolitan extension be continued to London Bridge, so tapping the commercial heart of London and the City across the river. The North Kent Railway was challenging the SER with a Waterloo Bridge to Dover line, but was agreeable to building only to Southwark Bridge and using LSW metals thence to Waterloo Bridge station. However, it surrendered its interests to the SER, which defeated it in the 1846 session, in which the SER-proposed line from Waterloo Road to the Greenwich Railway itself foundered.

The LSW was more fortunate, its London Bridge scheme being authorised on 26 August 1846 with the proposed terminus to be near Alderman Humphrey's wharf. Though expensive land was purchased, the depression caused the board's decision to observe how Waterloo influenced other lines before proceeding further. Loath to discard their dearly-bought powers, the directors applied to the Commissioners for extended time, but on 28 November 1849 the proprietors decided to abandon London Bridge. Waterloo was now established as a terminus.

The London Central Terminus prospectus reached the LSW board in February 1845. The object was to provide a station near Charing Cross financed and jointly used by many companies. The LSW, Richmond, and Brighton companies joined those participating, but the idea never left the ground. The Brighton company lost

L

NINE ELMS 1854

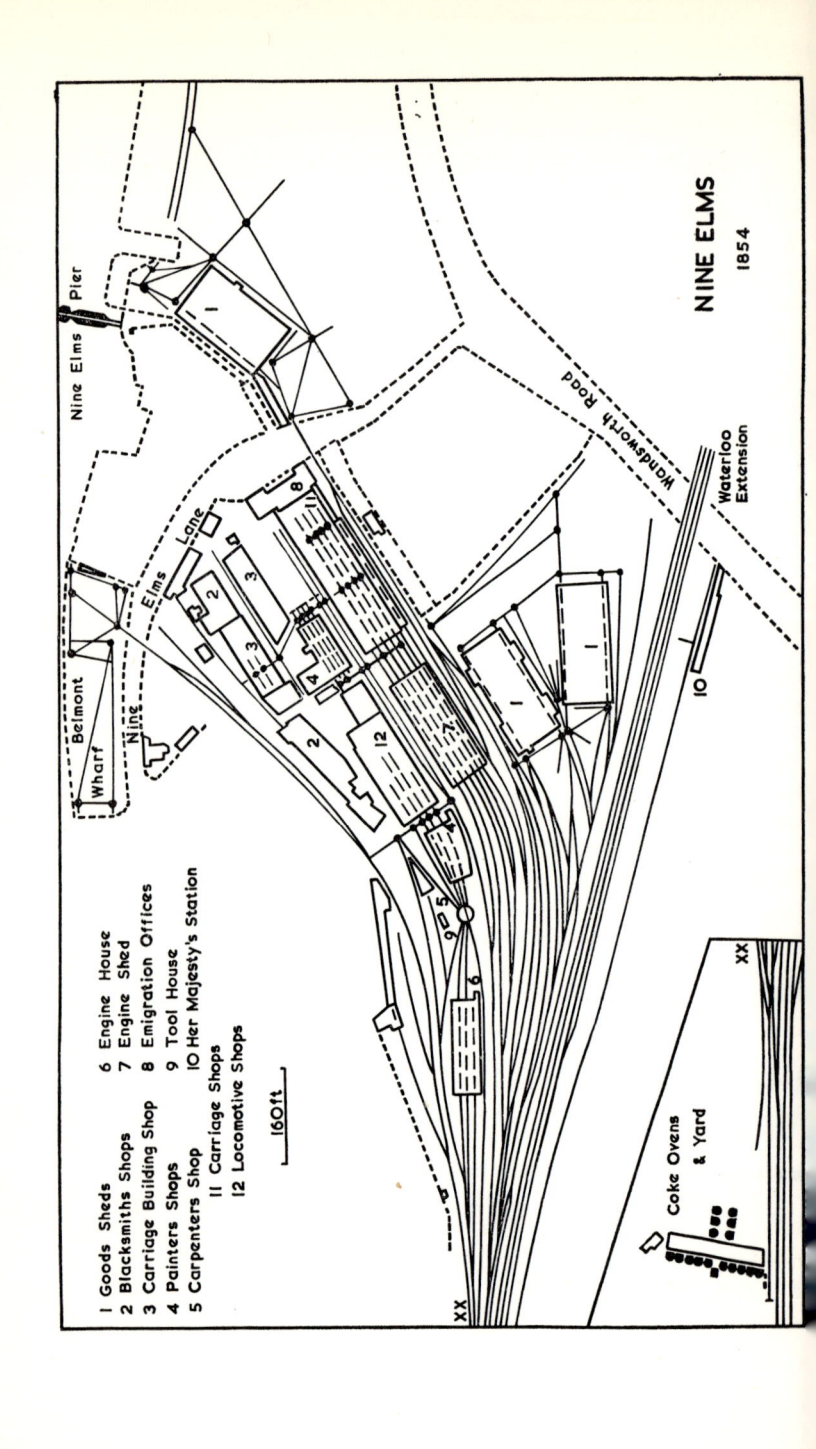

1 Goods Sheds
2 Blacksmiths Shops
3 Carriage Building Shop
4 Painters Shops
5 Carpenters Shop
6 Engine House
7 Engine Shed
8 Emigration Offices
9 Tool House
10 Her Majesty's Station
11 Carriage Shops
12 Locomotive Shops

160 ft

interest, and in November 1847 the LSW withdrew.

Nine Elms itself underwent many changes. By an Act of 19 July 1844, capital £12,500, a triangular site south of the terminus was acquired and a 2 furlongs 3½ chains branch built to Wandsworth Road, giving much needed room for expansion. Growing goods traffic, especially imports and exports through Southampton, made further riverside accommodation necessary, and improved access from the Thames to the coke ovens was desired, so powers were obtained with the Metropolitan Extensions Act, 1845, to cross Nine Elms Lane to Belmont Wharf. By 1853 it was announced that that 3½-acre site with long river frontage had been purchased for £11,200.

Despite imminent closure to passengers, some alterations carried out at Nine Elms in 1846 included segregation of first and second from third-class booking offices. After passenger traffic ceased, shareholders no longer suffered the indignity of attending general meetings in the goods shed because the boardroom was too small. The vacated booking offices and waiting rooms were converted into one large apartment seating 300, and the directors sat at those gatherings on a raised dais covered with crimson cloth. Workshops and goods accommodation was increased, the site in November 1854 being shown in the drawing opposite. The passenger shed became carriage shops (11 on the drawing), and the offices (8) were let to Emigration Commissioners until 1859. Incidentally, an 1844 plan of Nine Elms shows buildings 12, 2, and conjoined 2 and 3 existing, but their purposes then are not indicated.

By a further Act, 14 August 1855, the company acquired the land bounded by Wandsworth Road, Nine Elms Lane and the river.

On 21 June 1849, the way and works committee proposed '. . . to lay lines of rail along each of the platforms of the former arrival and departure shed, lowering the platform level to that of the other part of the shed, and provide a moveable platform which will preserve the facilities for the departure or arrival of Her Majesty'. In 1854, her private station was ready at Wandsworth Road, south of the main lines, but royal carriages were stored at Nine Elms carriage department until, in December 1857, Beattie was instructed to make room for them at the private station.

With powers obtained on 2 July 1847, a third line (the Nine Elms Widening) between Nine Elms and Falcon Bridge junction was opened in August 1848, the fourth, a down line, not coming into use until August 1860. On 3 August 1860, the Windsor line station opened at Waterloo, bringing that hard-pressed terminus towards

WATERLOO

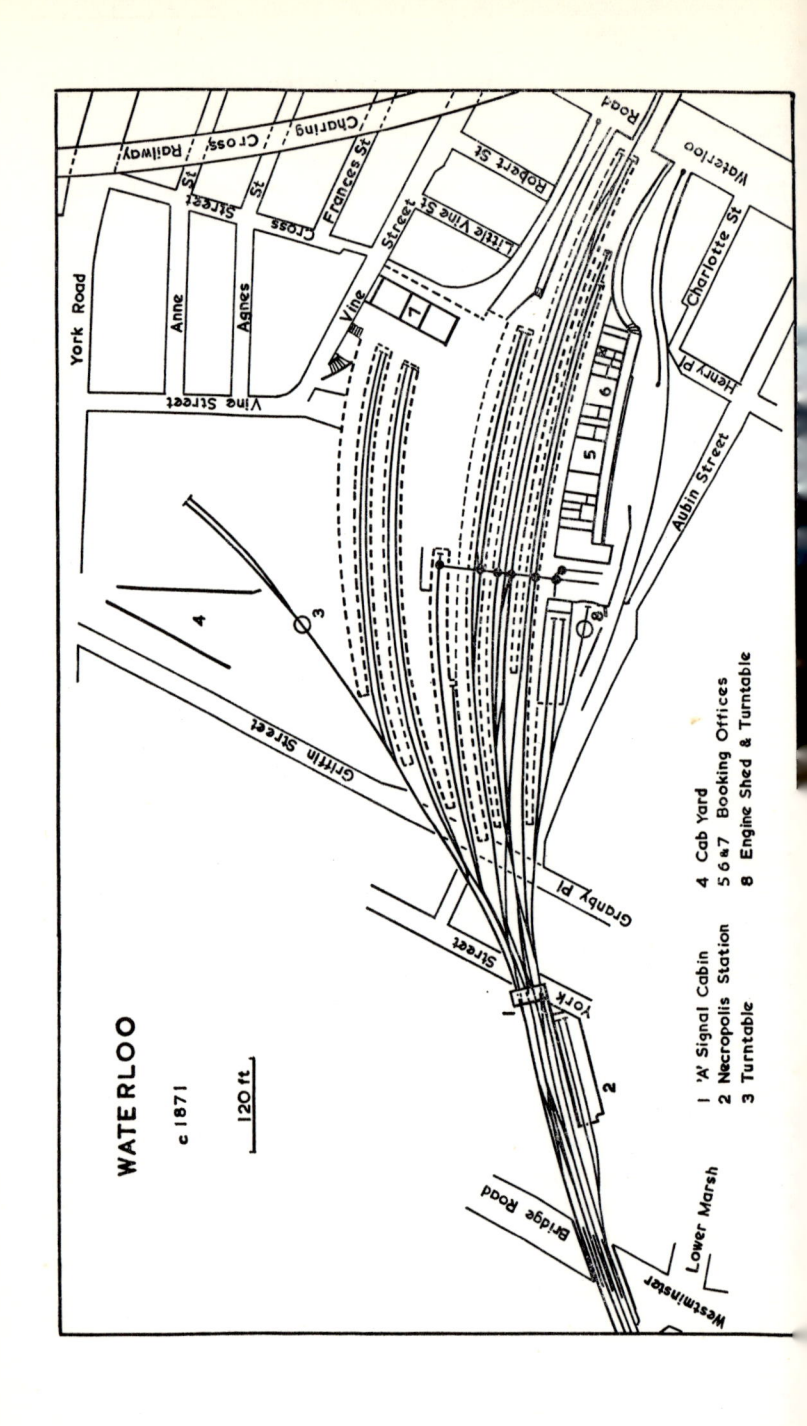

c 1871

120 ft

1 'A' Signal Cabin
2 Necropolis Station
3 Turntable
4 Cab Yard
5, 6 & 7 Booking Offices
8 Engine Shed & Turntable

its appearance in the diagram opposite. Main and Windsor line trains were now independent, but the Nine Elms Widening lines were for some time called Twickenham lines, because Twickenham became a semi-terminal station until the Kingston branch opened in 1863.

THE BATTERSEA KNOT

The stranger to Battersea might be perplexed by the entanglement of converging lines, or the size and heavy traffic of Clapham Junction. Many companies contributed, but our concern being the LSW we shall trace only those threads essential to our tale. Clapham Junction station was not opened until 1863, but the simple junction of LSW Southampton and Richmond lines was first augmented by the West End of London & Crystal Palace Railway, which itself took root from the Great Exhibition of 1851 in Hyde Park. Besides provoking that hideous period of repellent Victoriana bric-a-brac and artistic fantasy, the Exhibition bequeathed Paxton's showpiece, the Crystal Palace which, transported to a recreation centre at Sydenham, naturally encouraged a railway link with London's developing West End. Incidentally, the Exhibition gave London railways valuable traffic and hard work, and the LSW rewarded the efforts of its traffic staff with a shareout of £1,300.

The WE & CP Act of 4 August 1853 authorised a line to Crystal Palace Park from the LSW at Falcon Bridge, with a branch to a Thameside wharf near Chelsea suspension bridge then being built. The promoters had intended that the LSW should work them, and terms had been provisionally settled in April 1853, but when the LSW insisted on the WE & CP abandoning its Thames branch the latter refused, and as negotiations foundered it turned to the LBSC, whose line its southern end would join. This shortsighted defence of Waterloo cost the LSW its chance of controlling a railway route that was inevitable, sooner or later.

The LBSC came to terms and sought LSW consent on 6 October 1853: then WE & CP proprietors approved these working arrangements and submitted a Bill in 1854 for powers to sell or lease to the LSW, LBSC or SER, but after being savagely mutilated by Parliament it was withdrawn. Fresh negotiations brought agreement early in 1855 for WE & CP trains, worked by the LBSC, to go to an independent station the LSW would build near York Road, Waterloo. The WE & CP would abandon its Thames branch and pay the LSW seven-thirteenths of both its net receipts and of

£8,000 it would annually receive from the LBSC. Unfortunately, the LBSC decided Waterloo could not accommodate the heavy traffic expected and the idea was dropped.

The WE & CP, which subsequently became LBSC property, opened for traffic on 1 December 1856 from Crystal Palace to a temporary station on Wandsworth Common near the LSW. (The celebration trip was on 30 October 1856.) The Thames branch opened on 29 March 1858, concurrently with Chelsea suspension bridge, but rail access across the river only came when the Victoria Station & Pimlico Railway was authorised on 23 July 1858 to build from the WE & CP to a terminus near Victoria Street, and the LBSC, subscribing half the capital for half the station, began running there on 1 October 1860.

According to Oscar Wilde, Lady Bracknell would have been no more benevolent had Mr Worthing been deposited on the other side of Victoria station, jointly subscribed for by that most improbable alliance, the London, Chatham & Dover and the Great Western. The VS & P was laid with mixed gauge for GWR benefit, and the latter reached there via the West London Extension Railway which opened on 2 March 1863.

The West London Railway, ostensibly to link the GWR and London & Birmingham Railway with territory south-west of the metropolis, and with the Thames, got its own Act on 21 June 1836 as the Birmingham, Bristol & Thames Junction. The single line opened on 27 May 1844 from the L & B near Kensal Green cemetery to Kensington canal basin, but its trains were constantly delayed at the whim of the GWR, whose line it crossed on the level. It served such traffic-barren, rural country that *Punch* constantly lampooned it and called it his very own.

'Mr Punch's Railway' resented its discomfiting patron and hoped for lucrative traffic when the GWR and LNW co-operated in getting a GWR Act on 2 July 1847 to extend it over the Thames on mixed gauge where, after burrowing under the LSW at Battersea, it would join that company's Waterloo line near Wandsworth Road. However, the post-mania curtain drew across the scheme, despite protests by the WL board.

The extension idea reappeared in November 1858, and the LNW proposed it be continued to the SER at London Bridge. The LSW board disliked this threat to its own traffic and vacillated for weeks, but disturbed by other invasive schemes brewing in the area and believing in joining what you can't beat, it decided on 10 March 1859 to subscribe to the West London Extension (WLE).

LONDON, WINDSOR AND CONNECTED LINES

The WLE Act received Royal Assent on 13 August 1859, capital £300,000. In lieu of shareholders, the GWR and LNW each contributed £100,000 and each appointed four directors; the LSW and LBSC £50,000 and two directors each. The 4 miles 6 chains double line from the WL at Kensington was authorised to join the VS & P at Battersea (in fact, it joined the WE & CP approximately where Queens Road Bridge now is) with a branch under the LSW to the WE & CP near Wandsworth Road bridge, all on mixed gauge. Two narrow-gauge branches would join the LSW; one near Falcon bridge towards Richmond and one near Pouparts Lane bridge towards Waterloo, but the second would only be made with LSW consent Another mixed branch of twenty-seven chains was authorised to the Thames near the mouth of Kensington canal.

When the WLE opened, the now doubled 'Mr Punch's Railway' at last led somewhere. The LSW ran fifteen trains daily on the twelve-minute journey from Clapham Junction to Kensington, 3¼ miles, and sixteen back, all taking first, second and third-class passengers, while Sunday services were almost as frequent. Intermediate stations existed at Battersea, ¾ mile, and Chelsea, 1¾ miles. LSW service timetables, 1863, show freight trains, including a butter special on Wednesdays and Saturdays, still reaching Willesden from Nine Elms via Barnes and the N & SWJ.

The LSW Clapham station, called Wandsworth when opened in 1838, stood by Freemasons bridge and was closed on 2 March 1863 when Clapham Junction station opened to make interchange of passengers between the LSW and LBSC more convenient. Unfortunately, original records of Clapham Junction at the time do not seem to have survived, but it appears probable that there were in 1866 eight platforms with fourteen faces serving, from north to south, seven lines for WLE narrow-gauge trains, Ludgate Hill branch and Windsor trains; three LSW main lines; two WE & CP lines, and two WLE mixed-gauge lines. There was a booking office in what is now Prested Road on the south side, and another in the centre of the station reached by a long approach from Wandsworth Road (St Johns Hill), though this description may well be incomplete.

THE RICHMOND RAILWAY

In August 1844, the LSW board declared its readiness to help an independently-mooted branch from Wandsworth to Richmond, with extension of the LSW to Hungerford and Waterloo bridges included. However, the board urged LSW proprietors to consider making it themselves, for existing traffic was large and ninety-eight omnibuses went to and from Richmond daily.

As we saw, the Richmond promoters yielded the extension to Waterloo to the LSW. The Five Kings having approved the scheme, the independent Richmond Railway Act received Royal Assent on 21 July 1845, capital £260,000, the first board of fourteen including Chaplin, Eyre and Humphreys of the LSW.

The route from Richmond lay through Mortlake, Barnes, Putney and Wandsworth, with stations at each, to the LSW at Falcon bridge, the contract going to Henry Knill for £50,000, and Locke being the engineer. The only large works were (1) a viaduct over the river Wandle and the Surrey Iron Railway, 1,000 ft long with twenty-three arches, three having spans of 70 ft, and (2) a cutting at Putney. At Barnes, the company was compelled to build a bridge to take the Hammersmith Bridge Company's road over the line, and screen it against fright to horses.

Delay at the Richmond end resulted from difficulties with landowners, but the cutting and viaduct were quickly begun. The line took only nine months to build, costing £195,000, or just over £30,000 a mile. John Tombs' tender of £11,075 for Putney and Barnes stations was accepted, these to have 'tiles for the roofs instead of slates, chimney tops in character, and a small room in the roof'.

Waterloo being incomplete, Richmond trains terminated at Nine Elms when the line opened on 27 July 1846 with seventeen trains each way daily. A directors' trip on 22 July in a sixteen-carriage train drawn by the locomotive *Crescent* was augmented by celebrations at the Castle Hotel, Richmond. Station buildings at Richmond were also unfinished, but the directors were loath to lose the lucrative seasonal traffic, and worked by the LSW under 'satisfactory arrangements' receipts the first week were £476, and £536 the second. Full traffic development awaited access to Waterloo, but passenger figures for June and July 1847 give some idea of the line's immediate success:

Wandsworth	9,486	Mortlake	9,221
Putney	8,550	Nine Elms to Richmond	53,944
Barnes	4,738	Richmond to Nine Elms	50,571

Herapaths Journal considered the line 'wanting in the picturesque' though crossing beautiful country, a defect compensated on reaching Richmond. Certainly, pleasure-seekers bound for the park or the river continue to contribute much to its value, though today it relies chiefly on commuter traffic from its dense local population. Fares of 1s 6d express, 1s 4d first class and 1s 0d second class from Richmond to Nine Elms were announced prior to opening, but being unfavourably received were quickly reduced to 1s 0d first class and 10d second.

There was, apparently, too much haste in construction. *Herapath* reported two heavy jolts near Richmond on the trial trip, and within four days of opening Gooch reported the line unsafe, his enginemen complaining they could not maintain their times. Locke was called in to remedy it.

Shortly before the opening, negotiations for sale to the LSW began. On 4 July 1846 a Richmond deputation reported provisional terms by which Richmond stock (13,000 shares of £15 paid up, i.e., £195,000) would become LSW stock after paying construction expenses, qualifying for dividend from January 1847, but there would be no Richmond representative on the LSW board.

Many considered this unreasonable, including the *Railway Times*, which recommended shareholders not to accept. This so annoyed the LSW that that journal did not receive an invitation to the opening and could only briefly announce that event, with a protest over its exclusion.

Richmond proprietors were dissatisfied, for if traffic carried under existing disadvantages exceeded expectations, receipts on opening to Waterloo would justify a better offer. With the LSW forced to concede, the final agreement gave Richmond proprietors a choice of one LSW £50 paid-up share for three Richmond £15 paid-up shares, or £25 cash for each Richmond share surrendered. Dividend on converted shares would commence on 31 December 1846, with five per cent interest payable from 1 July 1846 until then. One Richmond director would join the LSW board, the Richmond board winding up by 31 December 1846.

When T. B. Simpson, the Richmond deputy-chairman, was nominated, he was promptly advised by the LSW that as no vacancy existed he should join the Southampton & Dorchester board, or another company in the Richmond, Staines or Windsor areas. Irate Mr Simpson immediately saw Chaplin, emerging with the promise of an LSW seat immediately a vacancy arose.

The line was not without accidents. On 17 November 1848 the *Vulture* engine used by Brassey for ballasting the Datchet line (see below) returned to Richmond at 5.0 pm. Instead of being properly disposed of, she was left attached to wagons in the old platform shed. When she loudly blew off steam, an investigating porter, discovering she had little water in the boiler, located her crew in a public-house. The fireman took the *Vulture* for water and returned her to the station. Soon, the over-refreshed driver and four companions returned, mounted the engine and drove her rapidly on a private trip to Barnes. Near the junction with the Datchet line, they collided with the 5.35 pm Waterloo to Datchet express, severely damaging both engines and slightly injuring some passengers. Doubtless because of the small compartments, most of the injuries were to their knees. The *Vulture* driver was seriously injured, and a companion, who was thrown against the gauge cocks and broke them with his skull, received over him the boiler's scalding contents and did not survive. Discipline at Richmond was promptly tightened after this affair.

The first Richmond station was a terminus on the London side of Kew Road, and the Datchet line diverged to the right about 635 yd before reaching Kew Road bridge from London. The circumstances of the accident lend weight to the belief that probably some temporary platforms were opened on the Datchet line when trains began running through, perhaps adjacent to the original terminus. In September 1849, Twickenham became a semi-terminal station and remained so until the Kingston line opened. On 7 March 1850 it was decided to move the engine house, turntable and water tank from Richmond to Twickenham, and after the way and works committee had visited Richmond and found it inconvenient and inadequate, tenders were invited in March 1852 for a new passenger station between the bridges over Parkshot Road and Kew Road. It probably opened in 1853.

WINDSOR LINE AND THE LOOP

The fertile Thames Valley, with variations of heath, parkland, nurseries, easy contours and close proximity to London, naturally attracted railway speculators. While railways made many places prosperous, others suffered acutely from them. Such was Hounslow which, situated on the Bath and Staines roads, had thrived on coaching traffic. Then the GWR bled it from the north and the LSW from the south until, in 1842, its distress was great and 'in a window at one of the chief inns is an inscription, that "new milk and cream is sold here", whilst another announces the profession of the chief occupier as that of "mending boots and shoes"'.

The Richmond proprietors had always looked towards Staines,

Brentford and Hounslow, and had encouraged the Staines & Richmond Junction Railway, whose prospectus for a ten-mile line from the Richmond Railway to the Thames at Staines had appeared in 1844. In August 1845 the rival London, Hounslow & Western Railway appeared with an intended line to start close to the present Clapham Junction, cross the Thames to Fulham. thence via Hammersmith, Chiswick, Brentford, Isleworth, Hounslow and East Bedfont to Staines. Its promoters sought terms with the Richmond Railway, which refused to abandon its own plans for Brentford and Hounslow or to negotiate unless the London, Hounslow & Western agreed to go no farther than Hounslow. In the 1846 session the latter company's scheme was thrown out by the Commons, while the Lords rejected the Richmond company's proposed branch from Mortlake to Kew. Concurrently, the Commons rejected the Staines & Richmond Bill, whose opponents included the Commissioners of Woods and Forests, and the GWR. The latter, however, received a setback to its Thames Valley surburban ambitions, as its Bill for a line from Ealing through Brentford and Isleworth, and between Twickenham and Hounslow to Staines, was also lost.

Another failure in 1846 was the Windsor, Slough & Staines Atmospheric Railway, despite its winning support from the ratepayers of Slough, who had earlier intended opposing all Windsor lines, lest their town, like Colnbrook, became 'a deserted village'. Opposition by the Commissioners of Woods and Forests, Eton College and the GWR was so strong that, after a Commons committee rejected the Bill, its promoters considered, on 16 July 1846, that they should accept the GWR amalgamation offer and allow it to make the branch. Cautiously, the Atmospheric promoters sounded the LSW for better terms, but the latter hestitated pending successful acquisition of the Richmond Railway. The Richmond company, however, promised that should its own negotiations with the LSW fail, it would lease the Atmospheric on terms better than those the GWR offered. Thus the ambitions of the Windsor, Slough & Staines Atmospheric were guided away from the broad gauge.

On 22 September 1846, most Atmospheric proprietors approved an agreement for amalgamating with the Staines & Richmond Junction to form a new company. The Atmospheric would provide £150,000 and three directors, the Staines & Richmond £200,000 and four directors. The LSW would make up the board to fifteen, provide the balance of the capital, guarantee four and a half per cent rent on the gross outlay and pay the company half the profits; but it would have the option of purchasing the new company with £15 LSW stock for each £20 of its capital.

The board of this new Windsor, Staines & South Western Railway first met on 9 October 1846 at Nine Elms, when Locke, its engineer, recommended making the line in two parts. On this principle two Bills were presented, and as Number One Act and Number Two Act were passed on 25 June 1847, the double incorporating powers making two companies within one organisation. Number Two Act and its line from Staines to Pirbright with a Chertsey branch we shall consider later, but Number One Act, capital £500,000, authorised a line from the Richmond Railway, through Twickenham and Staines to a Datchet terminus near Black Potts, about 1,100 yd north-west of Datchet bridge, with a loop from the Richmond Railway at Barnes via Brentford and Isleworth joining the main line near Hounslow. Bridges over the Thames at Barnes and Richmond were to give 21 ft clearance at high water. As the main line intersected the cavalry barracks review ground on Hounslow Heath, the company was required to construct a new entrance complete with lodge gates, and provide, if demanded, a platform for troops nearby. Any other station within 600 yd was forbidden.

The loop line would cross the Grand Junction canal, and where the Duke of Devonshire's estate was crossed at Chiswick, a station to serve it was obligatory.

The ultimate prize was Windsor, with the prestige of serving the Queen. On 11 June 1847, the Lords Committee had rejected the GWR Windsor branch Bill; and its Acton to Staines and Egham line, with Brentford, Isleworth and Twickenham branches also failed in that session. When the WS & SW made an agreement on 10 May 1847 with the Commissioners of Woods and Forests, involving a payment of £60,000 to the Crown, it had thought the prize secured. The money was earmarked for 'essential' improvements in Windsor Great Park before the Datchet line was extended, but on 15 June 1847 Lord Morpeth, the Chief Commissioner, informed the WS & SW that the improvements Bill had been postponed until the next session. The directors protested at the delay, but in vain.

The agreement with the Commissioners had been sanctioned by Number One Act and had provided for a GWR branch from Slough to be accommodated at the WS & SW terminus. On 19 October 1847 the WS & SW wrote to Saunders asking whether his company intended going to Black Potts, a project the WS & SW would not oppose. Saunders' reply of 22 October enquired, before answering, whether that terminus was permanent or, if the WS & SW was going to Windsor, what direction was it going to take? Hearing from Lord Morpeth that the GWR was concurrently promoting a Windsor branch almost like its earlier rejected one, the angry WS & SW board realised that Saunders' enquiry was sent merely to stall it. It therefore decided to promote its own 1¾-mile line from Black Potts to Slough, but was persuaded against seeking to cross Home Park to Windsor when Lord Morpeth signified the Queen's disapproval and GWR opposition.

The GWR was improving its influence at Court and organising stronger opposition against the WS & SW. In the 1848 session it transpired it had also made an agreement with the Woods and Forests, paying £25,000, and now the Commissioners supported its Bill for close access to Windsor and opposed the WS & SW Slough branch. Proceedings in the Lords were bitter, Lord Morpeth being accused of double-dealing and removing an advantage the WS & SW had dearly bought. Its Slough branch rejected, the WS & SW was induced to withdraw opposition to the GWR Bill by being promised that, should it succeed, the Queen would allow the WS & SW to cross Home Park.

The GWR Act was passed and Windsor was destined to have two termini. The £85,000 extracted from both companies went towards draining Home Park and improving approaches to the castle and town, including the construction of Victoria and Albert bridges and the destruction of Datchet bridge. The report of 25 August 1848 to LSW shareholders was obscure on these events:

> The company were compelled by the Commissioners of Woods in the session of 1847, to adopt a station, certainly not so convenient for the town of Windsor, as would otherwise have been selected; but it was then understood that the Commissioners would allow no other to them, or their competitors. The Windsor company therefore took measures for opposing the Great Western company's proposal to make a Windsor branch ending nearer to the town than the station prescribed last year, but Her Majesty having graciously consented to an extension of the Windsor, Staines and South Western Line from Datchet across the Home Park into the town of Windsor, every object of the Windsor company has thus been attained.

Brassey's successful tenders were £111,700 from Richmond to Datchet and £75,012 for the loop. The terrain being flat, work proceeded quickly, despite economies imposed after the mania, and the line to Datchet opened on 22 August 1848, following a directors' special on 19 August. The weekday service between

Datchet and Waterloo, operated by the LSW, was fifteen up and twelve down trains.

The WS & SW got powers on 26 June 1849 to extend by skirting Home Park to New Windsor, terminating 'near a certain lane there, called "Farm Yard" ', but Eton College and the Woods and Forests consenting, work had started early that year. Brassey's accepted tender was £30,000, and the extension expected to cost £80,000 was to be completed by 1 August 1849. It was ready on 9 August when, alas, two piers of the Thames bridge at Black Potts had settled since the track was laid. Locke admitted he had never before used cast-iron cylinders, but had done so here to avoid delay with coffer dams. He was now forcing down the cylinders with 150-ton weights.

The board was sternly displeased! 'They expect a well-devised, substantial, well-built, durable and complete bridge, and they impress on Mr Locke the necessity of having it constructed on the earliest possible day.'

Six weeks later, the board asked Locke to confirm information that the bridge over the Grand Junction canal had failed. He replied that when striking the centres the arch followed more than usual, though because of rapid construction and not defect. It had not moved since. Who, he asked, was informing against him? The board expressed concern that a defect existed, but refused to answer him.

The Black Potts failure allowed the GWR, building rapidly, to reach Windsor first, on 8 October 1849. The WS & SW extension opened to a temporary terminus on 1 December 1849. The Act contained conditions protecting Eton College similar to those imposed on the GWR. No building, station, yard, wharf, etc, could be erected ,and no passengers entrained or detrained, between Datchet and Windsor without the written and sealed consent of the Provost and College. This recalled the GWR London to Bristol line Bill which, strongly opposed, was passed with a clause forbidding any station within three miles of the college. The condition was faithfully observed, but nothing prevented trains stopping and taking up or setting down passengers at Slough. The furious Provost and Fellows unsuccessfully sought an injunction, but eventually so relented that a station at Slough was opened in June 1840.

The WS & SW Act gave the Provost and staff free access to the station, including booking offices, to seek scholars and demand information concerning their attempts to travel. Each refusal by the company incurred a £5 penalty.

LSW directors and Windsor inhabitants alike treated the opening with nonchalance, but the town resented the 'makeshift' station reached with difficulty along the narrow Datchet lane. Eight trains ran each way on weekdays, six on Sundays, the fastest reaching Waterloo in 50 min, while the Parliamentary took 85 min.

The permanent station opened on 1 May 1851 and had twelve large doors leading to the widened Datchet lane, doubtless intended for cavalry. There were two waiting rooms, the first-class one having the marble chimneypiece and fittings from the old royal station at Farnborough. The new Windsor royal station, with the Queen's waiting room and another for court attendants, was approached by an oranamental drive round a fine ilex tree. This palisaded forecourt faced a new private road from the castle, and Plate 24 shows the tower overlooking it from which warning was given of the Queen's approach.

The impulse of competition there being weaker, the loop suffered economies during the post mania slump, but opened from Barnes to Smallberry Green on 22 August 1849. The latter station was on the London side of Wood Lane, about a quarter of a mile east of the new station (now Isleworth) which replaced it on 1 February 1850 when the present Hounslow station also opened and the line was extended to the main Windsor line by the review ground.

LSW terms for leasing the WS & SW at four and a half per cent and half the surplus profits were accepted by WS & SW proprietors on 9 August 1849 when they met, but within six months so many had taken the alternative offer of £16 for each WS & SW £16 share (£12 paid-up) that the company was merged with the LSW from 30 June 1850.

THE NORTH & SOUTH WESTERN JUNCTION RAILWAY

Following the Manchester & Southampton failures of 1846-7, William Chadwick of the Richmond Railway and his supporters launched their alternative scheme for linking northern narrow-gauge lines with Southampton—a seven-mile North & South-Western Junction Railway between the LNW at Harrow and the LSW at Brentford. The LSW decided on 26 November 1847 to have nothing to do with it.

Calling it a 'railway hoax' and 'a little paltry line which we have really done honour to by noticing', *Herapath's Journal* devoted much valuable space to a vitriolic attack on this apparently minor railway, whose traffic, it said, was non-existent and its territory 'nearly as destitute of population as the wilds of America'.

> Except in brooms to make birches for the idle and naughty boys of Harrow School, we have no conception what traffic there can be in goods. This pretended line is to go near the Hanwell lunatic asylum, no doubt, either instinctively or to keep all in character. We venture to suggest that it would be very advisable to make the terminus at the asylum, if for no other reason, that it would ensure the promoters kind treatment and care, should they become inmates of that useful institution.

A similar scheme in '44 or '45 had failed through lack of support, said *Herapath*, doubtlessly meaning the abandoned Middlesex & Surrey Grand Junction atmospheric of 1844 for linking Harrow with Merstham, via the GWR near Southall and the LSW near Kingston.

Spurning discouragement, and despite GWR opposition because of its newly-acquired powers to extend the West London, the N & SWJ fought on to the Lords who, on 25 July 1848, decided it was 'inexpedient to proceed with the Bill' and threw it out. Chadwick was roughly handled under cross-examination, and indiscreet remarks during evidence earned the line the title of 'Little Go or Watercress Railway'.

The Watercress re-appeared in 1850 as a 3 miles 5 furlongs line from Brentford to Willesden, which the LSW and LNW would jointly work and guarantee. Besides merchandise between Southampton and the north, good tonnages were expected from distilleries, soap works, breweries, flour mills, cement works, etc, around Brentford. *Herapath* now delightedly expressed confidence in the line's ultimate success, and its Act was obtained on 24 July 1851, capital £50,000. Henry Tootal was chairman; George Berkley, engineer; two directors each were appointed by the guarantor companies who, on 16 August 1851, successfully insisted the line be made double, and Brassey got the contract for £20,549 0s 5d, the work to be finished by 31 August 1852.

Work progressed well, then when the opening was imminent troubles piled up. A wages dispute with sub-contractors' men and a large earthslip caused postponement until 14 October 1852; then the Board of Trade unexpectedly required additional by-laws, but when on 27 November 1852 it certified the line fit for passengers and goods, the LSW and LNW were immediately told. Those companies had agreed on 11 August 1852 to provide and work rolling stock for a third of gross receipts, and pay tolls of six miles for goods, minimum £2,250 per annum, and four miles for passengers, while the N & SWJ would have a six per cent dividend from net receipts and half the balance, leaving the LSW and LNW to share the remainder.

The N & SWJ was flabbergasted when both companies refused either to work the line (ostensibly because sidings and the junction with the LNW at Willesden were incomplete) or to start the payments due immediately the Board of Trade certificate was issued. Railway circles openly said they hoped to delay the opening because neither relished losing their lucrative cartage business in tranships between Euston and Nine Elms. To Captain Huish, that unscrupulous tactician and LNW general manager, sharp practice was the breath of life, and his trademark appears unmistakeably in the jiggery-pokery which followed. One wonders how far the LSW would have supported Huish, were Chaplin still in the chair.

Being short of rails, Berkley asked the LSW for those it had promised to sell him. He was told there were none to spare, although Errington privately assured him otherwise. He tried the LNW, where the person responsible for rails was 'not available'. Eventually, Henry Tootal ordered old rails from the Shropshire Union Railway, of which he was deputy-chairman, and switches and crossings from manufacturers in Staffordshire. Huish regretted the unfortunate shortage of wagons to collect them, but when that was solved they arrived so late as to suggest a deliberately protracted transit. Wide-eyed, Huish disclaimed all responsibility and blamed a misunderstanding.

As Berkley said, nothing during December need have prevented the companies adopting his suggestion of opening temporarily as a single line, using the other in lieu of unfinished sidings.

On 15 February 1853 the line eventually opened for goods, and complaints soon arose that the LNW was keeping traffic from it. Passenger services started on 1 August 1853, with four North London trains daily from Hampstead Road to a temporary platform at Kew, until a N & SWJ station was built there soon after. There were connections with Fenchurch Street. The North London, said the N & SWJ, gave it friendly assistance; the LSW treated it like a stepchild. Public complaints abounded until Sunday trains were introduced on 2 April 1854.

Tootal's target was Windsor, and the LSW reluctantly agreed to take trains on there experimentally from 1 June 1854, at times

M

convenient to itself and at fares not less than those from Waterloo, plus 3d first and 2d second and third class. Seven trains daily now reached Kew from the Watercress, three continuing via Brentford to reach Windsor at noon, 3.15 pm and 7.30 pm, returning at 12.15 pm, 4.00 pm and 8.00 pm. There were booked connections with Fenchurch Street but probably no through trains, and the North London authorised alterations to Hampstead Road platform to increase accommodation for changing passengers. Passengers travelling throughout had two-hour journeys, and the service was useless to London-bound Windsorians, almost certainly by Waterloo's deliberate design. During September 1854, the N & SWJ was told that it would end on 30 September, but on appeal it was continued until the end of October 1854 and then never resumed, despite every plea by the Watercress board. Tootal was convinced that the GWR had exercised backdoor pressure to protect its Windsor traffic, but it is more likely that the LSW acted on its own account.

On 28 June 1853, the Watercress got powers for a one and a quarter-mile branch from Acton across open country to growing Hammersmith, a project which Waterloo disliked. It opened on 1 May 1857, at first only for freight, but remained outside the arrangements with the LNW and LSW.

More menacing was the N & SWJ scheme to reach Richmond independently. The LNW disassociated itself and the railway press declared that the N & SWJ was biting the hand that fed it. Fortunately, the Bill for the 1854 session was dropped. Richmond, however, was attracting general interest. In 1857, the Watercress was disgusted because a Lords committee rejected an independent Richmond & Kew extension from the North London, and then the LSW fought hard against the broad-gauge Brentford & Richmond Railway, independently promoted as a branch from the GWR. The Lords rejected that on 7 July 1858. Waterloo decided these and subsequent threatening schemes should be countered by improvements to its own local services, and so, on 20 May 1858 by agreement with the N & SWJ, North London carriages began running to Twickenham by reversing at Kew and Barnes. while LSW carriages ran to Hampstead Road in approximately alternate trains. Some LSW carriages apparently worked through to Fenchurch Street, and on 11 December 1862 the LSW refused a North London request to fit them up for gas lighting. The timetable for September 1858 shows nine trains over the N & SWJ daily, eight on Sundays.

Opposition Bills for 1859 included, inter alia, (1) the Kingston,

and (2) the North London, Paddington, Richmond, Hampton Court and Kingston. The Kingston was a more lavish scheme of the defeated Brentford & Richmond promoters, to go from the GWR at Southall to the Wimbledon & Croydon at Merton via Kingston, and touching the LSW at Isleworth and Malden. The LSW defeated them by offering improvements at Kew and Barnes, and to make a porters, etc.
Twickenham to Hampton Wick branch. Consequently, on 1 August 1859 it was given powers for curves at (1) Kew, from the N & SWJ into the loop line towards London, forming New Kew Junction to distinguish it from the original or old Kew Junction and (2) Barnes, from the loop line into the Richmond line towards Windsor. It dallied over building them, despite the potential operating advantages, and they opened on 1 February 1862 with surprisingly little improvement to timings, as the LSW service timetables, 1862, show:

January (without curves)			March (with curves)		
Kew Junction	10.15	12.10	New Kew Station	10.18	12.18
Kew Bridge	10.17	12.12	New Kew Junction	10.18	12.18
Barnes arr	10.23	12.19	Chiswick	10.22	12.22
Barnes dep	10.26	12.22	Mortlake	10.29	12.28
Richmond	10.34	12.29	Richmond	10.34	12.34
Twickenham	10.40	12.35	Twickenham	10.40	12.40

The new route displaced the N & SWJ station at Kew, and so it used an extension of the LSW station facing the new curve. For this it paid £100 annually, including the services of booking clerks.

The value of the Watercress was unchallengeable. During six months ended 30 June 1854, 22,387 tons of coal and 10,787 of general merchandise passed over it, and today the original route continues as an exchange artery for freight between Feltham marshalling yard and other Regions.

The depressed passenger traffic was blamed on the LSW, because of its attitude over Windsor. The three weeks succeeding opening brought 1,347 passengers, and receipts during six months ended 30 June 1854 were only £2,023, but real improvement came with services to Twickenham.

THE KINGSTON BRANCH

Powers for the Kew and Barnes curves were concurrent with those for a branch from Twickenham to near the Middlesex foot of Kingston bridge in Hampton Wick. It stirred considerable local unrest. A Kingston deputation to the LSW requested that the line should terminate there. The LSW decided to cross the river, but when the Act was passed on 6 August 1860 the board was chagrined to find in it the following clause:

> Before the company shall open the railway hereby authorised for public traffic, they shall make and fit up and shall thenceforth maintain and keep open a passenger station at Hampton Wick in the county of Middlesex, with all conveniences proper and sufficient for the accommodation of the traffic thereat.

It demanded an explanation, and found the clause was inserted by the Lords committee, despite strong opposition by counsel. Hampton Wick inhabitants had scored in defeat!

The contract went to Brassey for £48,193, who constructed the three and a half-mile line with Ogilvie. It opened on 1 July 1863 with stations at Teddington for Bushey Park, Hampton Wick, and the terminus of New Kingston on the Richmond Road about 28 yd south of Canonbury Passage. Besides trains from Waterloo, North London carriages from the N & SWJ now worked into Kingston, fulfilling LSW obligations under the 1859 Act to take them to Hampton Wick, the place to which it was then empowered to build.

CHERTSEY, WEYBRIDGE, WOKINGHAM AND HAMPTON COURT

In October 1844, Locke suggested a line from Woking or Weybridge to Staines. The board, having just lost the Newbury Bill, wanted to go on to Colnbrook and link with northern narrow-gauge lines, but the London & Birmingham Railway would not co-operate by taking a branch there from Watford, so LSW surveys were confined between Weybridge and Windsor.

> By this branch, Her Majesty and the Court might have the advantage of a continuous line of railway from Windsor to Portsmouth, shorter by some miles than the present route (by road and railway) through Farnborough, or by any other projected line.

Incidentally, a royal waiting room at Farnborough was begun earlier that year, designed by Tite, its fittings, as already mentioned, being transferred to the new Windsor station in 1851.

An Act was obtained on 16 July 1846 for a branch from Weybridge through Chertsey to an Egham terminus south of the Thames near Staines bridge. It was built and opened on 14 February

1848, but only between Weybridge and a temporary Chertsey station, because the WS & SW (Staines to Wokingham) Act of 25 June 1847, Number Two Act, capital £300,000, required the LSW to abandon the remainder. The WS & SW line was from Staines, through Egham, to the LSW main line at Pirbright, with a branch to Chertsey to join the LSW branch there from Weybridge. The Commons had lopped the Wokingham portion from the Bill, but the Pirbright line was expected to ease pressure on LSW main-line stations. Alas, the post-mania depression claimed another victim; the WS & SW line was not built and powers expired.

Hampton Court Palace, close to the LSW main line and visited annually by 178,000, inevitably attracted a branch which Chaplin said 'will afford a fresh means of cheap and legitimate recreation to the poorer classes'. The Act was secured on 16 July 1846, when Locke immediately suggested extending to Windsor, joining at Staines with the line from Weybridge and making a branch from the latter at Chertsey to Ascot racecourse. This, of course, depended on the WS & SW Windsor Bill of 1847 failing, and construction to Hampton Court was postponed meanwhile. The WS & SW Bill succeeded as Number One Act, so work on the Hampton Court branch commenced in January 1848 and, despite severe restrictions because of the depression, the 1 mile 52 chain branch opened on 1 February 1849.

Its continuous embankment, 18 ft high, ran through Thames Ditton until, crossing the river Mole, the line reached level ground and terminated near the Thames at Hampton Court bridge in a station of deep red brick, in old English style with stone dressings. Five trains daily ran each way, taking about forty-five minutes from or to Waterloo. The line was electrified on 18 June 1916, and trains today take thirty-three minutes on at least a half-hourly service, while the palace, five minutes from the station, remains the great attraction for visitors. About 500,000 passengers now use the station annually, plus commuters from its surrounding suburbia or concerned with numerous local light industries, who account for about 10,000 seasons.

During inactive post-mania years, many communities which had expected to benefit from lines authorised to big companies watched time limits expire. Some salved their frustrations by independently renewing such powers, like those who, in October 1852, formed the Staines, Wokingham & Woking Junction Railway, securing an Act on 8 July 1853, capital £300,000, for a line leaving the LSW Windsor branch at Staines to a junction with the

RG & R at Wokingham. A five-mile branch to Woking, diverting nearly six miles from Staines, was to go through Chobham and join the LSW between Woking station and the Guildford branch, but was never built, despite pleas by local inhabitants. The main-line contract, first going to Earle & Merrett, was transferred to McCormack on 15 April 1854 after differences over prices.

The 17¾-mile line from Staines to Wokingham was double, opening only to Ascot on 4 June 1856 because track beyond was unfinished. The section to Wokingham did not open until 9 July 1856, so that the SER could not directly share in Ascot race traffic that year.

The LSW first worked the line under temporary arrangements until traffic requirements crystallized, but from 25 March 1858 under a forty-two-year lease giving it fifty per cent of gross receipts, minimum £7,000. For many years the line developed slowly and services were poor. Now, not only is it supporting a half-hourly service between Waterloo and Reading through attractive though expensive residential areas, but draws traffic from light industries at various points, of which Bracknell new town and its growing industrial estate are supremely important.

We shall study great SW & WJ ambitions at Reading and beyond in Chapter 7.

CHAPTER 7

Other Lines Outside London

THE ALTON BRANCH

Within its own frontiers, the LSW system developed comparatively quietly. On 9 August 1845, the proprietors agreed to provide a branch to serve the Alton area, and obtained an Act on 16 July 1846. The deposited plans showed two lines converging at Ash Green; one from the main line at Pirbright and the other from Guildford. Parliament authorised only the second, through Wanborough, Ash, Tongham, Bentley and Froyle, to a field at Alton near the road to East and West Worldham. The Reading, Guildford & Reigate Railway, as described below, got running powers between Guildford and Ash.

Farnham and Alton, barley-growing districts, would provide heavy traffic of locally brewed ale, 145,000 barrels of which annually went nine miles by road to Winchfield for rail conveyance to London. Hop-growing is an important occupation of the area today, and the brewing industry thrives at Alton, though the output of good English ale is augmented by the more sophisticated lager. Stone from quarries near Alton, unused through transport difficulties, was an expected traffic, with more coming from local agricultural activities.

Brassey's tender of £147,459 exceeded the lowest of £145,539 7s 5d, but when he reduced it to £143,667 3s 0d he secured the contract.

The line left Guildford just north of the station, first climbing sharply at 1 in 100 on a left-hand curve, to run parallel with and north of the Hogs Back chalk ridge and the ancient Pilgrims Way. It turned south-west through the gap between the ridge and the Hampshire Downs at Tongham to reach the pleasing Georgian town of Farnham, birthplace of William Cobbett, surrounded by farm and parkland, and bordered by wild country of pine and heather from which Crooksbury Hill rises with dark foreboding. Following the course of the river Wey, the line reached Alton, once important also for silks and wool.

This intensely rural route demanded no outstanding engineering feat, but earthworks were plentiful. Work proceeded well until October 1847, when the slump ruined hopes of completion by summer 1848. Reduced expenditure, now £2,000 to £3,000 monthly, was restricted to works between Guildford and Farnham, which portion opened on 8 October 1849 for LSW trains, double from Guildford to Ash, the remainder single.

A two-year extension was obtained on 26 June 1849, but Chaplin had an unenviable task in persuading proprietors on 25 October 1850 to proceed with its completion. These were days of demands to close the capital account, and any illusions that branches were profitable had been shattered. When work was suspended, Chaplin said, all land had been contracted for or taken, and abandonment would mean heavy settlements with landowners. Brassey had agreed to reduce his price, and by making these last nine miles single for £3,500 per mile, the cost of the whole line would be only £30,000 above that to abandon them.

Opposition was heavy. Sir R. Jervis considered branches to be exhausters rather than feeders, while Gaselee, in excellent form, thought the proposals the thin end of the wedge before doubling and endless expenses followed. Only ales would increase existing traffic, and he trembled at the fate of London brewers under the inundation. However, the meeting authorised the work, and the completed single line opened on 28 July 1852 between Farnham and Alton.

To be fair to Gaselee, we have seen only one side of his character. The *South-Western Gazette* described him as 'eccentric in many ways, but of a kind and generous disposition. A genius in talent and ability, and with all his sharpness in business matters, most truthful, most honest, and most upright'.

RELATIONS WITH THE READING, GUILDFORD & REIGATE RAILWAY

The Reading, Guildford & Reigate Railway, incorporated in 1846, relied on using LSW metals between Shalford and Ash to reach the broad-gauge boundary. The LSW hoped this strange intruder would bring it a share of the large London traffic to and from Reading and give it access, via Reigate, to all parts of Kent, Surrey and Sussex, besides approaching Ascot racecourse which 'comprises in itself a fund of traffic'. The arrangements between the companies were seized on by the LBSC in 1846 as one excuse for breaking its agreement with the LSW.

The LSW Act of 16 July 1846 for its Alton branch required the line between Guildford and Ash to be completed within two years to accommodate RG & R trains, though in fact extra time was required. Extreme portions of the RG & R opened on 4 July 1849, i.e. eight miles from Redhill to Dorking and sixteen and a half miles from Reading to Farnborough. On 17 August 1849, the SER (which supported the RG & R and acquired it in 1852) announced that the ten and a half miles from Dorking to Shalford for Guildford would open on 20 August, on which day its trains also started between Farnborough and Guildford, ten miles, causing the LSW to protest to the RG & R at the use of its line without notice. The unfit state of the Guildford to Godalming line meant SER trains did not run between Shalford and Guildford, (one and a half miles), until 15 October 1849.

The SER and LSW worked uneasily together. The RG & R paid the LSW thirty-five per cent of its gross receipts over LSW metals, but in September 1851 the SER partly dodged this by running a free omnibus between Guildford and Shalford. Stovin was instructed to discover the loading of SER trains, so that the toll avoided might be recovered. Lacking the direct route to London, the SER competed with uneconomic fares, compelling the LSW in 1852 to reduce its returns between Godalming and London to equal those from Guildford, i.e. 10s first and 7s second. In 1858, when the SER was subsidising an omnibus between Ash station and Farnham, the LSW could do nothing but protest.

When the Staines, Wokingham & Woking Junction reached Reading with running powers over the SER from Wokingham, the latter again displayed awkwardness by lowering its Reading to London fares to those charged from Reigate, thus compelling the GWR, LSW and SW & WJ to lower theirs. Such competition profited no contestant, and in 1858 they all reached agreement to charge equal and sensible fares and to share receipts.

The SW & WJ was small but ambitious, though its hope of 1853 to reach Oxford never took shape. An Act of 31 July 1854 required the GWR to add narrow gauge to its line between Oxford and Basingstoke, prompting the SW & WJ to seek its own extension from the SER at Reading to the GWR mixed-gauge line. The SER did not want to participate, but agreed not to oppose it. In January 1855 James Garrard, SW & WJ chairman, and two directors, saw Parsons and Fowler of the Oxford, Worcester & Wolverhampton Railway to seek support and access to the north via that line. In 1855, the Commons rejected the SW & WJ Bill for a junction with the GWR, its opponents including the GWR and, obviously after second thoughts, the SER; but the Board of Trade struck the death blow by refusing the level crossing over Caversham Road, Reading. Parsons had to admit in evidence that his company could not send an ounce of traffic over the line. The promoters gamely tried persuading the Commons committee to exact a pledge from the SER and GWR to make the line but, though sympathetic, it confined itself to the Bill before it.

In 1857, both the SER and SW & WJ deposited Bills for the junction, when the Commons committee passed the latter and rejected the former. Having taken its narrow gauge straight to the Berks & Hants line to avoid Reading station, the GWR obviously intended confining the SW &WJ when it offered to participate in making the junction east of Reading, provided neither company diverted or used traffic against the other.

Agreement being reached, the Reading Junction line, authorised on 27 July 1857, capital £40,000, was built by the GWR and SW & WJ. The intended opening on 1 September 1858 was delayed, first because the interested companies agreed that the line should be doubled, and then because the Board of Trade inspector was dissatisfied with the signals. It opened on 1 December 1858 for goods, and completely on 17 January 1859 after re-inspection. *Railway Junction Diagrams*, 1867, show the 71-chain line commencing just west of the GWR station, with the 62-chain GWR portion taking a wide easterly sweep before burrowing under the main line, south of which the SW & WJ built the remaining nine chains. The SER paid a one-mile toll for its equal rights over the line.

CHALLENGERS FOR SOUTHAMPTON

Among the most serious challengers of the LSW stronghold at Southampton was the Manchester & Southampton Railway. Its prospectus of 1845 showed Sir John Barker Mill of Mottisfont Abbey as chairman, and its strong committee included Cooke and Reed of the LSW. George Hudson, the Railway King, gave it his gracious support.

The line was to fling wide the southern shipping gateway to the world for the busy mills and factories of northern England. Chaplin doubted its prospects, with considerable southbound traffic having little returning north to balance it, while intense competition would come from parallel lines. The M & S proposed using existing lines from Manchester to Cheltenham, building its own thence through Cirencester, under the GWR at Swindon, by Marlborough and Ludgershall to Andover, and onwards to Stockbridge, Romsey and Redbridge down the delightful Test valley, whose clear waters meander quietly through the rich green Hampshire basin. A branch was planned to Salisbury, Ringwood, Wimborne and Poole.

The M & S got a bad press, and blamed the GWR and LSW. *The Times* forecast the Cotswolds would prove insurmountable—a strange prediction considering what railway engineers had already achieved, and Stephenson hotly disputed it.

In 1846, an LSW Bill for a 5 mile 5 furlong-line to link Redbridge with Romsey was rejected by the Commons because of its purely local nature, the committee being influenced by the M & S Bill which duplicated it. That Bill, however, foundered in the Lords on 22 August 1846 under fierce GWR opposition. To kill the narrow-gauge invader, that company promised through Russell to mix the gauge from Oxford to Basingstoke, thus completing a narrow-gauge north to south route. The M & S might have taken comfort when the committee said its decision should not impede a future application if there was a public need; more likely it found greater encouragement from an agreement with the LSW.

LSW opposition had at first been intense but, having lost the Redbridge to Romsey Bill, Chaplin sought to save the day by agreeing with the M & S on 7 August 1846 to take over its proposed line between Andover and Redbridge. The M & S would retain full user rights, use Southampton & Dorchester metals between Redbridge and Bletchynden, and be free to build independently from Bletchynden to Southampton pier and thence to the docks. The LSW might purchase half ownership of any independent M & S Southampton station. Accordingly, LSW opposition to the M & S Bill had been immediately withdrawn.

This agreement was kept simmering, but a fresh M & S application in 1847 failed Standing Orders through discrepancies in the revised levels, for which Stephenson accepted responsibility. The embittered M & S vented its fury on the GWR, accusing it of disowning this year Russell's undertaking of last, and not laying one yard of the promised narrow gauge to Basingstoke. Chaplin quickly consoled it with a revised agreement of 25 March 1847, by which the M & S would build its own line north of Andover, and the LSW south to Kimbridge Mill (three miles north of Romsey) for their joint ownership and profit: thence to Southampton would be LSW property which the M & S would use at a price. The LSW would adopt the M & S contract to acquire the Andover canal, and share M & S property purchased at Southampton. Clause 6 read:

> In case one Bill only be obtained this session, it is understood that this agreement shall not cease but shall be continued in force for another session providing the unsuccessful company produces on or before 1st September next bona fide evidence of its intentions and powers to apply again to Parliament for the same or a similar line.

The South-Western's own Parliamentary excursion yielded powers on 2 July 1847, capital £300,000, to make lines from Andover to Michelmarsh on the Bishopstoke to Salisbury branch; from Romsey to Millbrook, and to purchase the Andover canal. To perpetuate the agreement, the M & S gave notice of a Bill for a Cheltenham to Andover line, but alas, the depression killed it, and its property at Southampton held solely or jointly with the LSW was sold.

The economic blizzard also stopped the LSW building; neither did it acquire the Andover canal despite having paid £10,000 deposit. How bitterly it regretted wasting those powers when, in 1856, the GWR attacked Southampton with a broad-gauge extension from Salisbury, two-thirds of which would accompany the existing LSW branch. The Bill, to LSW relief, was rejected in 1857, but so was an LSW attempt to revive its 1847 powers between Romsey and Redbridge. Parliament felt neither scheme justified its cost and that another line between Salisbury and Southampton was unnecessary.

On 12 July 1858, an independent Andover & Redbridge Railway swept the board with an Act, capital £130,000, for a twenty-four-mile broad-gauge line from Andover to Redbridge through Romsey. The LSW, its sole opponent, had fought tooth and nail, but could not even win a narrow-gauge clause. Basking under GWR geniality, its promoters had quickly recruited Lord Palmerston's support in Parliament and persuaded him to turn the first sod, at Ashfield Bridge, near his house Broadlands, Romsey, on 20 September 1859. His patronising remarks that day encouraged the company to seek powers in 1860 to extend southwards to Southampton Royal Pier and northwards for fourteen miles to the intended Berks & Hants extension at Burbage. Now were LSW fears fulfilled and its opposition vigorous. It rejoiced when the Commons committee rejected the Bill, but the A & R directors, never contemplating failure, reeled with shock and charged the LSW with inciting and financing the opposition from landowners.

The respite was short, as the A & R produced another Bill for

1861. Preparing for battle, Mangles' board found in Hattersley, the A & R contractor, a Trojan horse for penetrating that company's meetings, by persuading him to sell shares he received in part payment of his £100,000 contract. Just now, the A & R was financially troubled and Hattersley, like many associated with it, consequently lacked money. He was also criticised for unsatisfactory work, especially concerning the Andover canal, authorised in 1789 and now acquired by the A & R for £25,000, half being in A & R shares. The A & R Act required three months public notice of intention to stop up the canal: this was given and expired on 18 September 1859. Instead of immediately draining it so that the residual mud might harden (as was usual), Hattersley waited until he was nearly ready to build, then removed the sticky mud from the canal bed, charging this unnecessary cost to the company. Hattersley's present mood well suited LSW purposes, and through him it discovered much it wanted to know of its rival's financial status, but was unable to outvote it.

The A & R Bill for extension to Southampton was presented, but was withdrawn during March 1861. Mangles now suggested that both companies should accept what Parliament had decided concerning them and reach agreement accordingly. He claimed he would have succeeded had not the GWR engineer explored from Basingstoke east of the LSW main line, seeking that autumn a route to Southampton. Eventually the GWR attracted the A & R into an agreement, by which it would lease the latter and extend it to Southampton and to the GWR system at Newbury. What obviously swayed the A & R was the promise of money to permit work to resume. Hattersley had been dismissed in May 1861 for scamping the work with the cognizance of Burke, the engineer, who himself resigned two months later, being succeeded by Collister. For a while Jackson, another contractor, had carried on; then everything had stopped.

The GWR incursion angered the LSW board, which tried dissuading it by offering to cut the existing rate for GWR traffic from Basingstoke to Southampton; to take GWR narrow-gauge carriages to Southampton, and to allow that company an office or 'touting shop' there, but all to no avail. Crombie, the LSW secretary, now wrote disclosing to A & R shareholders recent correspondence between the companies. This revealed an LSW offer of 10 October 1861 to assist in completing the A & R on narrow-gauge and to work it on reasonable terms. This offer Wyndham Portal, LSW director and A & R shareholder, was ready to explain to the assembled proprietors, and it was repeated in writing on 3 January 1862 to William Cubitt, A & R chairman, with a further offer to take unallotted A & R shares, guaranteeing existing shareholders four per cent for three years after the opening and four and a half per cent in perpetuity thereafter. The A & R declined, pointing to its sealed agreement with the GWR, whereupon Crombie alleged that the agreement was invalid unless the shareholders had approved it. (In fact, it had not been so approved but had been sealed at a board meeting on 29 October 1861 at Mansion House, London, presided over by William Cubitt, then Lord Mayor.)

Crombie ended his letter to A & R shareholders with an appeal to accept the LSW offer, as:

> The alternative proposition, viz, of alliance with the Great Western company and of continuing in unceasing hostility to the South-Western, is to come before Parliament with four Bills, two of which are to authorise the already condemned extensions from Andover northwards to the Great Western Railway, and from Redbridge southwards into Southampton. These proposals will, as this board confidently relies, be rejected by Parliament as heretofore, and even if sanctioned, they will at least lead you into a vast and most uncertain amount of expenditure, while their result will be to isolate your railway from the network of lines belonging to the South-Western Company now occupying the district, and to prevent that interchange of traffic with them which is essential to the public advantage.
>
> In order that the shareholders may have an opportunity of expressing their opinion upon these important questions, I am instructed to enclose a form of proxy which will be used in favour of the acceptance of the offer made by the South-Western board.

The 'four Bills' were (1) to join the A & R with the Berks & Hants, (2) to extend A & R time limits and increase capital, (3) to extend the A & R to Southampton, and (4) to authorise the GWR to lease the A & R. They were considered simultaneously by a Commons committee during one of those mammoth hearings which exhilarated lawyers and impoverished shareholders. Three more Bills concurrently examined were (1) the GWR Radstock & Keynsham scheme, (2) to authorise the LSW to make junctions with the A & R, and (3) for an LSW line from the S & Y near Gillingham to Bristol.

The last Bill was hardly serious, but rather a tit-for-tat against the GWR. You penetrate my territory and I'll penetrate yours! However, Mangles, Gaselee and other LSW notables had visited Bristol in December 1861 to stir support, attending a public meeting on 27 December at the Guildhall, chaired by the mayor, which unanimously resolved 'that this meeting considers the proposed extension of the London & South-Western Railway Company from Gillingham to Bristol most advantageous to the city, and deserving the unqualified support of its inhabitants'. Enthusiasm in Southampton for the A & R stemmed largely from desires to increase trade with Bristol, South Wales and the Somerset coalfields. It was this traffic that Mangles claimed the LSW would serve while avoiding the break of gauge, though admitting it would never have been projected had the GWR not invaded Southampton.

The day before the Bills were deposited, the GWR sought peaceful negotiations, but it was too late and the rival gauges struggled bitterly before the Commons committee. Much dirty linen received a public wash, including Hattersley's courtship with the LSW. It was revealed that his shareholding acquired by that company was broken down among numerous persons to create plenty of pro-LSW shareholders. On 16 May 1862, after all the money and energy expended during the thirty-eight days hearing, each Bill was rejected save that extending time and capital for the A & R.

The GWR had never relished paying for the contest, and now decided against financing further excursions to Southampton. Thus, some said, it betrayed its ally, the A & R. That broad-gauge concern, lonely and dispirited, was distinctly receptive when, in June 1862, the LSW wrote suggesting negotiations. There followed months of hard bargaining before amalgamation terms were accepted by the A & R on 12 December 1862, under which the LSW would take its debenture debt of £43,000; find £30,000 to liquidate its floating debt, and pay three per cent per annum on its capital up to £50,000, the latter being redeemable at LSW option at twenty-five years purchase.

Prospects now improved and hopes rose for the neglected works. In February 1862 the A & R had engaged another contractor, Brotherhood, to complete the line within fourteen months for £56,379 5s, including remedying the defects of his predecessors. He immediately deposited much equipment and commenced work with great gusto; then, in July, he stopped without notice and nothing had been done since. Now, the partly-finished brickwork suffered badly from exposure.

On 29 June 1863 Parliament authorised the amalgamation and a short line linking the A & R with the LSW at Andover Junction, while between Romsey and Michaelmarsh (Kimbridge Junction) the A & R, now narrow gauge, would use the Bishopstoke to Salisbury branch. Work proceeded well, and then the Board of Trade destroyed hopes of opening in 1864 and created unwarranted expense by insisting that the permanent way be strengthened beyond the limits it had previously fixed.

Eventually, after a directors' trip on 4 March 1865, the line opened on 6 March 1865 most inauspiciously. The first train from Southampton, due at 8.30 am, arrived carrying only five persons, including Mr Footner, apparently an Andover railway enthusiast, who had that morning walked to Clatford to take this trip back. The morning was damp, the rails were greasy, and the engine, having no sand-box, twice stopped while climbing to the junction. The first train to Southampton caused little more interest, and thereafter, said the *Andover Advertiser*, the only excitement was the hindrance to road users because the level-crossing gates were ever closed, due, it seems, to zealous interpretation of Archibald Scott's order to keep the line always clear.

Four through trains travelled daily each way, plus one from Southampton to Romsey. The one Sunday train departed from and returned to Southampton, to the disgust of Andover residents, who could not go out and back that day.

Traffic was most discouraging, and Stockbridge races never rivalled Newmarket for interest as the *Andover Advertiser* had predicted. However, the single line, which acquired the name of 'Sprat and Winkle', was doubled as follows:

			(As near as can be established)
Andover Town	to	Andover Junction	1 January 1883
Andover Town	to	Clatford	21 September 1884
Clatford	to	Fullerton	7 December 1884
Fullerton	to	Stockbridge	19 or 20 April 1885
Stockbridge	to	Horsebridge	19 November 1885
Horsebridge	to	Mottisfont	19 or 20 Nov. 1885
Mottisfont	to	Kimbridge Junction	13 July 1885
Romsey	to	Redbridge	16 or 17 March 1884

THE SOMERSET & DORSET RAILWAY

Few lines stirred more nostalgic emotion than the Somerset & Dorset*, which had preserved its identity under joint ownership of the Southern and London, Midland & Scottish Railways until nationalisation in 1948. The leisurely traveller might have rejoiced at the scenery of his trans-Mendip ride, especially the view from

---

*The Somerset & Dorset Railway is the subject of a separate volume in this series.

Masbury summit, 811 ft above sea level; but the business-like passenger would have fretted at the crawling, manoeuvring progress over this poverty-stricken but remarkably individual railway. The 'Pines Express', having for many years linked Liverpool and Manchester with Bournemouth, battled daily with its gradients until being re-routed in 1962 through Southampton, Reading and Oxford. It had been easily the Somerset & Dorset's most important train.

Preceding the ingredient companies of the Somerset & Dorset was the unsuccessful South Midland Union Railway, from the Bristol & Birmingham at Keynsham to Poole harbour by a route comparable with that later followed by the 'Pines Express'. The £1,000,000 scheme was too large for those difficult times and, with few subscriptions forthcoming, the 1853 Bill was abandoned.

The history of the Somerset & Dorset, that amalgamation of the Somerset Central and Dorset Central Railways, has been recounted elsewhere, but a brief review is necessary here. The Somerset Central, authorised independently on 17 June 1852, capital £70,000, was nurtured by the B & E and worked by it for four per cent shortly after opening in broad gauge between Highbridge Wharf and Glastonbury on 28 August 1854. On 30 July 1855 Parliament approved a Wells branch and an extension to Burnham; the latter, which opened on 3 May 1858, was largely for inaugurating a steamship link with South Wales which never really prospered. The Dorset Central, of 1855 vintage, sought prosperity by bringing coal from Radstock to the potteries centred near clay deposits at Poole, and conveying inland to Wiltshire, etc, the timber and other commodities landed at Poole harbour.

The Somerset Central, yearning to link the Bristol and English Channels, saw in the Dorset Central an ideal partner which it commenced to woo, suggesting a rendezvous at Bruton. The narrow-gauge Dorset Central, duly impressed but having a slender purse, made the journey in two stages, first getting powers for ten and a quarter miles from Wimborne to Blandford on 29 July 1856, capital £100,000, then from Blandford to Bruton, twenty-four miles, on 10 August 1857, capital £300,000.

The section from Wimborne to Blandford, heavily graded and sharply curved to economise on earthworks, opened on 1 November 1860 with five daily and two Sunday trains each way. The LSW supplied rolling stock, staffed, worked and managed it under a five-year agreement for fifty per cent of annual gross receipts or sixty per cent if those were under £600 per mile, but with a minimum of £360 per mile. To avoid installing a turntable at Wimborne, an LSW tank engine was used.

Another, and concurrent, agreement was reached because of a Dorset Central Bill of 1860 to extend from Wimborne to Poole and Bournemouth, its price for withdrawing it being running powers over the LSW to Poole. The LSW, highly alarmed, was reluctantly forced to agree to carry in through vehicles attached to its trains all traffic between Poole and Dorset Central stations, these being exchanged at Wimborne station which the Dorset Central used without charge. The LSW received a five-mile proportion of rates and fares and in return the Dorset Central withdrew its Poole Bill.

Incidentally, the LSW board had tempted the Dorset Central by promising to urge LSW proprietors to seek powers in 1861 for extending the Poole branch of the Southampton & Dorchester (today's Hamworthy goods branch) across the harbour to Poole town, but in fact improved access there was delayed until 1872.

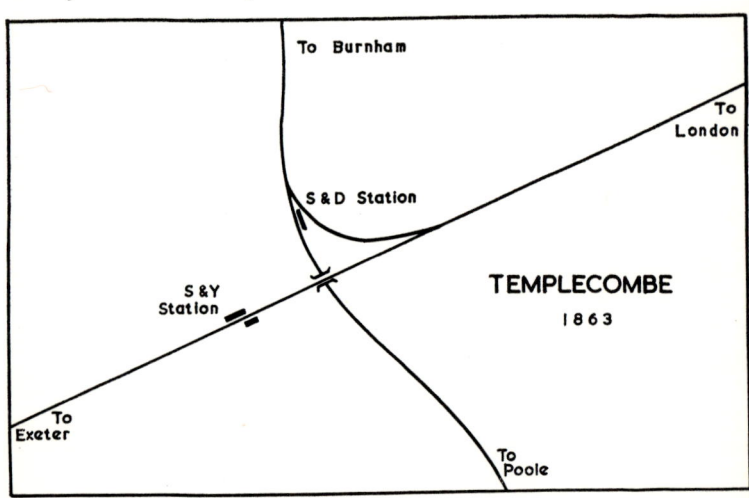

The Dorset Central line from Blandford to Cole, near Bruton, crossed the Salisbury & Yeovil line at Templecombe. In 1856, the latter company had considered a rival line from Gillingham to Bruton, but on reflection dropped it, having decided that the importance of its capturing prospective traffic was secondary to the LSW having a narrow-gauge link between the Bristol and English Channels and London. In 1861, the S & Y and Dorset Central agreed on a junction at Templecombe, authorised on 10 August 1857, and the Dorset Central opened from there to Cole on 3 February 1862. At that time the S & Y was single through Templecombe, and the relevant layout is shown on page 194. The LSW doubled the S & Y between its Templecombe station and the junction, at Dorset Central expense, and the latter sent a left-hand curve from its southbound line trailing into the S & Y line towards London, so Dorset Central trains reaching the S & Y had inconveniently to reverse into its station until a westerly connection was formed in 1870. However, for a short while an LSW shuttle service ran over the junction, commencing in 1863 after the Somerset & Dorset opened throughout.

3 February 1862 also saw the Somerset Central extend from Glastonbury to Cole, as authorised, on 21 July 1856*. That company had had trouble with its guardian, the B & E, which had firmly believed its ward was attracted to the WS & W. Indeed, the Act prescribed that the extension should terminate by joining the WS & W. Hints of Somerset Central intentions came with its Act of 1 August 1859 which allowed mixed gauge on its existing lines, and a Dorset Central Act of 3 July 1860 permitting it and the Somerset Central to use each others metals. In 1861 a Somerset Central Bill sought, *inter alia*, powers to abandon the broad-gauge rail, but the irate B & E (and other broad-gauge companies) successfully opposed such clauses, and the Act of 1 August 1861 forced its ward to mix the gauge to Bruton and construct the junction with the WS & SW. The broad-gauge rail, dutifully laid, was hardly used and entirely removed about 1870, but it is unlikely that metals ever topped the completed earthworks of the junction.

The B & E lease of the Somerset Central expired in August 1861 and was not renewed, but to avoid stopping traffic while mixing the gauge, rolling stock and locomotives were thereafter hired from and worked by the B & E. Weak Somerset Central finances delayed its purchase of narrow-gauge vehicles, and in July 1862 the LSW helped it by lending two first-class and four second-class carriages for two months.

The Somerset Central and Dorset Central having finally met at Cole, and Parliament approving their match on 7 August 1862, they faced life together as the Somerset & Dorset Railway from 1 September 1862.

The last sixteen miles, from Blandford to Templecombe, opened privately on 31 August 1863 and public services began on 10 September 1863. Anticipating this, the Somerset & Dorset and

*The printed Act shows 29 July 1856, obviously in error.

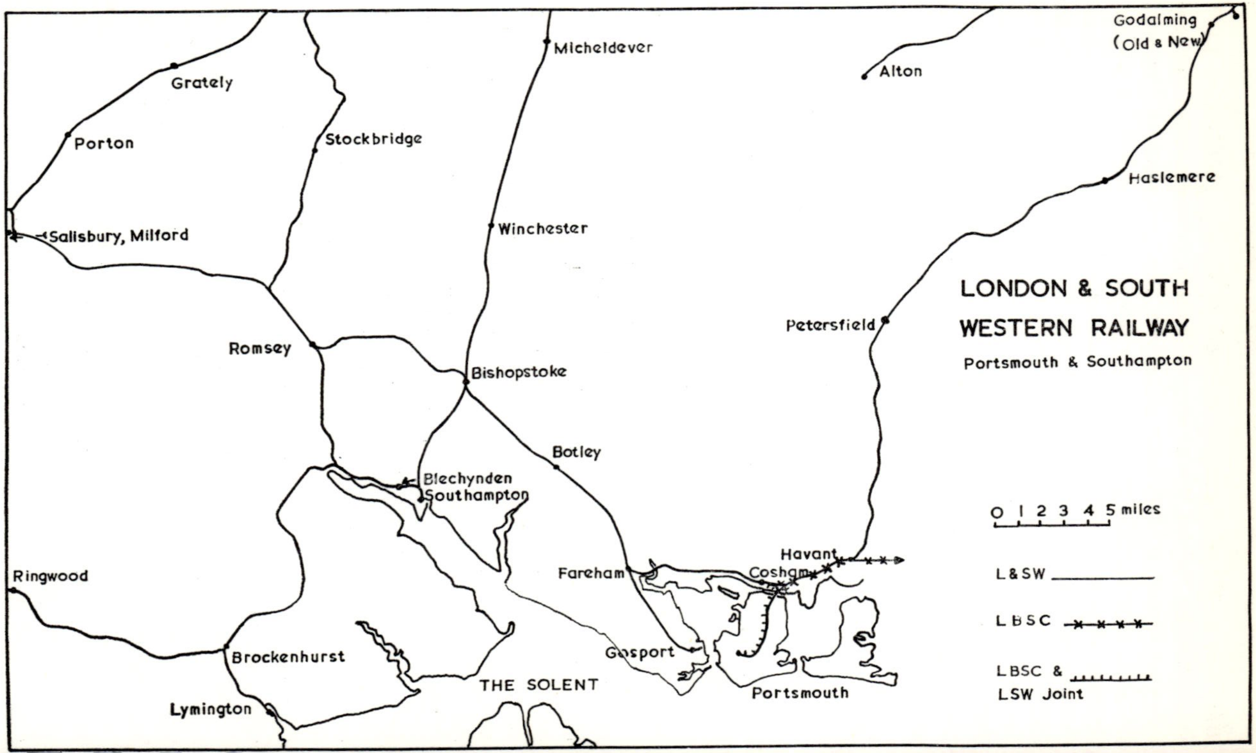
LONDON & SOUTH
WESTERN RAILWAY
Portsmouth & Southampton
0 1 2 3 4 5 miles
L&SW
LBSC
LBSC &
LSW Joint
Godalming
(Old & New)
Haslemere
Alton
Petersfield
Havant
Cosham
Portsmouth
Micheldever
Winchester
Bishopstoke
Botley
Fareham
Gosport
THE SOLENT
Blechynden
Southampton
Stockbridge
Romsey
Grately
Porton
Salisbury, Milford
Ringwood
Brockenhurst
Lymington

LSW had negotiated a fresh agreement to operate in perpetuity from that day, allowing Somerset & Dorset trains to use Wimborne, from whence to Poole LSW engines would take them with Somerset & Dorset guards. The Somerset & Dorset was allowed its own agent at Poole for collection and delivery of goods. On 14 September 1863, the LSW handed over to the Somerset & Dorset the section between Blandford and Wimborne, on which day through services between Burnham and Poole commenced. The Poole branch was doubled in 1864.

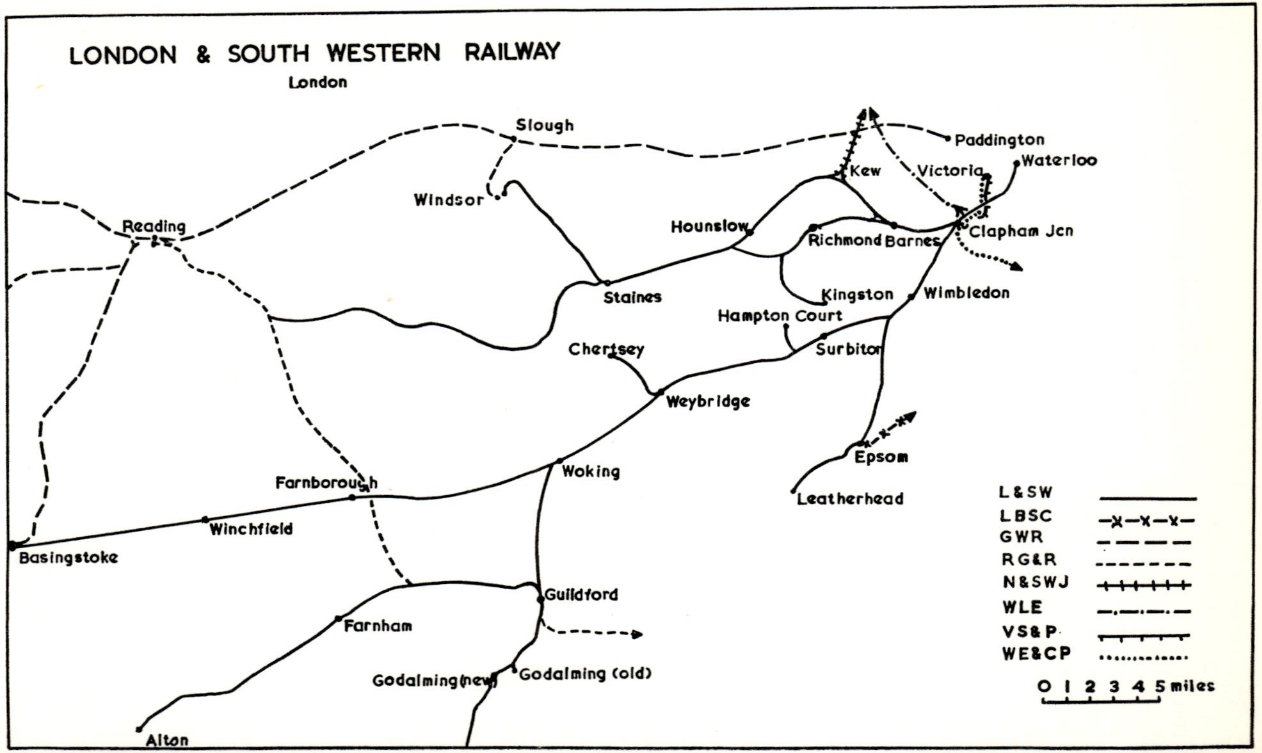
LONDON & SOUTH WESTERN RAILWAY
London
Slough
Paddington
Waterloo
Kew
Victoria
Windsor
Reading
Hounslow
Richmond
Barnes
Clapham Jcn
Staines
Kingston
Wimbledon
Hampton Court
Chertsey
Surbiton
Weybridge
Epsom
Woking
Farnborough
Leatherhead
Winchfield
Basingstoke
Guildford
Farnham
Godalming (new)
Godalming (old)
Alton
L&SW
LBSC
GWR
RG&R
N&SWJ
WLE
VS&P
WE&CP
0 1 2 3 4 5 miles

CHAPTER 8

The LSW and the Sea

DEVELOPMENT OF SOUTHAMPTON PORT AND AN
LSW FOOTHOLD IN FRANCE

The first sailors along Southampton Water were probably occupying Celts trading with France, followed by Greeks and Phoenicians seeking tin. Real prosperity came to the port with the Norman conquest, when Continentals favoured it for wine and wool traffic; while in the fourteenth century trade with Genoa, Spain, Venice and the east began. Docks were first seriously contemplated in 1803, and then, after the Southampton, London & Branch Railway & Dock Company opted out, the Southampton Dock Company was formed, getting its Act in 1836. The deplorable conditions Henderson described in 1831 were remarkable for a port so unique in natural advantages. Sheltered by the Isle of Wight, favoured with four high tides daily and a great depth of water at low tide, and approached by Southampton Water about six miles long and a mile wide, its development was long overdue.

On 12 October 1838, at the confluence of the rivers Itchen and Test, roughly south-east of the L & S proposed terminus, the foundation stone of the first dock (now Outer Dock) was laid. At first, capital shortage delayed work, but by August 1841 there were 1,800 men employed day and night, the scene after dark being lit by over 100 coal fires. The dock was opened on 29 August 1842, when the LSW decided on a direct link with the railway.

Railway and dock development soon established Southampton among shipping interests, but much impetus had come from steamships, which could use Southampton Water without the difficulties sailing vessels found in that sheltered stretch, and but for which the port would long since have surpassed Liverpool and Bristol. As evidence of its now remarkable growth, customs duties for three months of 1840 were £34,000, rising to £158,000 for the same period of 1841, and 'it only required that the flood gates of trade should be thrown open, to enable Southampton to take its proper position among English ports'.

Every effort was made to woo the steamship companies even before the tidal dock was opened: the Royal Mail Steam Packet Company, the Peninsular & Oriental Steam Navigation Company, and the West India Steam Packet Company adopted the port, being offered special rail freight rates by the L & S to and from Nine Elms. Robert Garnett, who had succeeded Easthope as chairman on 27 November 1840, said:

> . . . to show the facilities which the South-Western Railway presented, he might mention that on Saturday 14 August, the *Tagus*, Oriental Steam Packet, arrived at Southampton at 9 o'clock in the morning, and by 2 o'clock the same day, the private letters were received in London at Lloyds, whereas the public letters which had been taken to Falmouth were coolly delivered on Monday morning.

The rise of Southampton sounded the death knell of Falmouth, chosen in 1688 by the Post Office as the port for its mailboats sailing for Spain, and from which went vessels to the New World, etc, their passengers preferring a long coach-journey west to a slow, storm-tossed sailing down the Channel. As a naval port during the French wars, Falmouth was invaluable, and the Admiralty, it appears, empowered by an Act of 1818, placed naval officers in charge of the mail vessels, claiming them as training ships. From that time, Falmouth declined as a mail port, and eventually the traffic was transferred to Southampton.

The L & S sought, through Southampton, its own link with the Continent, and regarded a railway from the north coast of France to Paris as a necessary extension of its own. In 1832, therefore, it welcomed a line to start from Havre de Grace, with steam vessels linking the port with Southampton. The French government approved the scheme, and in 1839 its promoters asked for LSW assistance.

'We have an abundant traffic, and have no doubt that we shall be able to obtain means to make the road. We require, however, your practical experience, and wish to have your active cooperation.' Thus wrote Monsieur Laffitte during negotiations, shortly after Chaplin, Reed and Locke had visited France to examine the commercial possibilities, the physical features of the route, and problems of construction. The three visitors were much impressed. The line, now to run from Rouen to Paris, about eighty miles, and to cost approximately £2,000,000, presented no engineering problem. No gradient would exceed 1 in 330; no embankment be more than thirty feet high; no bridge of consequence would be needed, or other large work save a one and a half-mile tunnel through chalk. The work, except for the tunnel, could be completed within two years.

What struck them most was the extraordinary traffic potential, estimated at over 558,029 tons annually, producing £1,000,000 gross, which, compared with the capital of £2,000,000, said Locke, was a thing that must frighten almost everyone to speak of. Chaplin personally took 2,000 shares at £20 each, and when the revolution of 1848 reduced them to £10 from their £40 value in December 1847, he found himself unable to realise his investments and open to charges concerning payment of his calls on LSW stock.

On 29 February 1840, Laffitte wrote informing Garnett of the French government's favourable reaction. The Minister of Public Works had approved modifications proposed by Locke; adjusted French law more closely to English law, to satisfy English proprietors; published a tariff of tolls, and promised to induce the State to take one-third of the capital.

By August 1840 the Bill had been passed. The French government regarded the scheme as important, and would itself complete the line from Rouen to Havre if a company would not undertake it. By August 1841, work was in full swing, and surveys between Rouen and Havre were being carried out. Reed had relinquished secretaryship of the LSW to Alfred Morgan to become a director of the French company, and Locke controlled the engineering works, mostly built by Brassey, whose navvies astounded the local inhabitants by their energy and general performance.

No disturbance marred the rapid progress, and the line's prospects became increasingly attractive. Reed told LSW proprietors that:

> The directors of this company will not have discharged their duty fully until they have perfected every link in the great chain of communication, so that a passenger may be able to take his ticket for Paris at this station (Nine Elms), well assured that under the joint co-operation of all parties forming every link of the chain, that he shall be able to enjoy a continuous and an unannoyed journey from the capital of one kingdom to the other.

In 1842, with the Paris to Rouen line expected to open in May 1843, the French government sanctioned continuation to Havre, the most important French port, whose expanding facilities served a developing industrial hinterland. It had made a gift of £320,000, and a loan of £400,000 for fifty years at three per cent to complete the project. The line from Paris to Rouen opened with a directors' trip on 3 May 1843, traffic comencing on 9 May 1843. The extension from Rouen to Havre opened to the public on 22 March 1847, after a directors' trip on 20 March 1847.

THE RAILWAY AND STEAMER SERVICES

Early marine history affecting the LSW bristles with ambiguities and contradictions in surviving records. Cross Channel paddle-steamers operated from Southampton before the railway arrived, but experts express doubts concerning who owned which ships. However, newspaper advertisements by owners, like those quoted below and illustrated on pages 203-4, contrast sometimes with statements in standard works: the reader must accept or reject this evidence, which is mostly restricted to ships ultimately coming under LSW control, though other owners and ships were active.

The *Hampshire Advertiser* of 13 March 1830 showed that the General Steam Packet Company (i.e. General Steam Navigation) sailed the *Ariadne* to the Channel Islands and St Malo, and the *Camilla* and *George IV* to Havre. On 26 December 1835 a new ship, the *Lady de Saumarez*, was advertised on the Channel Islands run for the British & Foreign Steam Navigation Company, but the 26 May 1838 issue shows her going there for the Commercial Steam Packet Company (was this a new or renamed company?), which also ran the *Calpe* to Havre and the *Kent* from Southampton to Portsmouth and Poole. The Commercial advertised on 27 April 1839, in the *Hampshire Independent*, Channel Islands sailings by the *Lady de Saumarez* and the *Transit*, with the *Grand Turk* going to Havre. It had also acquired the *Camilla*. The 11 May 1839 issue carried advertisements by its rival, the South of England Steam Navigation Company, showing the *Monarch* sailing to Havre and the *Atalanta* to the Channel Islands.

The Commercial also ran the *Glasgow* and *William IV* between London, Southampton and Weymouth, and during 1841 the LSW forlornly tried making arrangements with that company for opening steamer services to and from Plymouth, by which it hoped to capture traffic before the broad gauge reached there.

To secure good cross-Channel services so vital to its interests, the LSW urged the South of England and the Commercial to unite, but being unsuccessful the directors appealed to LSW proprietors to subscribe £1 for every £50 LSW share held, to help launch a South-Western Steam Packet Company. The response was poor, the general meeting in February 1842 hearing that about six directors had taken 1,000 shares but proprietors only 330. Steamship com-

Southampton Steam Packets.

THE ARIADNE,
OF 197 TONS AND 74-HORSE POWER,
(Capt. Bazin,)
WILL LEAVE SOUTHAMPTON
FOR JERSEY & GUERNSEY,

ON TUESDAY, 30th of MARCH, at 6 o'Clock in the Evening, and will continue to leave Southampton EVERY TUESDAY EVENING during the Season, returning from the Islands every FRIDAY, excepting on the Weeks she proceeds to St Malo.

Main Cabin, £1 11s. 6d. | Fore Cabin, 18s. 0d.
Fore Deck, 10s. 6d.

☞ Passengers tak n on Board at Southampton Free of Expence.

The *ARIADNE* will proceed (weather permitting) to

ST. MALO ONCE A MONTH,

during the Season, viz.—on the Day after her Arrival in Jersey, after the 20th April, 4th May, 8th June, 6th July, 3rd and 31st August, and 28th September, leaving St. Malo the following SATURDAY for Jersey, Guernsey, & Southampton.

FRANCE & ITALY,
BY SOUTHAMPTON AND HAVRE-DE-GRACE.

Camilla & George IV.

The largest and Swiftest Vessels to FRANCE in the British Channel, will leave Southampton for Havre-de-Grace every WEDNESDAY and SATURDAY, during the Season.

The Camilla, (under the direction of an Officer in the Navy, one of the Proprietors,) will leave Southampton for Havre on the 7th of APRIL, and continue to leave Southampton every WEDNESDAY; and the *George the Fourth*, CAPT. WEEKS, will resume her station on the 1st of MAY, leaving Southampton every SATURDAY, and returning from Havre for Southampton the alternate Days, as follows:—

From Southampton. APRIL.	From Havre. APRIL.
Wednesday 7th, at 6 even.	Saturday 10th at 8 morn.
Wednesday 14th, 12 noon	Saturday 17th 4 even.
Wednesday 21st, 6 even.	Saturday 24th 8 morn.
Wednesday 28th, 12 noon	
MAY.	MAY.
Saturday 1st, at 2 after.	Saturday 1st at 4 even.
Wednesday 5th, 6 even.	Wednesday 5th 7 even.
Saturday 8th, 7 morn.	Saturday 8th 7 morn.
Wednesday 12th, 10 morn.	Wednesday 12th 11 morn.
Saturday 15th, 6 even.	Saturday 15th 4 after.
Wednesday 19th, 6 even.	Wednesday 19th 6 even.
Saturday 22nd, 7 morn.	Saturday 22d 7 morn.
Wednesday 26th, 10 morn.	Wednesday 26th 10 morn
Saturday 29th, 6 even.	Saturday 29th 4 alter.

FARES.
Each Passenger .... £2 2 0 | Servants £1 10 0
Carriages .... 4 4 0 | Horses 4 4 0

☞ FEMALE STEWARD ON BOARD.

. The *Camilla & George IV.* call at PORTSMOUTH an Hour and a Half after leaving Southampton, and perform the Voyage from thence in about 11 Hours.

PASSPORTS FOR FRANCE MAY BE HAD AT SOUTHAMPTON.

Particulars respecting these Packets may be obtained of W. J. LE FEUVRE, General Steam Packet Office, 71, High-street, Southampton; and of Mr. WHEELER, Broad-street, Portsmouth; or in London, at No. 6, Castle-court, Strand; and M. CHANOINE, Havre.

JERSEY AND GUERNSEY EVERY TUESDAY
THE BRITISH AND FOREIGN STEAM NAVIGATION COMPANY'S NEW AND POWERFUL STEAM PACKET,

THE LADY DE SAUMAREZ,
JAMES GOODRIDGE, COMMANDER, Will Leave SOUTHAMPTON for GUERNSEY and JERSEY on TUESDAY, the 29th December, at Six in the Afternoon; and Return from the Islands on the following FRIDAY, with Passengers and Merchandise.

FARES:
Chief Cabin........................ 25s.
Fore Cabin .... 16s.
Deck .... 10s. 6d.
Merchandise, 6d. per foot.

Particulars of Mr. N. M. PRIAULX, the Company's Agent, Southampton; or of Mr. DE BUCK, Secretary, 8, Fenchurch-street, London.

The Company's New and Superior Steam Packets will commence running early in January between London, Lisbon, Cadiz, and Gibraltar, calling off Oporto, with Merchandize and Passengers, of which further particulars will shortly be advertised.

THE COMMERCIAL COMPANY'S BRANCH OF Steam Packets, from Southampton,
Will leave the Royal Pier, as follow:—

THE LADY DE SAUMAREZ, Captain James Goodridge, FOR GUERNSEY AND JERSEY, June 1, 6, 11, 15, 20, 25, 29, at seven o'clock in the evening: returning from Jersey, June 4, 8, 13, 18, 22, 27.

The Calpe,
Captain FAIRBAIRN, (calling off Portsmouth,) for Havre-de-Grace, every Tuesday,—June 5th, at 7 Evening; June 12th, at 11 Evening; June 19th, at 7 Evening; June 26, 10 Evening;—returning every Wednesday.

The Kent,
From Southampton to Portsmouth and Poole, (calling at Ryde, Cowes, Yarmouth, &c.) leaving Southampton every Monday, Wednesday and Friday mornings, at nine o'clock; and Poole every Tuesday, Thursday and Saturday mornings, at eight o'clock.

The City of Glasgow,
From London, with Goods and Passengers, every Sunday morning, at seven o'clock, calling off Deal, Dover, Brighton, and Ryde, returning every Thursday at two o'clock. The City of Glasgow will leave Southampton for Weymouth, on Tuesday mornings, returning from thence to Southampton on Wednesdays, and will proceed to London the following day.

The above Vessels have this season been entirely refitted, and greatly improved, expressly for the above stations.

For further particulars apply to the Offices of the Company, 17, Fish Street Hill; Chaplin's Universal Offices, Regent Circus, London; Mr. Ranwell, Jersey; Mr. Barbet, Guernsey; Messrs. Vanden Bergh, and Son, Portsmouth; Mr. George Penny, Poole; Mr. Fooks, Weymouth; or Mr. N. M. Priaulx, Southampton.

REDUCED FARES.
MAIN CABIN, 10s.—FORE CABIN, 7s.

THE COMMERCIAL COMPANY'S Fast and Powerful Vessels, will leave the Royal Pier Southampton, during MAY as follows :—

For HAVRE-DE-GRACE, calling at Portsmouth,

THE GRAND TURK,

500 Tons, 150 Horse Power, fitted with a Splendid Saloon and Private Cabin, making up together 100 Berths,

CAPT. PERKINS WRIGHTSON

every Tuesday and Friday from Southampton, returning Monday and Thursday, as follows :—

FROM SOUTHAMPTON.	FROM HAVRE.
Tuesday, April 30 .. 9 Even.	Thursday, May 2 ... 2¾ Aft.
Friday, May 3 ..... 2 Aft.	Monday, May 6 ... 6¼ Aft.
Tuesday, May 7 .... 6 Even.	Thursday, May 9 .. 8 Even.
Friday, May 10 .... 7 Even.	Monday, May 13 .. 11 Even.
Tuesday, May 14 .. 8 Even.	Thursday, May 16 1½ Aft.
Friday, May 17 .... Noon	Monday, May 20 .. 5 Aft.
Tuesday, May 21 ....3½ Aft.	Thursday, May 23.. 7 Even.
Friday, May 24 .... 6 Even.	Monday, May 27 ..10¼ Even.
Tuesday, May 28.... 8 Even.	Thursday, May 30 .. 1 Aft.
Friday, May 31 .... Noon	

For GUERNSEY, JERSEY, and St. MALO direct, the well-known and favorite Steam-ship, the LADY DE SAUMAREZ, Capt. James Goodridge; The TRANSIT, Capt. James Goodridge, Jun., every Monday, Thursday, and Saturday, from Southampton, at 6 o'clock in the Evening, leaving JERSEY every Wednesday, Saturday, and Tuesday.

The "Lady de Saumarez" and "Transit," will proceed to St. Malo every Monday, returning every Wednesday.

NOTICE.

Passengers going to St. Malo or the South of France may proceed by the Commercial Company's vessels direct, without having to land and re-ship their luggage, carriages, or horses from one vessel to another, as with the Atalanta and Ariadne. Passengers are also cautioned against the false statements in circulation as to the difference of speed between the Atalanta and the Commercial Company's vessels, for taking the average passages, there is little difference between the Atalanta and Lady de Saumarez, or Transit; and it is well known, that on a late occasion the Ariadne was 10 hours going between Jersey and St. Malo, when the Lady de Saumarez did it in 5 hours, making on the whole passage from Southampton a saving of time, saving of expense, and saving of fatigue to the passengers who proceeded by the Commercial Company's vessels.

For the greater accommodation of the public, the Lady de Saumarez will call off Cowes for Passengers.

Fares to Havre-de-Grace, Jersey, or Guernsey:—10s. Main Cabin; 7s. Fore Cabin.—To St. Malo direct, £1 0s. 0d. Main Cabin; 14s. 6d. Fore ditto. Carriages and Horses per agreement.

For full particulars, apply to Mr. N. M. Priaulx, 78, High-street, Southampton; Mr. J. G. Jones, Bristol; Messrs. Vandenberg and Son, Portsmouth; Mr. Roper, Vine Inn, Cowes; Chaplin's Universal Office, Regent Circus; or 17, Fish-street Hill, London.

SOUTH OF ENGLAND STEAM NAVIGATION COMPANY'S PACKETS,

FROM THE PORT OF SOUTHAMPTON.

FRANCE AND ITALY,

BY SOUTHAMPTON, PORTSMOUTH, AND HAVRE-DE-GRACE.

THE MONARCH, 400 Tons, R. FORDER, R. N. Commander, will leave Southampton, for Havre as follows :—

Monday, May 13, 8 Morning.
Thursday, " 16, 8 Evening.
Monday, " 20, 3 Afternoon.
Thursday, " 23, 6 Evening.
Monday, " 27, 8 Evening.
Thursday, " 30, 9 morning.

calling at Portsmouth one hour and a quarter after leaving Southampton, and performing the passage from thence in ten hours.

Fares—Main Cabin £1 5 0. Second Cabin £1 0 0. Children under ten years of age, half price. Carriages £3 0 0. Horses, £3 0 0.

JERSEY, GUERNSEY, & SOUTH OF FRANCE.

The ATALANTA, 400 Tons, will leave Southampton for Guernsey and Jersey every Tuesday and Friday Evenings during the Season, at 7 o'Clock in the Evening, returning from the Islands Mondays and Thursdays.—FARES: Main Cabin, 10s.; Fore Cabin, 7s.

St. MALO and GRANVILLE—one of the Company's Packets will proceed to St. Malo every Thursday, and to Granville every Saturday, on arrival of the Atalanta from Southampton. Passports for France to be obtained of Mr. W. J. Le Fefeuvre, French Consul, Southampton, of whom further particulars may be obtained; also of Mr. Wheeler, Broad-street Portsmouth.

panies in those days were comparatively risky, and investors avoided subscribing to them unless liabilities, otherwise unlimited, were defined by Acts of Incorporation. It was, however, resolved 'that this meeting approves the steps taken by the directors in the exercise of their discretion for promoting steam navigation from Southampton in connection with this railway, and particularly their advance of £5,000 out of the funds of this company, on the security of two steam vessels to be especially employed between Southampton and other ports on the south-western coast of England.'

The establishment of the steamship company was hampered by lack of investment, and objections were made to the loan. Articles appeared in newspapers, and one writer, self-styled 'Scrutineer,' suggested that the £5,000 had been abstracted from railway dividends, but Chaplin told the August meeting of proprietors that it had been a loan, now terminated, which had earned £250 interest.

Chaplin and Locke strongly appealed at that meeting for early action. Cross-Channel traffic was competitive, and efforts were afoot to divert it from Southampton. Better-class ships were needed to attract passengers, who could otherwise choose the shorter Folkestone/Boulogne route, relieved also by the convenient knowledge of daily sailings thereon from memorising on which days ships left Havre or Southampton. An arrangement designed to overcome shareholders' fears called on holders of the 46,000 LSW £50 shares to subscribe £1 for each, against debentures issued on security of the steamers. Liability would not exceed £1 per share, and four per cent could be paid on the £46,000 before dividend on £30,000 already raised by the South-Western Steam Navigation Company, to whom the new capital would be loaned.

With money so far subscribed, the LSW had ordered a new iron paddle-steamer from Ditchburn & Mare of Blackwall, to be ready for the Paris to Rouen line opening. Built in 1843, of 204 gross tons and with speed exceeding twelve knots, she could reach Le Havre in nine hours, but seems to have operated extensively on the Channel Islands run. Named *South Western* and impressive for her time, she soon came under royal scrutiny.

> *South Western* took . . . passengers on her trip, and was the only boat that could keep up with the royal yacht, being so much faster that it was necessary to stop the engines frequently. This was noticed by the Queen and Prince Albert, who appeared to admire the vessel and repeatedly acknowledged the huzzaing of those on board.

So record LSW minutes, but she was soon outclassed, though

lasting until 1863 when she was sold to a Japanese firm who removed her paddles and rigged her as a sailing vessel for the journey home.

Chaplin's scheme did not attract sufficient capital, so steamship powers for the LSW were sought in a Bill for branch lines in 1844. Unfortunately, the attempt failed Standing Orders. Contrasting with his enthusiasm thirteen years earlier, Henderson had protested against the railway concerning itself with steamships, which he thought should be left to public competition.

Traffic through Havre decreased, despite increases through other Continental ports, and existing steamship services began running at a loss. On 14 February 1846, LSW proprietors approved the formation of a new company, with a board of fifteen LSW shareholders, at least ten being LSW directors. The prospectus of this New South-Western Steam Packet Company assured subscribers of five per cent dividend. By agreement in July 1846, the South of England Company ceased to exist, the new one purchasing its ships for £25,000 and taking its agencies in Jersey and Guernsey. On 17 November 1846 LSW proprietors authorised a loan of £50,000, if necessary, to make the new company quickly efficient, and on 12 July 1847, £25,000 having been advanced, the *Transit, Ariadne, Wonder, Monarch, Express, Camilla* and *Atalanta* were assigned to the LSW as security. (By now, the Commercial Steam Packet Company seems to have faded out.) Two new vessels, the *Courier* and *Dispatch*, were also assigned on 14 September 1848.

Patronage of steamers remaining low, the LSW again sought its own operating powers. Despite steam packet companies' opposition, Parliament authorised the LSW on 14 August 1848 to build, buy or hire steam vessels for fourteen years, working them between Southampton, Portsmouth, Gosport, Lymington, Poole, Weymouth, the Channel Islands, Havre and adjacent French ports. As Chaplin said, in principle Parliament opposed railways entering the steamship business, lest the monopoly created should endanger public services: consequently, some companies seeking similar powers had tried to prove that boats lost money, whereupon Parliament said that if it deprived the railways of steamships it was not denying them anything very desirable.

The LSW proposal to lease the ships and property of the New South-Western Company, on terms securing five per cent dividend for LSW shareholders, was opposed at the half-yearly meeting on 15 February 1849, because of there being no guarantee for the capital invested, the bad condition of the vessels, and lack of traffic. These objectors being defeated by a poll, the lease was concluded on 16 March 1849 for thirteen and a half years from 1 January 1849, and Tables 5 & 6 show the vessels involved. On 21 September, a special committee was formed to manage steamship affairs, Colonel Henderson becoming chairman, and on 2 November the board approved the establishment of a joint committee with the dock company 'for the purpose of acting on all matters affecting the mutual interests of the dock and railway, so that such mutual interests may be treated as one common interest'.

TABLE 5

Paddleships leased by the London & South-Western Railway in 1849

Ship	Length (a) in feet	Breadth (b) in feet	Depth (b) of hold in feet	Burthen tons	Engine tons	Room length in feet
Ariadne	121.6	17.4	10.8	116.7	80.6	46.6
Camilla	117.6	16.2	10.7	106 $\frac{156}{3500}$	66 $\frac{1750}{3500}$	35.5
Transit	126	19.6	13	160	107	38.9
Lady de Saumarez	127.2	20	12.85	157.1	116 $\frac{336}{924}$	42
Calpe	125.4	19.5	12.8	157	102	41.8
Monarch	137.7	21	13.15	174.3	140.4	47
Atalanta	138.1	21.9	13	171 $\frac{1538}{3500}$	137 $\frac{1369}{3500}$	44.4
Grand Turk	135.3	20.2	13	243.9	125.5	25.3
Robert Burns	132.1	19.4	10.5	184.7	124.7	56
South Western	143	18	10.8	131.6	71.9	34.2
Wonder	158	20.6	10.1	168.5	82.1	36.5
Express	159	21.4	10.4	152	103.4	43
Courier	167	22.5	10.8	195.8	118	45
Dispatch	166.7	22.1	11.6	197.1	123.4	44.4

(a) Measured from the inner part of the main stem to the fore part of the stern post; (b) Measured amidships.

These details have been copied from the Certificate of British Registry for each vessel.

TABLE 6

Paddleships leased by the London & South-Western Railway in 1849

DESCRIPTIONS

Ship	Built Year	Built Place	Decks	Construction	Bust, Shield or Billet head	Other items
Ariadne	1824	Rotherhithe	One	Carvel	Woman bust	Quar gallei
Camilla	1824	Rotherhithe	One	Carvel	Woman bust	No gallei
Transit	1835	Regent Dock Millwall, Poplar	One and a poop	Carvel	Man bust	Sham quart galler
Lady de Saumarez	1835	Millwall	One and a break	Carvel	Woman bust	Sham galler
Calpe	1835	Rotherhithe	One	Carvel	Man bust	Sham galler
Monarch	1836	Southampton	One main and one break	Carvel	Woman bust	Mock galler
Atalanta	1836	Cowes	One	Carvel	Woman bust	Mock galler
Grand Turk	1837	Greenock, Renfrew	One and a quarter	Carvel	Shield	Sham quart galler
Robert Burns	1838	Greenock, Renfrew	One and a quarter	Carvel	Shield	Sham quart galler
South Western	1843	Blackwall	One and a raised	Iron clench	Shield	Sham galler
Wonder	1844	Blackwall	One and a break	Iron clench	Billet	Sham galler
Express	1847	Orchard Y'rd West Ham	One and a raised	Iron clench	Shield	No galle
Courier	1847	Orchard Y'rd Blackwall	One and a break	Iron clench	Shield	Quar bridg
Dispatch	1847	Blackwall	One and a break	Carvel built with iron	Shield	Sham galle

All were two-masted, schooner-rigged, with standing bowsprits, and square sterns.
These details have been copied from the Certificate of British Registry for each vessel.

During the first months of the lease, New South-Western fortunes much improved, so that for six months ending 31 December

THE LSW AND THE SEA 209

1849 steamship earnings enabled it to meet the interest on the £50,000 loan, pay the five per cent guaranteed dividend, and carry forward £3,180. Old vessels were disposed of, among which the *Monarch* fetched £900 plus £180 for her machinery, and the new vessels operated much more efficiently.

Freight and mails were important traffics, the latter having been transferred from Weymouth in 1845. Through rates were arranged for goods between LNW stations and Paris via the North & South-Western Junction Railway, and likewise with other companies. Livestock was important, the New South-Western having two cow boats at Havre for shipping and landing it. Much traffic, however, travelled from the Continent to Folkestone and the South-Eastern Railway, whose shorter route made possible a quicker delivery in London, while traders did not have to pay separate port charges, the SER owning the port.

On 6 August 1860, Parliament made LSW steamship powers perpetual, but the Board of Trade could report in 1874 or any succeeding seventh year if public interests appeared injured, and the powers would cease twelve months after. On expiry of the lease, the LSW acquired the New South-Western Steam Packet Company, dissolved from 1 July 1862, for four per cent debenture stock having a cash value of £114,679 8s 7d.

SHIPS AND ROUTES

On 29 August 1846, regular sailings by the *Wonder, South Western, Robert Burns, Lady de Saumarez, Grand Turk* and *Calpe* were advertised, leaving the Royal Pier, Southampton, wind and weather permitting, for Guernsey and Jersey each Tuesday, Thursday and Saturday at 7.0 pm, returning Tuesdays, Thursdays and Sundays. Sailings for Havre on Wednesdays and Saturdays at 3.0 pm returned each Thursday and Monday, with calls at Portsmouth. Each Monday and Thursday at 5.0 pm, the *Transit* sailed direct from Portsmouth to Havre, returning Tuesdays and Fridays.

By January 1860, sailings for Havre were on Monday, Wednesday and Friday, from the Royal Pier by the *Alliance* and *Havre*, but without calls at Portsmouth. Some fares then were:

	1st	2nd
London to Paris	28s	20s
ditto return, valid one month	50s	36s
Southampton to Havre	21s	15s
Portsmouth to Havre, via Southampton	23s 6d	17s

O

During the same month, the *Atlanta* sailed for Jersey via Guernsey on Mondays from Southampton docks, returning on Wednesdays. The timetable does not name the vessels which left the Royal Pier on Wednesdays and Fridays for the Channel Islands. By February 1860, the *Atalanta* was withdrawn except for freight when required. She had sailed regularly at 4.30 pm, in contrast to the *Alliance* and *Havre*, whose departures varied constantly between 4.30 pm and 11.45 pm, an unsatisfactory arrangement for attracting passengers.

Combined rail and sea excursions proved popular. The 27 September 1841 was fine as a special train of twenty carriages left Nine Elms at 6.45 am with over 300 passengers, another 100 joining at Woking. Arriving at Southampton at 9.0 am they immediately embarked in the *Grand Turk* to sail round the Isle of Wight, returning to Southampton via Spithead at 5.0 pm. The train left at 6.0 pm, reaching Nine Elms in three hours, the party having covered over 220 miles by land and sea for 20s. For similar excursions in 1842 the vessel was the *Princess Victoria*, recently repaired and considerably altered after purchase from the Commercial Steam Packet Company by residents of Cowes and Southampton in conjunction with LSW proprietors. She averaged eleven knots.

Reported facts concerning some New South-Western vessels are interesting. The *Transit*, said originally to have belonged to the Weymouth & Channel Islands Steam Packet Company but which we know sailed for the Commercial Steam Packet Company, soon distinguished her New South-Western career by ploughing into the quay at Southampton, damaging her bows. The enquiry revealed that the chief engineer had been left ill at Guernsey, unknown to the captain, while the second engineer, ignorant of how to stop or reverse the engines, could not obey the order to go astern. The *Transit* ended up in the sixties as a coal hulk.

The *Wonder* was among the fastest ships of the time, logging fourteen knots. When, in 1857, the Weymouth & Channel Islands Steam Packet Company seriously challenged the Channel Islands service, she left the Southampton/Havre route for Weymouth to answer it. This unprofitable rivalry continued until 15 December 1859, when she returned to her original route, finally being broken up in 1875.

The *Grand Turk* went on charter to the Mediterranean from 1848 to 1850, but in September 1851 was recorded as running to Morlaix for the LSW. A year later she was making three return trips weekly to Havre with the *Wonder*, until a special committee on 23 November 1854 decided that, as the Board of Trade had condemned her for passenger traffic after 9 February 1855, she should cease in that service from that date. Her final fate is obscure. She was put up for sale, but on 16 August 1855 four offers up to £750 were refused and a minmum of £850 fixed. Her additional equipment for Mediterranean service included a chronometer, barometer, azimuth compass and stand, nautical almanac, quarantine flag, two six-pounder iron guns and wood carriages, one ladle and worm, rammer and sponge, four copper portable powder magazines, forecastle awning and foredeck awning, etc.

The *Dispatch*, a two-funnel ship, operated between Southampton, the Channel Islands and Havre, and logged thirteen knots. The *Express* was reputedly built in six weeks and given engines originally meant for a gunboat. She served the Channel Islands but found fame when, in 1848, with a naval captain in temporary command, she sailed to Havre to bring King Louis of France, in fisherman disguise and in flight from Paris, to Littlehampton. In 1855, she was offered to the South-Eastern Railway for £10,000 but was refused, then to the Government for £12,000 with the same result. She was wrecked on 20 September 1859 after striking a rock in Jailer Passage off Corbiere, Jersey, while her captain was off the bridge through sudden illness. Only three of the 200 aboard were lost. The *Courier* is reputed to have reached seventeen knots on one trip between Southampton and Guernsey, but her official speed was thirteen knots. She also served Havre and was broken up, it is reported, in the mid-seventies.

The *Alliance*, a handsome two-funnelled paddle-ship with clipper bows and sprit, named to commemorate Anglo-French union, was built by Mare of Blackwall in 1855. Replacing the *Grand Turk*, she cost £9,460, plus £10,000 for engines supplied by Seaward & Capel, Millwall. Her dimensions, taken from her drawings and a published description, were:

Length overall	201 ft
Length between perpendiculars	175 ft 4½ in
Length on keel for tonnage	161 ft 2½ in
Breadth for tonnage	23 ft 7 in
Depth amidships	15 ft 8½ in
Depth in hold	14 ft
Burthen in tons	476 and 76/94ths
Power	160 nhp

The drawing overleaf shows her cabin arrangements. Before

'ALLIANCE'
1855
CABIN PLAN

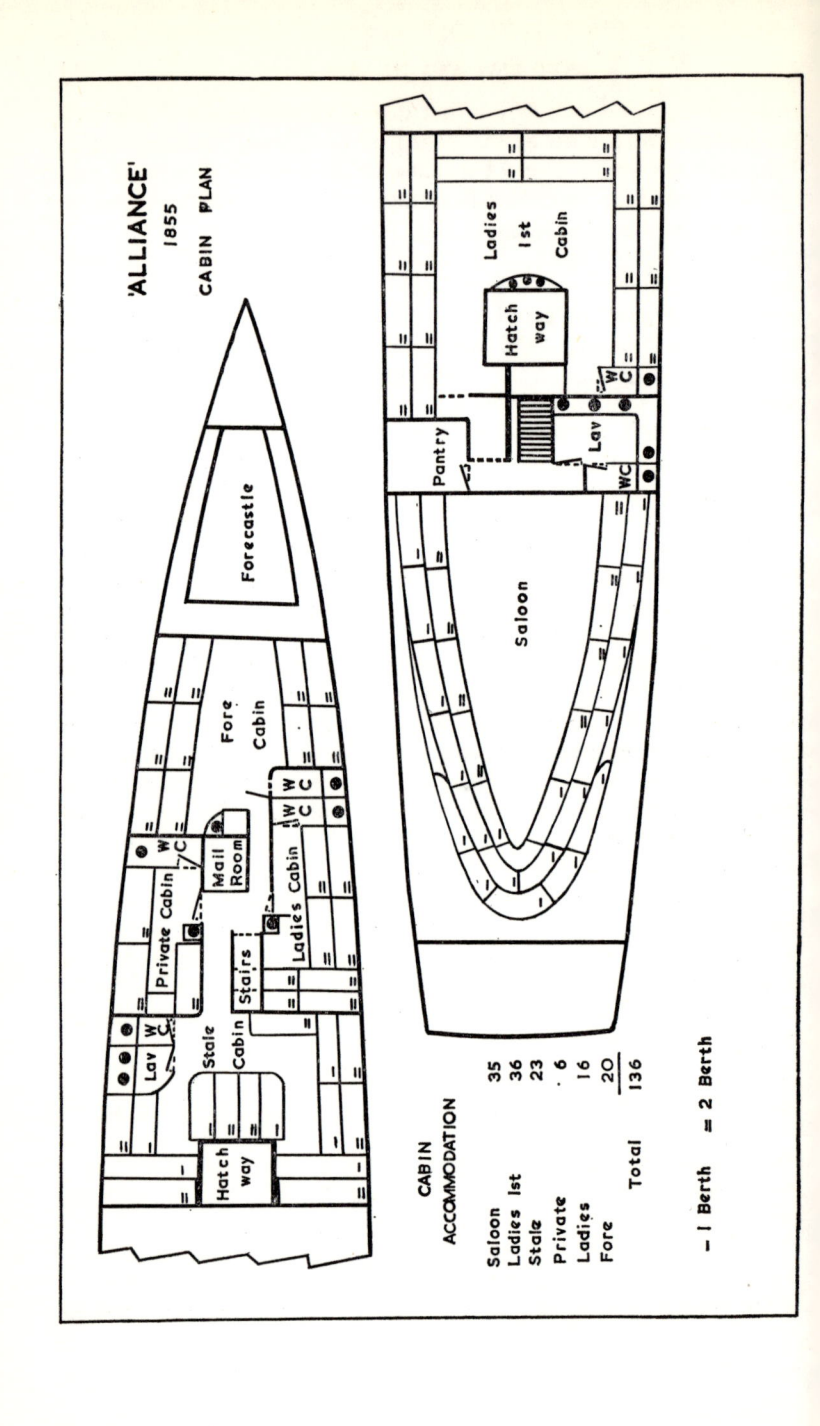

CABIN ACCOMMODATION

Saloon	35
Ladies 1st	36
Stale	23
Private	6
Ladies	16
Fore	20
Total	136

— 1 Berth = 2 Berth

being broken up in 1900, she transferred to the Jersey/Granville/St Malo service.

In 1856, the *Havre* joined the *Alliance* between Southampton and Havre. Also built by Mare, this two-funnelled iron paddle-ship, launched in May 1856, was announced as being:—

Length (?)	187 ft
Beam	24 ft
Depth amidships	15 ft 8 in
Burthen tonnage	517

Seaward & Capel supplied her 225 hp atmospheric engines, which had three open-top cylinders of 62 in diameter with 54 in stroke, making twenty-nine revolutions a minute. Her speed was 12.95 knots and she drew 9 ft of water. Her premature end came through striking rocks near Guernsey in hazy weather on 15 February 1875 while on passage from Havre. Her passengers and mail were taken off.

The last and largest of the New South-Western Company's vessels was the *Southampton*. Built by Palmers at Newcastle, she reached Southampton on 16 September 1860 after steaming 410 miles in 38 hr with heavy seas and strong headwinds. This two-funnelled paddle-ship measured 215 ft 5 in overall, 25 ft 7in beam, and 12 ft 7in, depth in hold, while her 475.55 gross tons included 175.58 for 'the engine room and its appurtenances'. Her 250-hp oscillating engines were made by Palmers, and ten furnaces fed her two boilers which, by the builders' contract, were restricted to 15 lb pressure.

Her trials on 24 September 1860 at Spithead were disappointing, for she only averaged just over thirteen knots, her engines making 28½ revolutions a minute. The builders blamed the restricted boilers. However, after modifications to the funnels, etc, she was accepted and performed the Channel Islands night sailing on 12 October 1860. After Palmers refitted her three years later, she reached fifteen knots. She was re-boilered in 1875, 1880 and 1889, and in 1880 she also received new engines and one new funnel to replace the two, besides being lengthened 20 ft. Thereafter she sailed mostly to Havre, but after going on the Channel Islands run in 1897 she was sold, ending her days in 1898 in a Dutch breakers yard.

A mid-nineteenth century Channel crossing, in cramped and segregated quarters and through boisterous weather, could play havoc with Victorian dignity, especially as the engines of the tiny paddle-ships, being necessarily amidships, kept passenger accommodation from what is normally the most comfortable part of any ship in rough weather. No wonder the long South-Western voyage found less favour than the shorter sea routes of its easterly competitors. In those days, a passenger might be booking a ticket to peril, while today luxury ships give a voyage of real pleasure, speedy yet leisurely. In 1964, private enterprise took over the Southampton to France routes which the railway abandoned, while Channel Islands passenger services were concentrated on Weymouth from 1961.

CHAPTER 9

Personalities and Policies

EARLY ORGANISATION

On Easthope's recommendation, three committees were appointed on 25 January 1839 to manage the newly-opened line; (a) Finance: controlling expenditure, receipts, dividends and securities; (b) Locomotive Engine: dealing with construction, use of and repairs to engines, and (c) Traffic and General Purposes: handling charges, fares, timetables, claims, carriages and all remaining matters. The board remained responsible for rates of pay, appointment and discharge of salaried staff, and establishment.

Easthope's dictatorship prevented departmental officers being able to define their responsibilities, and on 17 October 1840 Locke wrote strongly to the board:

> There is no strength in the executive. There is no officer of the company authorised to act as a head to keep men up to their duties. The system such as it is has not had fair play, for each person does his part as he best may without reference to the whole, and there is no one to keep the parts together.
>
> The officers of the company, instead of acting freely and energetically, are afraid to act for fear of giving individual offence. To such an extent has this feeling arrived that unless it be deeply eradicated it is vain to expect great improvement. You may appoint extra conductors and enginemen, increase the police and pointsmen, set one man to see that another does his duty, and multiply your expenses *ad libitum*, but unless you place the outdoor management under an efficient head, give him ample powers, and make him responsible solely to the court, you need not hope to be free from those casualties which have heretofor so frequently occured on this line. I have already offered you such aid as I can give in endeavouring to establish a better executive. I beg now to repeat the offer, and to repeat also my decided conviction that your system needs only a more uniform and a more determined course of action to make it work as well as on any other railway. Adding to the number of your servants is not the best way of curing your defects. Let every man feel that he has an eye upon him as ready to commend as to condemn, and he will be much more vigilant and attentive to your interests.

The growing rift between Easthope and the board caused him to leave the chair on 30 October 1840, an unfortunate event because his strong personality had done much to guide the company through its early difficulties. Space allows only short extracts from his letter of resignation:

> I make no pretentions to superior sagacity or discernment and it is very possible that I may sometimes have recommended or or supported plans or measures less advantageous than others that might have been suggested. But if at any time I have so acted, the error was one of judgement only. Ever since I have had the honour to be connected with the company my single object has been to promote in every way that my limited means and opportunities would allow, what I conscientiously believe to be its real and lasting interests . . . . . .
>
> I am not aware of any proceedings on my part that should have occasioned the withdrawal of any portion of the confidence you were formerly pleased to repose in me. But I perceived with much concern some months ago that that confidence was shaken and latterly it would seem, for what reason I know not, to have almost wholly disappeared.

Easthope claimed that the final straw was the board's appointment of Morgan as secretary, but his objection to that person is not clear.

Chaplin now became chairman for two weeks, then deputy-chairman to Garnett. From 28 November 1840, one committee replaced the three, to which were responsible Locke, the engineer-in-chief; Martin, general superintendent of the line; Stovin, general manager of traffic; and Gooch, superintendent of the locomotive department from 1 January 1841 in succession to Woods who had resigned in December. These officers had powers and duties carefully defined. Departmental committees were necessary, however, and returned after four months as Traffic Police and Goods; Locomotive Engine; Way and Works; and Finance Stores and Audit. This system of management, with variations in succeeding years, became established.

FINANCE AND AUDIT: THE STOVIN AFFAIR

The George Hudson scandal and the post-mania economic hangover ended the honeymoon between the LSW board and proprietors. Though the latter had cheerfully sanctioned over £6m new capital in 1846, a small minority in 1847 shuddered at the amended £2,462,766 13s 4d which surviving schemes, especially the Exeter line, required. However, a special general meeting on 27 November 1847 approved the issue of 147,766 third shares at £16 13s 4d each, in proportion of one for each £50 share held. The thirds would take seven per cent preferential dividend on the deposit and five per cent on calls until 1854.

Hoyes, the arch-rebel but shrewd business man, could see no return on his money and protested that his preferential would come from his ordinary dividend, a practice he called illegal. Vigorously opposed to the western extension, he wanted the capital account closed. At the half-yearly meeting in February 1848 he unsuccessfully tried to prevent Count Eyre, Messrs Smith and Uzielli being re-elected directors, for 'having sanctioned the attempted appropriation of the revenues of this company to purposes entirely unauthorised by the Acts of Parliament'. Likewise he failed to get the November 1847 meeting declared null and void, and the directors' actions were overwhelmingly approved.

Hoyes concurrently campaigned for auditors, a species Chaplin surprisingly detested because of some unfortunate early experience. However, the directors bowed to the proprietors' wishes, and Hoyes and Thomas Close were elected auditors on 25 August 1848.

A miserable year passed, and at the half-yearly meeting on 18 August 1849 some shareholders displayed an ugly mood when, despite higher net receipts, Chaplin announced a dividend reduced to three and a quarter per cent, because extra capital worth £2,814,033 raised during the mania was now participating for the first time. Alexander Kaye of Manchester began stirring what he thought were muddy waters, suggesting the directors held most of the seven per cent preference shares and that original shareholders' dividends were being slashed to pay them. He also criticised their general conduct, such as holding free passes and freely transferring them.

On 28 November 1849, while the proprietors were discussing the fate of the London Bridge extension, Gaselee, with expert timing, suddenly announced his lack of confidence in the directors and asked if it were true that any of them had borrowed the company's funds to pay their calls: if so, at what rate of interest? He understood they had paid five when twelve per cent was being charged elsewhere.

The effect was electric, and both auditors admitted there was evidence of loans which had made them uneasy. The board offered to resign if confidence in it had gone, but clearly some enquiry was essential and a committee, including Gaselee, Locke, Hoyes, etc, was appointed on 22 December 1849 to investigate. Meanwhile, rumours had multiplied of trickery with accounts; undue preferences by directors; Chaplin's interests in the firm of Chaplin & Horne being incompatible with his LSW directorship, etc. So serious did Chaplin consider the allegations that on 15 December he addressed his 'fellow shareholders' with a pamphlet of defence. He denied receiving dividends greater than the interest on his arrears of calls, and stressed his steady devotion to the LSW of time, mind and money, in good times and bad. He had always taken his proper proportion of new capital and no more, but in 1846 proprietors' applications for new stock were far below what was necessary and he took 3,000 additional shares reluctantly, for he already had enough. Other directors did likewise.

In 1845, he loaned the company £43,000 at low interest without security, which was repaid to him in cash or set-offs against calls. He found difficulty when his 2,000 Paris & Rouen £20 shares, worth over £40 each, fell to £10 because of the revolution in France in 1848. This prevented his realising them to expunge his arrears on LSW calls, but he paid the same interest as all LSW shareholders in arrears. His losses were heavy, but his actions, he said, were sincere and honest.

He admitted the management might wish much of the past undone, but:

> All of us may be wise after the event, but it is for fools or knaves to pretend that they had had such after-acquired wisdom from the beginning. I make no such pretension. We are all much sufferers, and I among the greatest; but if we make the proper use of our present depression, and, instead of quarrelling among ourselves, and making charges or casting imputations which had no justification in fact or fairness, we devote ourselves to the careful working and development of our property, there is yet prosperity in store for us.

The directors explained to the investigating committee that the loans Gaselee had referred to, totalling £50,000 at five per cent, were made to seven persons, including three directors, to employ temporarily idle capital and adequate securities were taken. The committee's report reached the half-yearly meeting on 27 February 1850. It found the directors had greatly exceeded their powers when acting, as they thought, for the company's benefit, but they were not corrupt. Wrong though it considered some of Chaplin's actions to have been, it was satisfied the company's interests were his first object.

Besides dealing at length with audit and procedural matters, the committee criticised the board (which it considered too large) on two matters of behaviour. First, it deprecated the liberal issue of general free passes, and recommended that they be limited to directors, auditors and principal officers. (It had, in fact, been the practice for servants accompanying directors to travel free, but some were found doing so when travelling alone.) Secondly, it decried directors who sent their parcels free, for this was a bad example to every employee. '. . . we cannot look for rigid honest discipline in a widely-spread executive, so long as it is known that such practices are adopted by the directors themselves.'

In all, it had discovered much to blame and regret, but unanimously agreed nothing had come before it affecting the integrity of the directors. Thus generally vindicated, Chaplin was re-elected to the board, and it was moved by Currie, the committee's chairman, and carried unanimously that the board be assured of the entire confidence of the proprietors.

Unhappily, some of the company's staff were more blameworthy. Cornelius Stovin, an old coaching man, was an unlucky choice as superintendent of the traffic department from 23 February 1839 at £250 per annum. Redesignated general manager of traffic on 30 September 1840, he had the entire management of goods traffic, except while actually in transit, and from December 1840 his authority at Nine Elms extended to passenger traffic as well. In coming years his responsibilities increased with the confidence placed in him. Introduced by Chaplin, who stood surety for him, his beard, fierce countenance and unpopularity earned him the title among the staff of 'Black Prince.'

His tactics were hard with staff and customers alike. In April 1839 a watchman left something in Merton Lane without lights or warning, which damaged a passing gig. Stovin caused the watchman to negotiate a settlement with the owner, the sum he agreed being deducted from his wages. In 1840, after paying £10 for a parrot killed in transit, he insisted on the stuffed remains being surrendered to the company as salvage by its sentimental owner.

These, however, were minor matters! The LSW, like other companies, carried much freight brought to it by independent carriers, allowing them a rebate from the carriage charges they collected, and three months credit facilities. Stovin was responsible for their accounts, which were poorly kept, and in June 1851 his attention was drawn to the heavy arrears. That August he was instructed to see that Ford, a West of England carrier, quickly reduced his outstanding debit to £5,000.

Early in 1852, Stovin took sick leave during which, in March, he vanished to America. His accounts were investigated, a task found so complicated that not until July was it established he had a shortage of £2,921 11s 8d. In addition, station agents' bad debts amounted to £651 5s 7d.

Stovin shouted his innocence from America, but ignored Chaplin's offer to pay his fare if he would return and explain matters. The repercussions were enormous, especially as Ford became bankrupt in July. His debt of £8,051 10s 7d, including authorised credit, had to be written off over five years, while Stovin's sureties being only £500, the balance of his was similarly cleared over two years. The fifteen station agents involved received various punishments up to dismissal.

The affair revealed the company's generally unsatisfactory accountancy arrangements: it probably never knew its true losses over many years. In 1849, a cashier suddenly died leaving a deficiency of £2,802 8s, while another loss, of £380, was discovered at Vauxhall in January 1852, only five months after six clerks at Waterloo had been responsible for £295—and other cases occurred. Severely shaken at last by Stovin's affair, the board made the treasurer solely responsible for collecting monies from carriers, and as several sureties for employees had defaulted, a fund was established to which all servants required to find sureties, such as officers and clerks handling money, had to contribute.

The company's capital, following piecemeal and sometimes anomalous growth, was reorganised by the Consolidation Act of 14 August 1855 as follows:

Preference shares under the Act of 1839	£ 14,400	0s 0d
Preference stock created by this Act	£ 171,276	13s 4d
Ordinary stock	£5,737,879	13s 4d
Ordinary shares	£1,616,770	6s 8d
New share capital for works under this Act	£ 9,000	0s 0d

Borrowing powers of £2,403,416 made the total £9,952,742 13s 4d, excluding £1,000,000 for the Exeter extension which this Act compelled the company to promote.

ARCHIBALD SCOTT: THE GOODS BUSINESS

Archibald Scott, who succeeded Stovin, had served the Edinburgh, Perth & Dundee; Edinburgh & Glasgow; and North British Railways, having been goods manager of the latter. At the LSW half-yearly meeting on 17 August 1852, the day he took office, one proprietor questioned his sureties and objected to directors standing security for officers; to which Chaplin replied, 'You may be sure, I'll never go security again'.

Scott quickly justified his excellent reputation. A sound, perceptive manager with an excellent sense of judgement, he was strong but patient in negotiation and, unlike Stovin, not needlessly agressive. He placed the LSW in a strong commercial position, especially by arrangements with other companies to secure through traffic.

The goods business he now controlled was yet immature. The LSW had so far relied on the network of carriers who fed it traffic, while in London its agents were Chaplin & Horne, the city's chief parcels carriers, who likewise served other metropolitan railways from receiving offices dating from coaching days. Cattle, coal, timber, agricultural necessaries and produce; these were LSW main traffics, yet it had recognised in 1844 that the growing imports and exports through Southampton offered good payloads.

> In order to confer those advantages in the manner most calculated to meet the object, and also most likely ultimately to produce the largest amount of benefit to this company, the directors have determined on the adoption of a very low scale of charge for great quantiities, the charge per ton decreasing as the tonnage increases, until at fifty tons, in one consignment, the charge is as low as 10s a ton for carriage of import and export goods, the whole length of the railway.

In general, LSW freight receipts were low; about £1,000 weekly in 1844. When in 1845 it reduced its charges to attract extra traffic, the effect on freight was astonishing, but while the tonnage carried during the second half of that year was 108,950, or 31,500 above the same period of 1844, earnings were only £1,000 up.

In 1849, Chaplin invited proprietors' views on whether or not the company would profit by doing its own cartage and excluding carriers. He personally thought carriers valuable among the farms and villages in the west, where they 'by constant attention and assiduity, pick up a trade about the country which a large company would have great difficulty in doing'. By becoming its own carrier, the company might economise with wagons but sacrifice speed, for 'when people had a little monopoly they were not inclined to use so much exertion as when they were subject to competition'.

His analysis of 63,408 tons through Nine Elms in six months at that period is interesting:

Dealt with by Chaplin & Horne	7,687
Dealt with by general carriers	17,162
Dealt with by the public's own wagons	23,003
Dealt with by barges and boats at the wharf	7,473
Coal and timber by barges and boats	8,083

A committee appointed to examine the question reported in August 1849 and July 1850. It recommended continuing with Chaplin & Horne in London, but for elsewhere it was undecided. LSW inland traffic came in small quantities from numerous and often distant sources, while northern companies got large originating tonnages. As Stovin said, '(the carriers) now work for us, although they pack into large parcels to the detriment of the company, and get their goods, under 5 cwt to them, carried at the wholesale or tonnage rate which the public do not, and if unable to break these peccadilloes they might divert the goods they bring into other channels. They might then work against the company through the canals, roads and Great Western and Brighton railways'.

The committee settled for retaining the carriers for the time being, while at Southampton the company experimented by doing its own cartage. In 1853, after four successful years at Southampton, the board decided on purchasing vans and horses and doing its own London cartage from 1 July 1853. The Eastern Counties Railway gave the LSW room at its Receiving House, Blossoms Inn, Lawrence Lane, 53 King William Street, City, for use as a central depot fed by branch offices.

Mr Horne objected to the LSW opening new offices, Blossoms Inn excepted, so on 1 February 1854 the LSW and Chaplin & Horne signed an agreement retrospective to 1 July 1853 by which, *inter alia*, LSW carts collected goods and parcels accepted at Chaplin & Horne's offices for a booking fee not exceeding 1s per consignment. It also opened an office at their new premises in the Borough, for £50 annually.

THE PASSENGER BUSINESS

The LSW and other railways from London encouraged the conurbation we call Greater London, for residence away from the working environment of the city appealed to many who could now easily travel to and fro daily. In February 1840 the *Railway Times* reported a new town rising between Kingston and the railway. 'Already nearly two hundred houses, snug and aristocratic villas are finished, or in the course of finishing', from whose first-floor windows five royal parks could be seen.

The company delayed its decision to issue season tickets until October 1848, and then conceded first class only, within five miles of Waterloo, for £2 10s per mile yearly, £1 8s half-yearly and 16s quarterly. Suburban traffic, of course, was the portion of business least affected during the post-mania slump, and in 1849 the 1,500 or so season holders made 691,513 of the 2,348,613 journeys, while thereafter their numbers grew rapidly.

The LBSC and SER were doing very well in persuading people to live in their territories, so in 1850 the LSW countered by offering a seven-year renewal of seasons, with ten and fifteen per cent discounts to the second and third holders respectively in a household. Children under fourteen could have them at half price 'to facilitate education', but ladies were refused seasons altogether.

In March 1852, the company announced:

> Residential Tickets. In order to encourage the erection of houses at moderate rates, viz, from £20 to £50 per annum, adapted to the wants of clerks and similar classes of society, on the suburban lines of this company, which traverse the most healthy and attractive portion of the neighbourhood of London, the directors are prepared to arrange terms for the issue at a reduced rate, and for a given number of years, of Residential Tickets, with persons encouraging to erect twenty houses or more of the class referred to, on specified conditions, for the use of the occupiers of such houses, and their families.

Such occupiers were given twenty per cent discount for seven years.

By 1853, seasons were available over the whole LSW system. Passengers were encouraged by frequent and convenient services, rather than speed, and in the early 1840s trains were run in excess of demand to allow traffic to build up. The policy succeeded, and as local journeys multiplied short-distance trains were introduced to supplant frequent stops by long-distance trains. In 1851, higher fares for express trains were stopped, because few were willing to pay them for saving so little time on the LSW short main line.

On Saturdays in June 1842, excursion tickets were issued at Nine Elms for Southampton or Gosport. For 28s first or 16s second class, passengers could leave London and return 'during the same or two following days'. Three years later fares by two trains were reduced by twenty per cent, while day tickets saving thirty-three per cent appeared, being available to Isle of Wight residents for two days.

These reductions increased passengers in three months by 52,195 (or thirty-five per cent) and receipts by £5,375.

On 1 May 1846 came further reductions, with second-class passengers taken on expresses, and first and second carriages on Parliamentary trains. Many trains were accelerated, and the press applauded the LSW as the first to provide 'locomotion for the million'. It thought others would follow, but 'to the South-Western, however, belongs the honour of being the first to fairly carry out the intentions of the legislature in favour of cheap and rapid travelling for the poorer classes'.

Overall, the LSW considered its services excellent, and in 1847 said 'they might look in vain in *The Times*—that great redressor of grievances—for any complaint in connection with the London & South Western Railway'.

Self-praise is ever unwise, and on 18 December 1848 some dissatisfied passengers held a meeting at Lambeth, their main complaint being the fare increases the company was then implementing.

Well-meaning but hopeless opponents of Sunday travelling had protested from earliest L & S days. Sir Thomas Baring wrote on 21 October 1834 'calling upon the directors to propose at the general meeting of proprietors tomorrow, a bye-law to forbid travelling on the Sabbath day'. The reply has not survived.

Henry Weymouth left the board on 7 June 1838 over Sunday trains, and when Mr Barney, a proprietor, raised 'this breach of the Divine ordinances' at the meeting that August, Easthope congratulated him for 'such decorous and religious zeal', but rejected his plea, for:

> ... there must be an enormous proportion who would not be able to obtain at all that healthy exercise and relaxation which was essential to them if they were to be entirely debarred from it on the Lord's day. There was an immense number of persons who felt that if this species of restraint was to be rigidly enforced on the Lord's day, the practical effect would be to increase vice and misery rather than to promote those feelings of religion and decorum which all well-disposed minds must desire to witness the spread of.

A year later, in concession to Sabbatarians, Sunday trains between Winchester and Southampton were limited to four each way. This followed some acid correspondence between Easthope and the clergy of Winchester. The latter had written protesting 'that the day of religious rest is continually desecrated by the running of the trains upon the railway under your superintendence and with your sanction' and lamenting 'that a large body of men in your employ are practically altogether prevented from enjoying that season of cessation from worldly business which of right belongs to them, and are precluded from attending the worship of God with their fellow Christians'. They were also concerned 'that our parishioners are drawn away from attendance upon the service of the Church, and our congregation diminished by the absence of many, who, until this temptation allured them, were accustomed to attend their respective churches'.

Easthope's journalistic experience as proprietor of the *Morning Post* invigorated his reply.

> You charge us with sanctioning the systematic desecration of the Lord's day, and thereby exposing ourselves to the displeasure of Heaven, which you suggest to be likely to lead to the failure of the enterprise in which we are engaged. We feel these accusations to be very severe, coming as they do from a large number of dignified clergymen, who may be expected to mingle charity in the expression of their opinion. We deem your accusations unjust . . . .
>
> The company is, by Act of Parliament, compelled to run trains on the railway on Sunday for the convenience of the Post Office. We view the railroad as a substitute for public highways and therefore feel that it would not be just toward the public, or within the discreet exercise of our duty, to stop travelling by railway on Sunday, seeing that the public conveyances cease to afford the accommodation formerly given. It is also manifest that travelling by railroads greatly reduces the animal labour formerly employed on the public roads, and consequently reduces the quantity of human labour required for conducting the employment of horses.
>
> We further submit to you that the whole question of Sunday travelling is one that justly and properly belongs to the Legislature of the Kingdom to determine, and ought not to depend on the caprice of railway companies.

The subject recurred over many years. Had the London Bridge extension been built, its Act would have prevented the LSW operating trains at that terminus on Sundays from 10.0 am to 1.0 pm, and 3.0 pm to 5.0 pm, to avoid disturbing services at St Saviour's, the parish church which, in 1905, became Southwark Cathedral.

In September 1848, to mollify Sabbatarians, the company stopped running Richmond and Windsor line trains from Waterloo during the hours of the Sunday morning services and ran only a minimum during afternoon services.

P

AMALGAMATION MOVES

During September 1848, the railway world heard of a peace meeting between the LNW, GWR and LSW, but under such secrecy that all *Herapaths Journal* could solidly report was that the deputations had 'made havoc with a cargo of sandwiches and sherry'. When further meetings followed, it transpired that a mammoth amalgamation was intended, the spectre of which made the country tremble. One rumour said competitive trains would give way to fast services making few stops.

While talks continued and rumours multiplied, difficulties arose over GWR shares and Brunel's desire to extend his broad gauge; then the GWR and LSW quarrelled over Windsor, where the gauge war then raged. The proposed amalgamation terms barred new financial activities by individual participants, except for discharging existing liabilities, but the LSW insisted the WS & SW should seek its Windsor terminus Act next session, having got royal approval. The GWR opposed it as now unnecessary, and was only quietened by being left free to fight the Bill in Parliament. Nevertheless, deadlock in the talks came in November 1848, principally through LNW demands for majority representation on the new board, consistent with its largest capital. The whole operation was, of course, intended for economy with capital, especially by eliminating competitive projects. Chaplin personally disfavoured the amalgamation, and feared LSW fortunes under it.

At the time of the talks, the individual companies stood as follows:

	Main line, miles.	Branches. miles.	Lines in which they have interest—miles.	Total	Capital paid, round figures
LNW	438	62	641	1,141	£14,000,000
GWR	198¾	41½	513½	753¾	7,000,000
LSW	215	22	—	237	6,000,000

CHAPTER 10

Working the Railway

STAFF MATTERS

The Christmas-card coach, shown racing through impassable snow to the genial inn where travellers might quaff merry pots of ale, ignores reality. Coachmen were hardy fellows, required to drive or guard with brief stops, through gale-swept rain, frost, sun, fog or other variation by day or night. Between London and Exeter, for example, the rolling Wiltshire chalklands offered no shelter, but dwarfed the swaying vehicle and its exposed passengers, while the coachman struggled constantly to observe a strict and non-generous time.

By using many displaced coachmen and guards when meeting expanding LSW needs, Chaplin combined plain commonsense with loyalty to old colleagues. Proved in stamina, they could conveniently adapt their transport experience to the new medium. Thomas Miller, stationmaster at Woking from 1839, had served Chaplin for twenty-five years, while Thomas Cooper of Thatcham, whose own coaches had rolled between London and Bristol before he became manager when Chaplin acquired them, was Richmond's first stationmaster. From whatever background, employees were appointed after nomination by individual directors.

Of the guard, the 1847 rule book required that 'from the moment the train is set in motion, he will be responsible for its regularity, punctuality and safety', no easy task from his ineffectual perch where he suffered a shorter but more intense exposure than his coaching companion. Despite more carriages with inside brakes, such miseries continued until, in May 1858, Guard Baker fell from his roof seat when near Wimbledon and was run over. The coroner's jury recommended that outside brakes be abolished, and under Board of Trade pressure the company converted each such carriage for the guard to operate the brake from inside.

Guards' duties, besides operating matters, included preventing smoking or nuisances by passengers, and ensuring that luggage did not fall from carriage roofs. Head guards were responsible for

P*

train lamps and equipment, while second guards took charge of parcels, stopped passengers leaving their seats after accidents or detention, and kept locked all carriage inside doors.

Perhaps rain, fog and cold dripping tunnels disfigured their scarlet coats, for about 1847 they donned blue with scarlet collars, and blue trousers with a double row of scarlet piping. In 1855, they wore dark blue cloth and silver collar badges, plus belts with pouches for fog signals and watches, those for first-class guards having silver badges. Goods guards and brakesmen received no uniforms until successfully appealing in 1842. Guards of the royal train were issued with scarlet coats in 1863.

The 1847 rule book said:

> The duties of the police may be stated generally to consist in the preservation of order in all the stations and on the line of railway. They are to give and receive signals; to keep the line free from casual or wilful obstructions; to assist in the case of accident; to caution strangers of danger on the railway; to remove intruders of all descriptions; to superintend and manage the crossings and switches; to give notice of arrivals or departures; to direct persons into the entrance to the stations or sheds; to watch movements of embankments or cuttings; to inspect the rails; to guard and watch the company's premises; and to convey the earliest information on every subject, to their appointed station, or superior officer.

Policemen at stations received two extra shillings weekly and wore silver embroidered collars. From 1853, iron ceased to burden the brims of their silk hats, and in 1855 they, too, donned dark blue uniforms. Their numbers diminished as specialist staff grades assumed many more duties.

> ... a class of men who have always been noted upon this line to be sober, careful and intelligent enginemen. The safety of the public, and the punctuality and efficient working of the trains, are the paramount objects to be attended, and whilst any deviation from the strict line and course of duty will always be punished, merit will meet with encouragement and reward.

Thus Beattie in 1856 summarised the attitude to enginemen, after announcing the dismissal of the crew of the *Atlas*. When working the 1.45 pm Dorchester up train the driver had, between certain stations, travelled on the train while the fireman worked the engine; then at Brockenhurst both deserted to a public-house. Such irresponsibility by LSW enginemen was extremely rare, and the pioneers among them had little enough to celebrate. Standing on the small, open, rolling footplate behind the coke fire and unpredictable boiler, watching primitive signals and awaiting the ever-likely mechanical failure, they, too, faced every kind of weather. At first, their employers issued coats, then in 1850 leggings, capes, caps and southwesters were added. In 1854, Beattie was ordered to fit shields on the engines, giving protection at least against the effects of forward driving.

Strict regulations for enginemen were enforced with fines for non-observance. Failure to take over an engine half an hour before departure cost a day's pay, while 1s was exacted if a man's completed coke ticket were not promptly handed to his foreman. Rule 72 of 1847 stated:

> There shall be delivered to every engineman a time-bill, showing the time he has to keep on his trip, and every engineman who shall arrive at any station more than three minutes before the proper time will be fined, in addition to the loss of his trip money for the journey. In all cases where special trains are required, the engineman must take care that the distance between Nine Elms and Southampton is not performed in less time than two hours, unless by special orders.

The 'utmost exertions' were expected of porters in the company's interests, but they (and all staff) were forbidden to accept gratuities. In 1855, dark green uniforms were decided on, with white collar badges. In addition to obvious tasks, station porters apparently shared point operating duties until July 1841 when, after an accident at Andover Road (Micheldever), pointsmen were experimentally appointed there and at Kingston, receiving distinctive badges and extra pay. A resolution of 30 December 1842 extended this to all stations. In 1859, pointsmen at Waterloo and at crossing stations on single-line branches were given shelters—'small sentry boxes, similar to those on the Dorchester line' until it was doubled.

Guards, policemen and porters received boots, costing the company in 1854 13s 6d, 11s 6d and 6s 10d per pair for those respective grades, to which no man over thirty-five and under 5 ft 8in was appointed after 1842.

Surviving records show various hours of work. In June 1843, enginemen did an average week of fifty-four hours, while workshops men in February 1848 worked from 7 am to 4 pm on Monday and Tuesday; 7 am to 5.45 pm on Wednesday, Thursday and Friday; and 7 am to 1 pm on Saturday, taking half an hour for breakfast and one hour for dinner. Then, in 1874, we read, carriage cleaners and carpenters at Clapham Junction were refused a reduction from fifty-nine to fifty-four hours without wages being proportionately reduced.

Clerical life at Waterloo is revealed in a minute of 18 July 1859:

> .... that the hours required for attendance at the offices at Waterloo station, except in the case of the booking clerks, have always been from 9 to 5 o'clock, and there is no report to the contrary. That all books shall be out on the arrival of the first clerk, and any clerks not present by 9.30 am shall be fined one shilling and every apprentice sixpence.
>
> That no books shall be put away until 5 o'clock has struck. That half an hour between 1 and 2 o'clock may be taken for refreshment, and the head of the office is held responsible for one half of the clerks of the office being present, and for no longer time being taken for this purpose, and to report in the attendance book against the name of any clerk or apprentice transgressing.
>
> That the fines shall be entered in the Book of Attendances against the names of the persons fined, and that such book shall be laid on the respective committee's table, in whose department the office may be, at each meeting of the committee.
>
> The fines to be deducted from the salaries before payment, and to be carried to the Superannuated Clerks Fund.

Between 1842 and 1859, lads started as clerical apprentices at £25 per annum, then that system was replaced by educational examination, successful youths beginning at £60 (£70 in London).

Clerks' salaries were individually negotiated before the first classification of 1 October 1843 introduced four classes, viz, class three (clerks), £70-£100; class two (senior clerks and junior superintendents), £100-£150; class one (senior superintendents), £150-£250; and special class (chief officers), £180 plus a house-£500. By 1861, there were ten classes below special. In 1844, clerks were granted one week's annual holiday.

Staff relations were comparatively good, and discipline was maintained in the Victorian manner of rewarding merit and punishing neglect. The scales of justice may seem tilted in these examples, but they must be judged against the general attitude and economic background of the day.

1. 24 January 1840. Policeman extinguished a fire in an engine house. Reward, one week's wages.

2. 17 November 1843. Policeman with a fatal disease worsened his condition when fighting a robbery. Regarded as 'a most deserving object for consideration'. Reward, £5.

3. 11 August 1859. Enginemen of a down train found a man asleep across the up metals, and removed him to a station. Reward, one day's wages.

4. 5 May 1859. Guard discovered a broken rail in a tunnel. Porter discovered an embankment slip. Each rewarded 20s.

5. 8 July 1842. Box worth £2 lost from a train. Guard made to pay and fined one week's wages.

6. 3 December 1847. Chief clerk of the transfer office seen with a gun on Battersea Fields while on sick leave. Punishment, dismissal.

7. 17 November 1859. Porter left sidings points open, causing an engine derailment. Prosecuted, and received two months hard labour.

8. 21 April 1859. Employee left the company's service without notice. Prosecuted and received three weeks hard labour, and warning given to all other staff.

Interruptions to staff routine were rare, such as on 10 April 1848 when the Chartist movement, then at its height, staged a monster meeting on Kennington Common led by Feargus O'Connor. The Government had declared the gathering illegal, and its venue being close to the LSW, with a march on London to follow, the board mustered 800 men to protect its property and aid the authorities, of which number those agreeable were sworn in as special constables, commanded by the secretary, Mr Campbell. Though the company was officially thanked for offering to accommodate troops on its premises, the object was probably to gain greater safety by their presence. Fortunately, the expected disturbance did not occur.

At least workshops staff enjoyed annual outings, until minority misbehaviour during that of 1857 stopped them. Thereafter, 'deserving men' and wives received free passes at varying times, which avoided closing the works for the day.

Staff welfare blossomed with the Nine Elms (or South-Western) Friendly Society for relieving sickness among uniformed staff, which 600 of 695 eligible had joined by February 1844. It was severely taxed during 1849 when cholera raged and mortality was high in Lambeth. The company's annual contribution was augmented by proceeds from lost property sales and staff fines. In 1852, the directors reported that most men had joined a casualty fund, paying one penny weekly which the company matched, and qualifying for £50 on death, £25 for loss of a limb, or 'suitable compensation' for permanent inability to work. About that time, superannuation for clerks was begun, and for the needy retired the distastefully named 'Decayed South-Western Clerks Fund' was established.

According to Chaplin in 1844, London had sufficient schools, churches and houses not to require the LSW to provide them, like other companies, for its staff. However, a night school for children of the staff, financed by the Friendly Society, opened about 1850 in vacated station buildings at Nine Elms. The men organised their own institution, providing a library, reading room, lectures and evening classes. The company gave £100 for purchasing books, and £30 annually towards expenses. The first, well-attended meeting on 19 July 1850 attentively listened to a lecture on astronomy. Wyndham Harding, the LSW secretary, who showed great interest in the institution, took the chair at the men's request.

On 1 August 1856, Doctor Beamen, the company's medical officer, began attending all London staff and their families (except for midwifery or syphilis). He provided all medicines, making no charges but receiving £300 from the company, plus staff contributions of 1d weekly from those earning up to 25s; 2d from those earning more, and ½d from boys.

The post-mania depression hit South-Western staff hard. In 1849, a rigorous 'economical enquiry' began, wielding its axe heavily on clerks. Many guided shaky pens while anticipating three months notice, while the survivors could rejoice only to suffer reduction of earnings common to all staff, but were hardly encouraged by the directors waiving their own fees. The reduction was generally ten per cent, but larger salaries took greater knocks and efforts were made to mitigate individual cases of hardship.

Factory shortcomings are largely hidden by four walls, but transport undertakings produce their unsubtantial commodity under public gaze, consequently receiving unlimited criticism ranging from ridiculous to highly constructive. Shareholders are especial onlookers and not easily ignored, particularly when, like Puncher, they comment at general meetings. In 1849, this well-travelled proprietor was dissatisfied with LSW economies. At Datchet, he said, twelve were doing the work of five: at Wandsworth he found one porter to each carriage, and at Fareham 'the only employment four or five servants had during the time he remained there was helping a fat lady into a carriage'. However, during 1848, station staff had been reduced by over eighty, despite openings to Waterloo, Windsor and Hampton Court. At small stations, too, police were abolished, though some were made porters.

THE PASSENGERS' ENVIRONMENT

Passengers were more numerous on the LSW than on many other lines. Chaplin claimed, in 1841, that 7,000 more departed annually from Nine Elms than from Euston. We saw, in Chapter 2, their earliest experiences, and many years passed before real comfort eased the journey of the ordinary man.

L & S stations, practical but austere, reflected the company's mood, and even behind the restrained grandeur of Tite's facade at Southampton, still preserved, platforms did not properly protect passengers from weather, and improvements were ordered in 1841 and 1844. Micheldever (formerly Andover Road) up side buildings today remain unchanged, showing the level canopy on simple pillars surrounding the rectangular L & S country station structure.

Companies absorbed by the LSW often expressed distinctive architectural tastes with local materials. The high-gabled stone building at Barnstaple Junction, surviving North Devon days, blends naturally into its background, though the whole station today hardly pleases the aesthetic eye.

At least the famished using Southampton station soon had refreshment rooms, at first small but subsequently enlarged and let to a tenant in 1849 with a licence to sell spirits. By then, similar establishments were being opened at other suitable stations, and whatever the quality of their fare, at least they lacked the notoriety of Swindon.

Having paid his fare, the first-class passenger was the darling of the company, whose weatherproof and ventilated carriage cushioned his anatomy and gave him an unimpeded view. However, early compartments were small and low, and while in 1847 Chaplin lauded the legroom of new luxurious Richmond line coaches, most passengers affected in the collision there in 1848 had knee injuries.

In contrast, third-class passengers moved on open and miserable display until Gladstone's Bill became law on 9 August 1844, requiring railways to run at least one train daily over each line at a minimum speed of twelve miles per hour, including stops at every station, carrying third-class passengers seated in carriages protecting them from weather, at fares not exceeding 1d a mile. These obligations challenged the imaginative ingenuity of those companies who considered third-class travel should be made uncomfortable enough to scare off those who could pay higher fares.

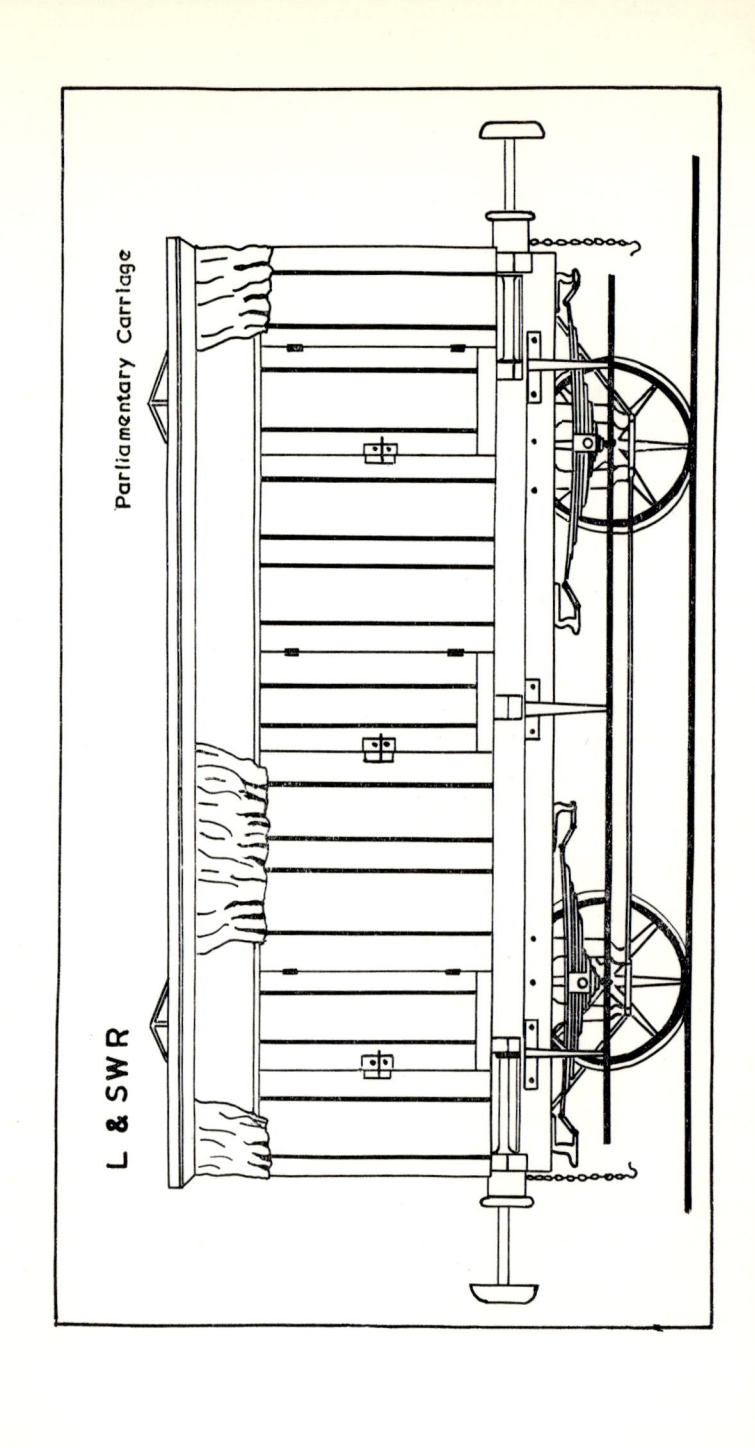

Parliamentary Carriage

L & SWR

The LSW produced a vehicle resembling a cattle truck with tarpaulin curtains across the window spaces, but when the Board of Trade insisted passengers should not travel in total darkness, two small skylight windows were provided. One by-product of this Parliamentary horror vehicle was a complaint from the senior collector of difficulty in collecting tickets, which at certain stations was done at platforms ahead of where passengers detrained. Doubtless, fare-dodgers skulked triumphantly in the vehicle's dark corners.

Having observed the law, the company continued open carriages on other trains until, it said, sufficient covered ones were built. In October 1852 they were ordered off long-distance trains, and on 10 April 1856 the board decided to abolish them. Weather apart, passengers in open vehicles faced hot cinders from locomotive chimneys, and claims for burnt clothing were frequent.

The Board of Trade in December 1854 forced the LSW to provide third-class closed vehicles with windows at the sides, ventilators near the tops, and lamps at night. Even so, passengers frequently fainted during hot weather, so that in August 1858 it was decided to make the windows to open, and to replace fixed ventilators in doors with moveable glass. Roof ventilators were improved to prevent rain entering.

Of course, the brake on improvements to third class was the expenditure on other classes which followed. The *Windsor & Eton Express*, 17 May 1851, criticised second-class carriages with wood in the doors where other companies had glass, and said 'the small windows by the sides are comparatively useless—people see with their eyes, not with their ears'. Glass replacements were not ordered until 12 October 1854.

During 1858-9, as second-class carriages entered shops, leather cushions and backs were fitted. On 10 March 1859 it was reported that those in a compartment of Coach 258 were cut to pieces—the seat slasher had arrived! The nuisance spread, and in April 1859 a disfigured carriage was publicly exhibited, with a warning that cushions would be removed if the habit continued. We well know that the cure still eludes us. That other vandal, the stone thrower, made a much earlier debut. At Gosport in 1842, two juveniles got one and three months imprisonment for this offence against trains, the tender years of the first having moved the magistrates to mercy. The lad who, at the same time, got fourteen days at Wandsworth where the habit was frequent, was singularly fortunate.

Returning to official discomforts, lack of heating was most

dispiriting. In October 1858, after much hesitation, the board agreed to supply small feet-warmers at 6d each to first-class passengers on trains travelling over twenty-five miles (subsequently increased to thirty) from Waterloo, Dorchester, Guildford, Southampton, Portsmouth, Gosport, Weymouth and Salisbury, where boilers provided hot water for these tin cannisters. The charge for feetwarmers was abolished on 18 December 1875. The LBSC objected, doubtless finding Portsmouth area passengers flocking to the less chilly route. In January 1861, Mr P. Salmon's system of heating 'by means of the exhaust steam from the engine, conveyed in tubes' was declined. Concurrently, sheepskin rugs (presumably first class only) were replaced by coconut, but following complaints the warmer sheepskins were restored to long-distance trains.

Initially a first-class luxury, oil pot lamps gave the only artificial light for many years, but not through tunnels during daytime. In 1858, J. W. Wilkins' offer to provide Knapton's patent gas lighting, as tried on the North London, was declined on Beattie's recommendation as too expensive. We must await Volume Three, when carriage design will be surveyed, before real lighting improvements are found.

The best carriages usually served the longest journeys, especially where competition flourished, e.g., to Weymouth. In April 1861, Scott reported using ten large cushionless second-class carriages for third class on Exeter trains, because LSW thirds were so disliked at Exeter and Yeovil in comparison with GWR broad gauge. Bodily anxieties on long journeys from lack of facilities could cause an uneasy conscience. On 26 March 1857 an anonymous writer sent the board 10s for 'having misused one of the company's carriages in a case of urgency'.

AN OPERATING MISCELLANY

At first, the London & Southampton relied only on strict timekeeping for train safety, and so frowned equally on early or late running. Drivers, who had no watches, were timed by station staffs and told if preceding trains were late, a system which gave no protection against breakdowns. After the Nine Elms accident of 17 October 1840, station clocks were given two faces, one visible to train crews, and were regulated daily by the guard of the first train. In December 1841, Mr Walker undertook to maintain all clocks on the system for £20 per annum.

Locke opposed anything mechanical relieving human respon-

WORKING THE RAILWAY 237

sibility for train safety. Sir Frederick Smith, the government inspector, reporting on the accident referred to, suggested machinery for turning the signal lamp at Nine Elms. Locke commented 'I believe the introduction of machinery will tend to lessen the attention of the men whose daily duty it would otherwise be to attend to the lamps. If the machinery be allowed to get out of order and the man becomes careless an accident would be more likely to occur'. Sir Frederick apparently shared this fear when, after a similar accident at Kingston (Surbiton) on 16 October 1841, he recommended a warning by steam whistle and red light on the foot plate operated from the lineside, adding that in case of failure someone should be there to give the ordinary signal.

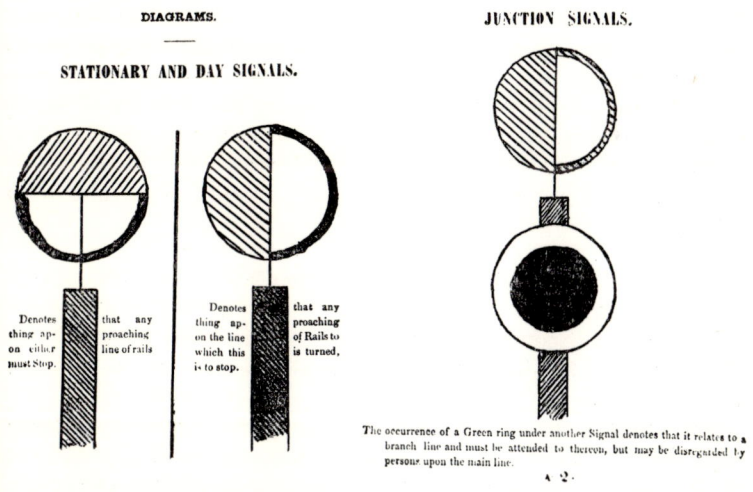

DIAGRAMS.

STATIONARY AND DAY SIGNALS.

Denotes thing approaching on either must Stop.

that any thing approaching line of rails

Denotes thing approaching on the line which this is to stop.

that any thing approaching of Rails to is turned,

JUNCTION SIGNALS.

The occurrence of a Green ring under another Signal denotes that it relates to a branch line and must be attended to thereon, but may be disregarded by persons upon the main line.

LSW Rule Book, 1847. Instructions concerning disc signals. The 'green ring' referred to is that surrounding the black circle, lower right

The LSW introduced fixed signals from 1840, mostly the disc variety whose indications shown in the 1847 rulebook are reproduced above. The disc was turned by an endless rope round its grooved edge, and indicated 'alright' when its supporting rod pivoted it to appear edge-on to the driver. In 1848, 'distance signals' appeared at Weybridge, Farnborough, etc, which could be worked over 600 yd away, showing colours by day and lamps by night from 20-ft high posts. 'When it will be required to stop a coming engine, the red will be instantly displayed; when to slacken speed, the green is shown; and when to pass the white is conspicuously observed; the one required being shown in the segment of a circle.' Stovin claimed credit for them, but apparently the idea originated on the Midland Railway.

In February 1860, the LSW decided on semaphore signals for the new Exeter extension, but economy prevented their immediate erection on the rest of the route from London, and the S & Y erected discs. During subsequent years semaphores gradually triumphed throughout the LSW system, but had existed on the Epsom & Leatherhead from its opening.

On 15 February 1854, the company 'resolved upon Mr Beattie's recommendation that the stationary signals at Southampton be fitted for the use of gas instead of oil, the cost of which is estimated at £64'. Minutes of following years show similar conversions at Richmond, Clapham, Winchester, Gosport, etc. On 10 February 1859, the traffic committee considered an 'application for ladders to the high signals at the gates on the Dorchester line. Recommend these to be placed where required, owing to gatekeepers being lame or old men'. Life previously must have been difficult!

Hand signals in the 1847 rule book were:

All right. An arm extended horizontally by day, or a white lamp by night.

Proceed with caution. Green flag by day, or green lamp by night.

Stop instantly. Red flag by day, red lamp by night, or any signal of any colour violently waved.

The person becoming aware of an accident went back at least 600 yd with a red flag or light, placing detonators not more than 100 yd apart.

The Kingston accident impelled the company to place a red lamp each side of the last carriage of every train, but the *Railway Times* of 15 January 1842 said these were as near as possible to the centre of the train and indicated clearly to following trains which line the preceding one occupied. Side lamps were abolished in 1854. On 29 September 1843, powerful reflecting lamps were ordered for mail trains. Goods trains apparently had side lights showing red behind only, until these gave way in 1854 to lamps on the rear vehicles showing red back and white forward, allowing drivers to know their trains were complete.

The 1847 rule book made head guards responsible for side and tail lamps, and for seeing trains also carried two hand lamps, two flags, two detonating signals, three fog signal lights and two spare coupling chains.

The inherent dangers of 'time interval' were mitigated by the intelligence transmitted by the electric telegraph, which appeared on the LSW in 1845, as described below. However, with or without it, Gunnell, the Southampton agent, was unjustified and reprimanded in October 1843 for instructing an up train driver to go slowly because Lady Holland was a sick passenger. At that time private special trains were discouraged because 'they are always attended with inconvenience and some danger unless ample notice be given of their intended despatch'. The train preceding a special carried a red tailboard by day and an extra tail lamp by night; a poor safeguard relying on infallible alertness by operating staff and the uninterrupted passage of the special. A special carrying royalty was preceded by a pilot engine.

The greatest contribution to public safety was the block system of signalling, which maintained a positive space between trains. A LSW minute of 30 March 1865 reads:

> Working of trains. Mr Scott reported that the working of trains under the Block or Electric system had been in operation between Clapham Jcn and Barnes since 6 March and that the working had been satisfactory, and he recommended that the system should be extended. 1. From Barnes to Twickenham. 2. From Barnes to Kew and thereafter to Hounslow. 3. From Clapham Jcn to Waterloo for Windsor line trains. Approved.

Later that year, the board ordered its introduction between London and Woking, Bishopstoke and Southampton, and Cowley Bridge and Crediton.

The system was adopted following a serious collision at Egham on 7 June 1864 during Ascot Races, when six passengers were killed. The driver of the 7.15 pm special from Ascot, first stop Staines, was unaware the 7.10 pm special was stopping at Egham. Fourteen carriages, plus two brake vans each with a guard, was the formation of each special, and with no turntable at Ascot both train engines ran tender first. The 7.10 pm was held at Egham while some pestilent cardsharpers were removed, and when the 7.15 pm driver found the distant signal 'on' (513 yd before the station) he whistled for brakes, but with a crowded train and falling gradient he could not avoid hitting the 7.10 pm as it moved out of the station. Colonel Yolland, inspecting officer, deplored the lack of continuous brakes and the block system, acidly suggesting that the LSW found it more expedient to risk human lives and pay compensation than to use a safer though more expensive system. Scott suggested the block system, with more signals and staff, increased the risk of human error, but the Queen having written on

27 December 1864, asking the board to take equal care for her subjects' safety as for her own, it was installed eventually throughout the line.

For many years reliable communication between drivers and guards was sought, which absence of continuous brakes made essential. Experiments in 1852 with bugles were unsatisfactory, then in 1853 the Hon Francis Scott invited proprietors to visit Waterloo and 'witness the guard from his own box sound at his pleasure the driver's whistle on the engine'. From an *Illustrated London News* description of LSW apparatus in January 1856, we find that when the guard operated a pump, a gutta-percha tube along the train conveyed air which was expelled at the other end in 'a very loud and shrill whistle'. One whistle meant 'look out', two 'caution' and three 'danger'. A minute of 30 January 1865 recommended that 'the cord communication between guards and drivers should be carried along the sides of the carriages instead of underneath as at present, with a gong to each tender . . .' Ultimately came the decision in September 1864 to adopt the deep-toned engine whistle for drivers to signal for brakes, the ordinary whistle remaining for other purposes.

The LSW tried a number of improved brakes. Captain Robin's brake, called self-acting, was tested on four carriages for four months in 1852, then Major Robin's (presumably the promoted captain) brake was tried in 1855 and subsequently fitted to forty-one carriages. Next came Newall's mechanical continuous brake in 1856, which the company told the Board of Trade it was well pleased with and had adopted generally. It had been tried on Windsor trains.

The company was offered many useless inventions, among which we must note the following:

> 9 August 1844. Read letter from Mr Curtis stating that he has discovered a mode by which passengers can be taken up and set down by a train in full speed, which was referred to Mr Beattie.
> 20 September 1844. Read Mr Beattie's report upon Mr Curtis's invention for fixing and detaching carriages without any stoppage of the train . . . which it appears is ingenious but inapplicable.

Nevertheless, on 1 June 1863 the 7.0 pm Waterloo to Portsmouth train began slipping a carriage at Weybridge, and by 1876 two trains slipped carriages there daily for the Chertsey branch. LSW slip carriages ceased on 2 June 1902.

On 1 January 1859 starting bells were discontinued at stations except terminals, but were 'to be rung as usual when the train is seen approaching the stations'.

Many early LSW passengers remembered road journeys by mail coaches, with rapid changes of horses at each stage and punctual arrivals unless emergency intervened. Post Office inspectors had insisted on strict timekeeping by coaching contractors. Small wonder those passengers and the Post Office were exasperated by unreliable trains, not least those of the L & S. The first L & S engines lacked size and power and frequently failed, yet Chaplin, a coaching veteran, apparently belittled complaints:

> If, therefore, they looked at the pressure on particular trains, they would not feel surprised that a good deal of time was occasionally consumed on the road. The parties who frequent the South-Western Railway were not principally commercial men, with watches in their hand and punctual to the minute, but ladies with children and bonnet boxes, who require, and I hope, receive every attention—so that it was really wonderful that, under such circumstances, so little delay occurred.

Actually, this complacent facade hid real concern. An investigation was eventually ordered, and 532 passenger trains run in May 1841 were said to arrive:

Before time (?)	474
10-20 min late	32
20-30 min late	17
Over 30 min late	9

Presumably, trains under ten minutes late were conveniently among the 474!

Delays occurred as traffic increased and extra carriages needed adding during journeys. Longer trains meant more double heading, and time was lost as a train engine moved up to take water after a pilot, with attendant risk to passengers joining the carriages they hauled. Many trains were detained awaiting mails coming to Basingstoke station by coaches from western territory beyond the railway. Possibly resentful coachmen, with nothing to lose, hoped to discredit their hated usurper in Post Office eyes by causing late arrivals in London.

While manufacturers basked in the high summer of demand, defective locomotives, hastily built and late delivered, were losing time or failing completely in traffic. Their unreliability greatly influenced the company's ultimate decision to build its own. Broken axles and tyres caused accidents besides delays, but Gooch blamed bad track for broken springs. In 1842, he recommended a maximum of twelve carriages to a train in summer, ten in winter, nine for a Mail, and double heading over difficult stretches against strong winds or on slippery rails. Despite the accumulated experience and improvements of years, delays remained a constant headache.

Speed was at first avoided while new earthworks settled, yet progress thereafter was not spectacular, as witness these examples:

July 1840 (fast train)		July 1866 (Express, 1st & 2nd class)	
Nine Elms	11.00 am	Waterloo	11.00 am
Woking	11.46 am	Basingstoke	12.15 pm
Farnborough	12.12 pm	Winchester	12.50 pm
Winchfield	12.29 pm	Bishopstoke	arr 1.03 pm
Basingstoke	12.50 pm	Bishopstoke	dep 1.05 pm
Andover Road	1.17 pm	Southampton Docks	1.20 pm
Winchester	1.34 pm		
Southampton	2.00 pm		

Quoted speeds in 1846 were 40 mph for expresses, 23 for mixed, 20 for thirds, and 16 for Parliamentary trains. Puncher thought even 25 mph too fast, and that lower speeds would encourage more ladies to travel who were meanwhile too timid. His appeal was ignored.

GOODS TRAINS

Fay tells us that goods traffic was first carried in wagons attached to the last passenger train each day, 'but upon opening to Basingstoke a goods train was run, conducted by three boys from fourteen to sixteen years of age'. These unpredictable lads were soon replaced by a man who, however, had no brake to work, the engine brake being the only one. On 24 March 1843 guards were ordered to ride in the last vehicle, being provided with moveable seats to take from wagon to wagon as train formations changed. Fay says:

> A vehicle called a Noah's Ark was placed at the guard's disposal; it had two swing doors on one side and a sloping roof, and carried small packages for roadside stations. Ordinary goods waggons were about twelve feet in length, very roughly finished, with dead buffers, and minus side chains and springs to the drawbars. In consequence of weak engine power some little difficulty was experienced in starting a heavy load, especially on an incline. Under such adverse circumstances the guard resorted to the expedient of placing a scotch under the last pair of wheels, so that the engine driver might put back to get all his waggon chains slack, and then take it with a run. This manoeuvre very often resulted in a portion of the train being left behind through chains breaking.

After June 1840 goods wagons had three, instead of two, chains. In May 1849 spring buffers were ordered for wagons, and in February 1853 proprietors heard covered wagons had arrived to reduce expenditure on tarpaulins.

Goods trains travelled 'at a regular and proper pace of fifteen miles an hour', but delays were frequent and operating practices sometimes alarming; as in October 1842 when one train lost an hour going back for goods it had dropped. Dissatisfied customers, especially butchers, complained in October 1840 of lost markets through delays, threatening to take to the road unless things improved. On 29 December 1840 they met at Salisbury and invited 'any party to a spirited undertaking, to transmit their goods per road carriage the whole of the way, and pledging themselves to give such a party their most strenuous support to such an undertaking'.

THE ELECTRIC TELEGRAPH

In July 1842, the LSW refused Wheatstone and Cooke's offer of their electric telegraph; then on 15 September 1843 it agreed with service chiefs to test the apparatus invented by Lieut Wright and Mr Bain, with a four-mile line from Nine Elms to the Wandle, 'so that by plunging the line and copper plates respectively into the rivers Thames and Wandle, the question of the generation of the electric wire and its transmission might be investigated'. Apparently the experiment failed.

The Government wanted telegraph communication with Portsmouth, and it reached agreement with the LSW and Wheatstone and Cooke for a line along the railway, connecting Whitehall with the Commander-in-Chief's house in Portsmouth dockyard. The Government would pay the inventors £1,500 annually for twenty-one years, while those persons would share construction costs and profits with the LSW and would maintain the line. The LSW, whose clerks would work it at Nine Elms and Gosport, had another line for railway purposes. 1 April 1845 was fixed for the opening of what then was the longest telegraph line in the country. The public paid 3s for single and 5s for double messages, maximum forty words, plus a delivery charge.

Once the board realised the value and scope of the invention, it installed it throughout the system as opportunity and capital allowed.

ACCIDENTS

Some noteworthy accidents have already been mentioned, but others still merit attention. On 17 May 1840 the engine *Mercury*, hauling the 10 am from Nine Elms, was derailed near Winchester, killing the driver and stoker who were thrown from it. Its speed was estimated at 20 mph, and though the track was suspected no cause was established.

A collision on 1 June 1840 between an engine and train at Farnborough, in which two horse-boxes were destroyed and some passengers injured, provoked a letter in *The Times* of 6 June censuring the company and charging its servants with unfeeling conduct towards the injured. This caused one casualty to leap to their defence by writing to the directors, 'I take the earliest opportunity of saying that no more could be done on the spot than was done on that occasion.'

On 16 October 1841, a luggage train from Southampton stopped near Kingston, and being unable to move the whole train, the driver left eight carriages with the guard while he took the rest to Nine Elms. The guard placed a red light on the last carriage, but hearing an approaching mail train he ran back, calling on it to stop and showing a red flag. His warning was unheeded and collision followed, but luckily damage was slight. Obviously the lesson of 14 August 1840 (see page 46) had not been absorbed.

This type of accident was repeated early on 18 May 1844 after the 8.30 pm up goods, heavily loaded, reached Wimbledon. Having insufficient water to take on the whole train, the driver continued with some wagons of fish for early delivery, leaving the brakesman with the rest and a warning to watch for the pilot engine's return from assisting another train down the line. It was now 4.0 am and daylight, and although the tail lamps were alight the brakeman's flag was inaccessibly resting in his box covered with goods, while he stayed near the train instead of going back 600 yd. Up came the pilot with its crew not watching out, resulting in the collision.

On 11 June 1846 an up goods from Guildford hit a down goods at Woking junction, overturning and damaging some empty wagons and slightly damaging an engine. The up goods driver was relieving the regular man who was sick, and was quite properly looking for a lamp on the high signal post. It was not displayed and he failed to see the signalman's comparatively insignificant hand signal.

At Bishopstoke on 20 June 1858 an excursion returning from Portsmouth was partly derailed while joining the main line, killing one passenger and injuring others. In recording 'accidental death', the coroner remarked he had held office since the railway opened, and this was his first inquest on a passenger, although a large part of the line ran through his district.

The company's generally good record was shattered on 28 January 1861 when the 5.10 pm train from Waterloo to Portsmouth was derailed at Raynes Park near the Epsom line junction, and descended the 20 ft embankment. Nineteen passengers were injured, and Dr Baly, principal physician to the Queen, was killed. The Board of Trade inspector presented a critical report. The prime cause was the track, consisting of bridge rails and longitudinal sleepers. It was in poor condition, with gauge variations up to ¾ in, and remedial work had been going on. The train consisted of an engine, tender and ten vehicles without continuous brakes, and the inspector attacked the company for running it at 42 mph with the only brake other than that on the engine being in the middle instead of at the end of the train. The guard had stopped the following train 300 yd from the wreckage, and so impressed were passengers with his conduct and that of the engine crew that they presented all three with watches. The board gave them medals and cash up to £10, with promises of early promotion.

On 5 June 1861, the 8.30 pm up goods from Salisbury, with a brake van at each end, left Grateley after shunting there and was found to be incomplete when reaching Andover. The driver consulted the guard, who had travelled in the front van, and they set back along the single line for the missing portion. At Grately, where it had been left, the stationmaster decided to take it on, using gravity for the descending first four miles and hoping for sufficient impetus to climb the next mile before a one-and-a-half-mile descent to Andover. So this unorthodox expedition set off, the stationmaster and brakesman riding in the second wagon and a porter in the brake van at the rear. The two portions met violently in a cutting on a sharp curve, and the stationmaster was killed.

Finally, an accident at Hampton Court junction on 20 June 1861. Like that of three years later at Egham, a race train was involved, also consisting of fourteen carriages sandwiched between two brake vans and hauled by an engine running tender first. Fortunately this train was empty when, returning along the Hampton Court branch, it hit an up passenger train on the main line. One passenger and a guard were injured. It seems that the race train

R

ran past a signal, but the inspector again criticised engines running tender first and trains with inadequate brake power.

MAINTAINING THE TRACK

The London to Southampton line was first maintained by Brassey for £24,000 per annum under a ten-year contract signed in 1840. As other lines opened, he or other contractors assumed their maintenance, too. Locke thought the company had made a bargain, but before the contract expired the board found the fixed price was denying it the financial reward of improved methods of working learned by experience. However, the close of 1850 saw the work relet at a more realistic price to those two responsible contractors, Brassey and Taylor, but in 1856 the company began doing its own maintance and claimed that improvements were the result.

Sleepers first laid were not all Kyanized. In 1842, instructions were given for all new ones to be so treated and untreated ones to be replaced. Unfortunately the process was unsuccessful, and decay began about four or five years after laying, so the method was discarded in favour of Paynes process. In 1846, sleepers were said to consist of 'scotch fir, beech, elm, and all the varieties of wood found in plantations and the thinning of parks in the vicinity of the line'. Semi-circular ones were now 9 ft long and 10 in diameter, and flat ones 10 in by 5in. They cost 4s 6d each.

Over sixty miles of the original 15 ft rails were still in use in 1858, many being fit for several more years. More were purchased, but in 1848 Locke had recommended trying bridge rails, of which 5,000 tons were purchased at £6 per ton and laid on longitudinal sleepers. Spacing between cross-sleepers on parts of the line was too great, and as relaying began in 1854 additional sleepers were provided. The whole of the Southampton & Dorchester line was so treated, and on that line, Errington reported in 1858, the large timber bridges were in good condition but were being replaced wherever possible with solid embankment. The half-yearly meeting on 9 February 1860 agreed rails should be fish-jointed and work began at once.

On 16 April 1851 it was decided to instal labels throughout the line, showing the gradients and their lengths.

A fall in Wallers Ash tunnel, near Winchester, on 2 April 1842, killed four workmen. A vein of clay in the chalk above was damaging the brickwork, and a conical shaft had been sunk from the surface and the clay removed. Material was then laid evenly on the tunnel arch and the shaft refilled, but on 28 March a watchman had reported the bricks were slipping. It was decided to reopen the shaft, and on 1 April timbers were put in to support the tunnel before removing the damaged bricks. Next morning slipping recommenced, and 23 ft of arch collapsed with fatal results. During repairs, passengers went by road between Andover Road and Winchester, but on 4 April trains were running again. Another fall occurred in this tunnel on 15 December 1852, but one line was cleared for traffic by next day.

Some ballast for the line was obtained in Surrey, powers being obtained from Parliament on 10 August 1857 to use lands in Wandsworth and Walton 'for getting therefrom stone, gravel and other materials for the repair and maintenance of the railway'.

BROOKWOOD NECROPOLIS

A service the LSW performed for many years was carrying deceased Londoners to the peace of Woking cemetery. When first asked to do this in October 1849 it agreed, provided coffins travelled in luggage trains at night and were brought just before the train started. The charge was 5s each, minimum four, and mourners travelled second class at single fare for the return journey.

In 1854, the London Necropolis & National Mausoleum published its prospectus. Because 'the Board of Health has reported (1) that the London graveyards are all bad, differing only in degrees of badness', that company had purchased nearly 2,200 acres of land near Woking. Arrangements had been made with the LSW for a 'reception room' near Waterloo with a junction with the main line (Necropolis station on the plan), and maximum charges for conveyance thence to Necropolis Junction (Brookwood) were:

For each corpse of the pauper class		2s 6d
For each corpse of the artizan class		5s 0d
For each other corpse	£1	0s 0d
For the conveyance to and from the cemetery of the mourners, not exceeding six persons for one funeral:—1st class, each person		6s 0d
2nd class, each person		3s 6d
3rd class, each person		2s 0d

In July 1854, Beattie was instructed to build one second and two third-class hearse carriages for use by the Necropolis company. LSW service timetables for 1863 show that a funeral train left

Waterloo daily at 11.35 am and reached Necropolis Junction at 12.25 pm; on Sundays the times were 11.20 am and 12.20 pm. Every day the return journey was performed in exactly the hour, leaving at 2.30 pm. In June that year, the LSW agreed to requests from local inhabitants and the Necropolis company for a new station near the cemetery, for which the Necropolis company provided the land, formed the approach roads and built the stationmaster's house. On 1 June 1864 the new station, Brookwood Necropolis, opened for trains on the main line to call, but the funeral train continued to run daily into the cemetery.

ROYAL PATRONAGE

Royal patronage of early railways was invaluable for dispelling fears among lesser mortals, yet even contemporary heroes were reluctant; like Hardy, fearless at Trafalgar but unable to face a train journey. The Duke of Wellington failed to use the LSW special train ever at his disposal, though this apparently was through prejudice against railways. In a speech in 1840, he said that he derived no advantage from the railways which passed near his house (i.e., GWR and L&S), and had been almost obliged to establish a stage coach for his own use. Easthope wrote to him in a tactful but hurt manner, asking for details of his complaints. He got no reply.

On 15 June 1842 Queen Adelaide, widow of William IV, left Nine Elms at 10.30 am, her special train of a guard's van, two firsts and a decorated state carriage reaching Southampton at 1.05 pm. Driven by Gooch, accompanied by Martin and Stovin, and attended at each terminus by directors, she enjoyed her easy and rapid journey, returning a few days later from the Isle of Wight for an equally successful trip to London. The only stop was at Winchfield, the half-way point, where the locomotive took water.

Perhaps her experience influenced Queen Victoria, for on 28 August 1843 she went by train to Southampton accompanied by the Duke of Wellington. Both expressed high pleasure with their experience and Chaplin predicted Her Majesty would thenceforward 'include in her arrangements one of our stations'. Until she could travel direct from Windsor to Southampton or Gosport, she went by road to Farnborough station, where private rooms prepared for her in 1847 cost £131 18s 9d.

The LSW provided Her Majesty with a royal carriage in 1844, designed by Joseph Beattie and described by the *Illustrated London*

News as 17 ft long and 7 ft 4 in wide, with Beattie's patent wooden wheels. The body was dark maroon with the royal arms in the centre panel, matching the Queen's private carriages. Commode and door handles were 'massive silver' with the royal arms liberally chased, windows were embossed and ground glass, and a 'crown and cushion surmount the centre of the body, and along its entire length is an elegant scroll cornice, the carriage itself being similarly decorated'.

The compartment for the Queen and Prince Albert occupied two-thirds of the length; the second compartment was for their children and suite. These were 'accessible by an almost imperceptible door, opening into either compartment and slung on a patent self-adjusting hinge'. The compartments were lined with light drab flowered-silk damask, having crimson and white silk trimmings and embossed pile figures. White damask embroidered with crimson covered the ceilings, having silver-embroidered national emblems encircling a golden crown at each corner. A carved and painted crown with shamrock and thistle surrounds commanded the centre of each ceiling. 'Immediately over this crown is placed one of the improved lamps, made by Miller & Son of Piccadilly; each crown, by an ingenious contrivance, being removable, so as to admit into both compartments an agreeable light.'

A white and gold cornice surmounted richly lined draperies of crimson and white figured satin damask; blinds were of peach blossom silk with crimson silk and silver tassels. Beneath the centre window, near seating for the Queen and Prince, were marble slabs on white and gold consoles. Axminster carpets covered a layer of cork and india-rubber composition (Kamptulicon) to prevent vibration.

As the royal family grew, another carriage was needed and built in 1851, an adapted ordinary carriage serving until its completion. The royal family also used two saloons, ordered in October 1858 as ordinary stock but kept locked. These were also available to Cabinet Ministers and for extraordinary occasions.

The Queen disliked speed, and complained of excess of it on the LSW in 1858. Thereafter, the LSW royal train did not exceed 40 mph. In March 1861, the board agreed to the Queen's request for a semaphore signal on her carriage, an apparatus she had on her GWR carriage to enable her to communicate her wishes to the train crew.

Probably the first event for using the royal carriage was the state visit of King Louis Phillipe of France. On 8 October 1844 he sailed into Portsmouth harbour, and at gaily decorated Gosport station was received by Colonel Henderson and Chaplin, before departing with Prince Albert for Farnborough and thence by road to Windsor. When he returned on 14 October, Locke drove the royal train and Queen Victoria also accompanied her guest to Gosport in the royal carriage. The triumphal arch and other decorations there were already soaked by rain, which increased to a torrent to greet the royal party, with hurricane winds and lightning flashes accompanying ominous rumbles from across a heavy sea.

This was enough to daunt the bravest cross-Channel passenger of the time, and King Phillipe decided to go home via Dover and Calais. The Duke of Wellington and Colonel Bouverie hurried to London by special train to make arrangements, and at 7.45 pm, after bidding the Queen and her Consort farewell, the King once more took LSW metals and reached Nine Elms at 10.35 pm. He crossed London to the SER at New Cross (where the station buildings were a mass of flames), reached Dover at 2.30 am and crossed the Channel later that morning.

Appendices

1: ARCHES TO WATERLOO

Usually reliable publications of the day described a viaduct of 300 arches to Waterloo, but original documents show only 235 as given below. Those underlined were arches or bridges across the roads named. The embankment west of Wandsworth Road was not replaced by arches until widening in 1877-8.

1		129	Lambeth Butts
2	Wandsworth Road		
-		130— 163	
3 — 18		164	Mill Street
19	Miles Street		
		165—174	
20 — 38		175—176	Lambeth Road
39	Archer Street		
		177—187	
40 — 43		188	Carlisle Street
44 — 46	South Lambeth Road		
47	The Creek	189—203	
		204	Homer Street
48 — 56			
57	Bridge Street, Vauxhall	205—207	
		208	Allen Street
58 — 65			
66	Spring Gardens Walk	209—213	
		214	Carlisle Street
67 — 74			
75	Vauxhall Walk	215—220	
		221	Upper Marsh
76 — 86			
87	Glasshouse Street	222	Westminster Bridge Road
88 — 120		223—231	
121	Salamanca Street	232	York Street (Leake St)
122—128		233—234	
		235	Granby Place

2: COMPANY ABBREVIATIONS

A & R	Andover & Redbridge	M & S	Manchester & Southampton
B & B	Basing & Bath	N & SWJ	North & South Western Junction
B & W	Bodmin & Wadebridge		
B & E	Bristol & Exeter	ND	North Devon
C & DC	Cornwall & Devon Central	P & O	Peninsular & Oriental (Steamship Co)
D & ECE	Dorchester & Exeter Coast Extension	RG & R	Reading, Guildford & Reigate
E & L	Epsom & Leatherhead	S & Y	Salisbury & Yeovil
E & C	Exeter & Crediton	SY & E	Salisbury, Yeovil & Exeter
E & E	Exeter & Exmouth	SER	South Eastern Railway
EY & D	Exeter, Yeovil & Dorchester	SW & WJ	Staines, Wokingham & Woking Junction
GWR	Great Western Railway	TV	Taw Vale
L & BR	London & Birmingham Railway	VS & P	Victoria Station & Pimlico
		WE & CP	West End of London & Crystal Palace
L & B	London & Brighton		
L & C	London & Croydon	WL	West London
LNW	London & North Western	WLE	West London Extension
		WS & W	Wilts, Somerset & Weymouth
L & S	London & Southampton		
LSW	London & South Western	W & C	Wimbledon & Croydon
LBSC	London, Brighton & South Coast	W & D	Wimbledon & Dorking
		WS & SW	Windsor, Staines & South Western
LS & Y	London, Salisbury & Yeovil		

Author's Note

This book could not have been written without the help of many people, too numerous to name individually. However, special thanks are due to the Archivist, British Railways Board, and his staff for their patient assistance over many years; the Council and Librarian of the Institute of Transport, and the Trustees of the British Museum. To my railway colleagues of various departments I am especially grateful for painstaking enquiries into obscure details and willing offers of material assistance. My chief, Mr C. F. Sanders, who has read much of the manuscript, has mingled helpful criticism with invaluable encouragement. Mr H. W. Hart gave me free access to his material and allowed me to photograph the Bodmin & Wadebridge tickets. At Wadebridge itself, Mr J. M. Taylor gave much on-the-spot assistance and supplied the picture of the opening train. My friend, Monsieur A. Kieken of SNCF, has checked my research into the Paris & Rouen railway, and Mr H. V. Borley has willingly drawn on his fund of knowledge and spent much time and trouble to help clarify doubts or ambiguities, especially concerning the London area. To each of these and to the host of other helpers, my gratitude is sincere.

I am aware of gaps in the story so far told. Unfortunately, many original records were lost or damaged during the London 'blitz', but what is readable of the surviving portion has been read. Some legends have regretfully been contradicted, and where good authority for certain familiar stories has not been discovered, they have been omitted.

The dates on station plans refer only to the years of the surveys from which the details have been taken, and do *not* indicate when changes took place. The area maps are incomplete, inasmuch as they show only those lines dealt with in this volume. Dates of agreements must be treated with caution: where the original has survived its date can be accurately quoted, otherwise it is only possible to give the provisional date, or the date of approval or sealing by one of the parties.

I am indebted to the Director of the Science Museum, South Kensington, for photographs 5, 6, 8 and 13; the Curator of the British Transport Museum, Clapham, for photograph 1 and the scene of Southampton station on the dust jacket; the Borough Librarian, Wandsworth Public Libraries, for the view of Clapham Junction; Mr F. C. Morris of Guildford for his copyright picture of Guildford station, and to Mr H. J. Compton of Woking for the scene at Wenford Bridge. The remainder of the photographs were taken by the author.

Staines, Middlesex R. A. WILLIAMS
October, 1967

Bibliography

GENERAL

LSW Reports and Accounts for shareholders
LSW minutes of directors and various committees
Prospectuses of various companies
Private and public Acts of Parliament
LSW service and public timetables
Bradshaw's Railway Timetables
Bradshaw's Railway Manual
Board of Trade Reports
Railway News
Railway Record
Railway Chronicle
Herapath's Railway & Commercial Journal
Illustrated London News
The Times newspaper
Fay, S. *A Royal Road*. W. Drewett, 1883

CHAPTER 1

Hadfield, C. *The Canals of Southern England*. David & Charles
Hampshire Advertiser
Deposited Plans for London & Southampton Railway Bill, 1834
Parliamentary evidence concerning London & Southampton Railway Bill, 1834

CHAPTER 2

Parliamentary evidence concerning London & Southampton Railway Bill, 1834
Deposited Plans for London & Southampton Railway Deviations Bill, 1837
Appendix to Working Timetables, Southern Railway
Hampshire Telegraph & Sussex Chronicle
Devey, Joseph. *The Life of Joseph Locke*. Richard Bentley, 1862.
Helps, Arthur. *Life and Labours of Mr Brassey*. Bell & Daldy, 1872.

CHAPTER 3

Parliamentary evidence concerning the Great Western Railway Bill, 1835
Minutes, Southampton & Dorchester Railway
      London, Salisbury & Yeovil Railway
      Salisbury & Yeovil Railway
      Chard Railway
Appendix to Working Timetables, Southern Railway
Salisbury & Winchester Journal
Hampshire Independent
Hampshire Advertiser

Western Times, Exeter
Nowlans Weekly Chronicle. Chard
Lymington Chronicle, Isle of Wight Gazette
MacDermot, E. T. (revised by C. R. Clinker), *History of the Great Western Railway*. Ian Allan, 1964.
Ruegg, Louis H. *The History of a Railway*. David & Charles, 1960. (reprint)

CHAPTER 4

Minutes, Cornwall Railway
        Bodmin & Wadebridge Railway (including Day Books & Accounts)
        Exeter & Crediton Railway
        Taw Vale Railway Extension & Dock Company (later North Devon Railway)
        Bristol & Exeter Railway
Tram & Railway World
West Briton & Cornwall Advertiser
South-Western Railway Gazette
Devonshire Chronicle
Cornwall Royal Gazette
North Devon Journal
MacDermot, E. T. *History of the Great Western Railway*. Ian Allan, 1964.
Lewin, H. G. *The Railway Mania and its Aftermath*. The Railway Gazette, 1936.

CHAPTER 5

Minutes, London, Brighton & South Coast Railway
        Brighton & Chichester Railway
        Portsmouth Railway
        South-Eastern Railway
        Wimbledon & Croydon Railway
        Wimbledon & Dorking Railway
        Epsom & Leatherhead Railway
Agreements, LSW and LBSC
Hampshire Independent
Hampshire Telegraph
Appendix to the Working Timetables, Southern Railway

CHAPTER 6

Minutes, West End & Crystal Palace Railway
        West London Extension Railway
        Richmond Railway
        Windsor, Staines & South Western Railway
        North & South-Western Junction Railway
        North London Railway
        Staines, Wokingham & Woking Junction Railway
Railway Gazette
County Chronicle & Surrey Herald
British Railways Magazine
Windsor & Eton Express
Deposited Plans for the Staines, Wokingham & Woking Junction Railway

CHAPTER 7

Minutes, South-Eastern Railway
        Staines, Wokingham & Woking Junction Railway
        Andover & Redbridge Railway
        Salisbury & Yeovil Railway
        Somerset Central Railway
        Somerset & Dorset Railway
Railway Junction Diagrams, 1867. Railway Clearing House
Andover Advertiser

CHAPTER 8

Agreement, signed and sealed, between LSW and New South-Western Steam Packet companies, containing copies of Certificates of British Registration for each vessel included in the lease.
Appleby, H. N. *Southampton Docks*. Southern Railway Company, 1930.
Burtt, Frank. *Cross-Channel and Coastal Paddle-Steamers*. Richard Tilling, 1934.
Grasemann, C. and McLachlan, G. W. P. *English Channel Packet Boats*. Syren & Shipping Ltd, 1939.
Hampshire Advertiser
Hampshire Independent
Southampton Times

CHAPTER 9

Agreement, LSW and Chaplin & Horne.
South-Western Railway Gazette

CHAPTER 10

Harris, Stanley. *The Coaching Age*. Richard Bentley, 1885.
Rule Book, 1847, of the London & South-Western Railway.
Minutes, Salisbury & Yeovil Railway
Prospectus, London Necropolis & National Mausoleum, 1854.
Windsor & Eton Express
Agreement, Wheatstone & Cooke, LSW, and Admiralty

Index

Illustrations are indicated by heavy type

Accidents: Bishopstoke, 245; Egham, 239; Farnborough, 244; Gosport, 123-4; Grateley, 245; Hampton Court, 245-6; Kingston (Surbiton), 238, 244; Nine Elms, 46-7; Raynes Park, 245; Richmond, 169-70; Southampton, 210; Wadebridge, 102; Wimbledon, 244; Winchester, 244; Woking, 244; Worgret, 63-4

Acts of Parliament: Andover & Redbridge 1858 and 1862, 188, 191; A & R and LSW amalgamation 1863, 191; Andover Canal 1789, 189; Bideford Extension 1853, 117; Birmingham, Bristol & Thames Junction 1836, 166; Bodmin & Wadebridge 1832 and 1835, 101, 106; Brighton & Chichester 1845, 133; Brighton & Chichester (Portsmouth Extn) & LSW 1847, 138; Bristol & Exeter 1845, 60; Chard Canal 1846 and 1847, 97; Chard Railway 1860, 97; Chard & Taunton 1861, 98; Cornwall 1846, 100; Direct Portsmouth 1846 and 1854, 137, 141; Dorset Central 1856, 193; 1857, 193; 1860, 195; Epsom & Leatherhead 1856, 152; Epsom & Leatherhead and Wimbledon & Dorking 1859, 154; Epsom & Leatherhead (LSW & Brighton) 1860, 154; Exeter & Crediton 1832 and 1845, 107, 112; 1850, 115; Exeter & Exmouth 1846, 1847 and 1855, 96; 1858, 97; Exeter, Yeovil & Dorchester 1848, 72, 97; Frome, Yeovil & Weymouth, 73; Great Western 1835, 52; 1845, 60; 1848, 72, 173; 1854, 185; Guildford Extension and Portsmouth & Fareham 1846, 137; Guildford Jcn 1844, 126; London & Brighton 1837, 125; London & Southampton 1834 and 1837, 20, 32; London & South Western 1839, 122; 1844, 54, 163; 1845, 159, 163; 1846, 70, 161, 180, 181, 183, 185, 225; 1847, 139, 159, 163, 188; 1848, 72, 206; 1849, 72, 184; 1853, 85; 1855, 86, 163, 220; 1856, 87; 1857, 151; 1858, 97; 1859, 179; 1860, 180, 209; 1863, 97; LSW and Southampton & Dorchester Amalgamation 1848, 65; LSW and Portsmouth Amalgamation 1859, 149; London, Brighton & South Coast 1846, 135; 1856, 151; 1858, 152; Lymington 1856 and 1859, 98; North & South-Western Junction 1851 and 1853, 176-178; North Devon Ry & Dock, 1851, 116; Portsmouth 1853, 142; 1854, 142-3; 1858, 144, 149; Reading, Guildford & Reigate 1846, 184; Reading Jcn 1857, 186; Richmond 1845, 168; Salisbury & Yeovil 1854 and 1857, 85, 91; Salisbury Ry & Market House 1856 and 1864, 96; Somerset Central 1852, 193; 1855, 193; 1856, 195; 1859, 195; 1861, 195; Somerset & Dorset 1862, 195; Southampton & Dorchester 1845 and 1847, 60, 64; Southampton Dock 1836, 199; Staines, Wokingham & Woking Jcn 1853, 181; Surrey Iron 1801, 128; Sutton Pool Harbour, 118; Sutton Harbour Improvement 1847, 119; Taw Vale 1838 and 1845, 107, 108; Taw Vale Ry Extn & Dock 1846, 108; 1847, 111; Victoria Station & Pimlico 1858, 166; West End & Crystal Palace 1853, 165; West London 1836, 166; West London Extension 1847 and 1859, 166, 167; Wilts, Somerset & Weymouth 1845 and 1854, 60, 65; Wimbledon

& Croydon 1853, 151; Wimbledon & Dorking 1857 and 1860, 152, 156; Windsor, Staines & South-Western 1847 and 1849, 172, 174, 181; Cheap Trains Act 1844, 233; Gauge Act 1846, 108; Regulation of Railways 1844, 53
Adelaide, Queen, 248
Albert, Prince, 205, 250
Alton branch, 136, 183-4, 185
Amalgamation proposals, 141, 225-6
Andover, 72, 75, 85, 86, 187, 188, 191
Andover & Southampton Canal, 75, 188, 189
Andover Road, *see* Micheldever
Arundel, 121, 156
Ash, 183
Atmospheric traction, 57, 99, 126, 133, 171
Auditors, 217
Axminster, 76, 77, 86, 95

Ballast, 22, 247
Baring, Sir Thomas, 17, 31, 35, 224
Barnes, 168, 172, 175, 179
Barnstaple, 101, 107, 108, 112, 116, 117-18, **plate 16**
Basingstoke, 72, 85, 187, 189
Basingstoke Canal, 37-8
Bath, 48, 49, 50, 51
Battersea, 14, 18, 20, 165, 167
Battle of Havant, 145-6
Beattie, J., 105, 163, 236
Beaulieu Road, 64
Bells, station, 240-1
Berkley, G., 151, 176, 177
Berks & Hants line, 53, 59, 67, 70, 71, 72, 186, 188, 190
Bidder, G.P., 151
Bideford, 108, 116, 117-18
Bircham, J., 81, 160
Bishopstoke, 54, 120, 122, **55**
Black Potts, 172, 173, 174, **plate 26**
Blandford, 64, 71, 193, 196
Bletchynden, 61, 62, 66, 187
Block telegraph, 239-40
Board of Trade, 66, 67, 69, 176, 235; inspections, 123, 141, 159-60
Bodmin, 99, 100, 101, 102, 105; *and see* Railways, Bodmin & Wadebridge

Bognor, 138, 156-7
Bonham-Carter, J., 142
Boots, 229
Bradford Abbas, 72, 85, 87
Brakes, 45, 124, 227, 239, 240
Branches, opposition to, 82, 184
Brassey, Thomas, 84, 116-17, 143, 169; *and see* Contractors, Brassey
Brentford, 172, 175, 178
Bridges: Barnes, 172; Black Potts, 174, **plate 26**; Grand Junction Canal, 174; Hungerford, 127; Northam, 40; Richmond, 172; Staines, **plate 25**
Bridport, 66, 67, 72, 74, 76, 77
Brighton, 144, 147, 151, 157
Bristol, 48, 49, 51, 190-1
British & Foreign Steam Navigation, 202, **203**
Brookwood: Necropolis, 247; station, 248
Brunel, I. K., 49, 92, 100, 126, 226
Brunton, W., 48, 49, 51
Bruton, 71, 193
Buller, J. W., 107, 110, 111
Burnham, 193, 196

Camel, river, 101
Campbell, P. L., 231
Canal, ship, 11
Capital re-organisation, 220
Carriages: First, 44, 233; Second, 44, 235, 236; Third, 44, 233, 235, 236; Parliamentary, 233-5, **234**; Bodmin & Wadebridge, 103, 105, **plate 13**; construction, 44-5; hearse, 248; heating, 235-6; lighting, 236; outside seats, guards, 45-6, 227; Richmond line, 233; royal, 163, 248-9; train formation, 241-2; vandalism, 235; ventilation, 235
Carriers, 221, 222
Cartage, 221, 222
Cash deficiencies, 219-20
Castleman, C., 57, 58, 63, 65, 74, 85
Central line, 73-96, 97, 99
Central Terminus scheme, 159, 161
Chadwick, W., 127, 175, 176
Channel Isles, 202, 205, 206, 209, 210, 211, 213, **203-4**
Chaplin & Horne, 34, 218, 221, 222

INDEX

Chaplin, W. J., 33, 34, 52, 56, 57, 58, 68, 73, 75, 76, 77, 78, 80, 83, 85, 92, 114, 118, 133, 136, 161, 181, 200, 201, 216, 218-19, 221, 226, 250
Chapman, J., 84, 85
Chard, 71, 97-8
Chard Canal Company, 97
Chartist demonstration, 231
Cheap Trains Act, 233
Chertsey, 172, 180-1, 240
Chichester, 127, 128-9, 130, 132, 157
Clapham Junction, 127, 165, 171, **plate 17**
Clerks, 230, 231, 232
Clocks, station, 236
Close, T., 217
Clyst, river, 97
Coaching, road, 24, 124, 126, 170, 227, 241
Coast line, 74, 75, 79-80, 86-7
Commercial Steam Packet Co, 202, 206, **203-4**
Committees, LSW management, 215, 216
Communication, train, 240
Contractors: Brassey, T., 34, 42, 75, 85, 116, 117, 122, 123, 138, 142, 152, 173, 174, 176, 180, 183, 184, 246; Brotherhood, 191; Collister, 189; Earle & Merrett, 182; Hattersley, 189; Hoof & Hill, 54; Jackson, 189; Knill, Henry, 168; Lee, 159; McCormack, 182; McIntosh, 34; Nicholson, David, 122; Peto, 61, 64; Peto & Betts, 151; Stannard, Robert, 21; Taylor, 91, 97; Tombs, John, 168; Treadwell, 21
Cooke, T., 24, 186
Cooper, E., 109, 110
Cooper, T., 227
Cornwall extension, Locke's advice, 113-14
Cosham, 149
Cowley Bridge, 107, 112, 114
Crediton, 107. **plate 15**
Crewkerne, 91
Crombie, L., 190
Cross-Channel steamships, see Ships
Crystal Palace, 165
Cubitt, J., 126, 132
Cubitt, W., 132, 190

Dalhousie, Earl, board of, 53, 59, 60, 67-8, 69, 99, 100, 107, 132-3, 168
Datchet, 172, 173, 174
Davis, I., 42-3
De Blauquire, Hon, 16, 49
Decayed South-Western Clerks Fund, 231
Delays, 241, 243
De Mauley, Lord, 69
Directors: Accusations against, 75-6, 217-19
Discipline, 229, 230-1
Ditchburn & Mare, 205, 211, 213
Dorchester, 57, 58, 59, 60, 66, 67, 76; station, 65
Dorking, 153, 154
Doubling: Andover & Redbridge, 192; Exeter, Central line, 95; Guildford Junction, 138; Portsmouth Ry, 149-50; Southampton & Dorchester, 65
Drivers, engine, see Enginemen
Dutton, Hon Ralph, 92

Earthworks, damage by weather, 39
Easthope, Sir John, 56, 121, 122, 224-5; dispute with Locke, 215, 39-40; resignation, 216
Egham, 180-1, 239
Electric telegraph, 238-9, 243
Eling tramway, 65
Enginemen, 46, 228-9
Epsom, 125, 126, 127, 133, 137, 154
Errington, J. E., 77
Eton College, 171, 174-5
Excursions, 103, 210, 223
Exeter, 54, 59, 66, 74, 79, 80-1, 86-7, 91, 92-4, 95, 96, 99, 107, 113, 118
Exmouth, 96, 97

Falcon Bridge, 127, 168
Falmouth, 99, 200
Fareham, 120, 122, 127, 138
Fares, 36, 56, 104-5, 140, 147, 160, 169, 178, 185, 209, 247; excursion, 210, 223; express, 223; season ticket, 223
Farlington Jcn to Cosham Jcn, 140, 149
Farnham, 183, 184
Farquhar, Sir Walter R., 153

Feet-warmers, 236
Fenchurch Street, 177, 178
Firemen, see Enginemen
Fires: New Cross, 250; Nine Elms, 158; Salisbury, 89; 'Five Kings', see Dalhousie, Earl, board of
Ford, carrier, 219-20
Fortesque, Earl, 108
Fotheringham v Southampton & Dorchester Railway, 62
France, 42, 200-2
Fremington, 107-8, 112, 113, 117
Funeral trains, 247-8

Garnett, R., 44, 201, 216
Gaselee, Serjeant, 74, 75, 76, 81, 82, 83, 85, 92, 156, 184, 217
Gauge, broad and mixed, 20, 52, 54, 61, 65, 71, 72, 73, 75, 89, 97-8, 99, 100, 111-12, 117, 166, 185, 186, 187, 226
Gauge Commission, 108-9
General Steam Navigation Co, alias, General Steam Packet Co, 202, **203**
Giles, Francis, 14, 17, 21, 22, 26-31, 48, 49
Godalming, 133, 138, 141, 142, 143, 150, **plates 21 and 22**
Gooch, D., 44-5
Gooch, J. V., 44, 216
Goods business, 221-2, 243
Goods trains, 44, 242-3
Gosport, 120, 122-4, 235, 243, **plates 18 and 19**
Gradient labels, 246
Grand Junction Canal, 173
Great Exhibition 1851, 165
Grissell, T., 153
Guards, passenger, 45-6, 124, 227-8, 229
Guernsey, 206, 209, 210, **203, 204**
Guildford, 126, 153, 156, 183, **131, 134, plate 20**

Hammersmith Bridge Co, 168
Hampstead Road, 177, 178
Hampton Court, 181, 232
Hampton Wick, 179-80
Hamworthy Goods, 194
Harding, Wyndham, 232
Harrison, T. E., 146

Havant, 138, 142, 143, 147, 149; battle of, 145-6
Hawkins, G., 145-6
Havre, 200, 205, 206, 209
Heathcote, Sir William, 83, 85
Heathfield, R., 25
Heating, train, 235-6
Helps, Mr, 74, 75
Henderson, G., 11, 14-16, 21, 25, 48, 83, 206, 207, 250
Hendford, 91, 96
Herapath's Journal, 175-6
History of a Railway, 69-70
Honiton, 73, 77
Hook Pit Deviation, 56, 57, 59
Hopkins, R., 101
Horsham, 151, 152
Hounslow, 170, 171, 172, 174, 175
Hours of duty, 229-30
Hoyes, A., 72, 217
Hudson, George, 186, 216
Huish, Capt., 111, 177
Hungerford Bridge, 127, 159

Institution, Nine Elms, 231
Isle of Wight, 98, 124, 150, 210
Isleworth, 172, 175, 179

Jersey, 206, 209, 210, **203, 204**
Jessop, William, 120, 128
Joint Line, Portsmouth, 138, 139, 141, 144, 146, 147

Kay, Alex, 76, 217
Kelly, Capt., 127, 129
Kew, 171, 178, 179
Kingston branch, 165, 170, 179-80

Lacy, H., 33, 75, 76
Laffan, Capt., 141, 159
Laffitte, Monsieur, 200-1
Lamps, train, 47, 238-9
Lancashire proprietors, 24, 25, 28-9
Lardner, Doctor, 142
Launceston, 99, 100
Leatherhead, 125, 152, 153, 154
Lennox Lodge, 138
Lennox, Lord George, 138
Lighting, carriage, 44, 236, 178
Locke, Joseph, 19, 29, 34, 39-40, 74, 75, 77, 92, 100, 109, 113-14, 118,

INDEX

126, 151, 152, 156, 168, 172, 174, 180, 200, 201, 215, 216, 236-7, 246
Locomotives: *Atlas* (1840), 103; *Atlas* (1853), 228; *Britannia*, 92; *Camel*, 101-2, 103, 104, 105, **plate 7**; *Chaplin*, 40; *Crescent*, 168; *Eclipse*, 47; *Elephant*, 103, 104; *Mars*, 40; *Mercury*, 244; *Minos*, 145; *Montrose*, 92; *Pegasus*, 38; *Pluto*, 103; *Rhinoceros*, 56; *Venus*, 40; *Vulcan*, 92; *Vulture*, 169-70; *Windsor*, 145; Double-heading, 241; failures, 241; **plates 5 and 6**
London & Southampton Railway: First moves, 11-17, **12-13**; Bill before Parliament, 17-20; construction, 21-42; openings, 36, 38, 40-2
London & South Western Railway: Organisation, 215-16; shipping interests, 202-14; style, 122
London Bridge, 142, 153, 161, 225
London Central Terminus, *see* Central Terminus
London Necropolis & National Mausoleum, 247
Lymington, 57, 64-5, 82, 98

Mangles, C. E., Capt., 92, 146, 147, 156
Mangles, F., 128
Mare, shipbuilders, *see* Ditchburn & Mare
Martin, A., 39, 160
Medical service, 232
Metropolitan Extension, 127-8, 130, 132, 133, 159-61
Micheldever, 42, 229, **plate 3**
Midhurst, 156
Millbrook, 188
Miller, T., 227
Mills, Sir J. B., 63, 65, 186
Misterton embankment, 91
Mitcham, 150-1, 156
Moorsom, Capt., 57, 74, 77, 100
Morgan, A., 67, 68, 201, 216
Morley, Earl of, 74, 76
Morpeth, Lord, 172, 173
Mortimer, C. S., 74, 75, 76, 83, 85

Nanstallon, 101
Necropolis stations, 247, 248

Newall's brake, 240
Newbury, 52-3
New South-Western Steam Packet Co, 206, 209
Nicknames: 'Black Prince', 219; 'Castleman's Corkscrew', 58; 'Mr Punch's Railway', 166; 'Parsons and prawns', 23; 'Sprat and Winkle', 192; 'Watercress', 176; 'Watersnake', 58
Nine Elms, 14, 17, 36, 46-7, 127, 158-9, 160, 163-5, 221-2, 233, 243, 248, **162, plate 1**
Northam, 38
Northam Bridge Company, 40
Notman, H. W., 85
Notman, R., 85

Ogilvie, A., 180
Okehampton, 99, 101, 118
Onslow, Earl of, 126
Openings (chronological order): Bodmin & Wadebridge 1834, 102-3; Nine Elms to Woking 1838, 36; Woking to Winchfield 1838, 38; Southampton to Winchester 1839, 38; Winchfield to Basingstoke 1839, 38; Basingstoke to Winchester 1840, 40 and 42; Bishopstoke to Gosport 1841, 122-3; Paris to Rouen 1843, 201; West London Ry 1844, 166; Woking to Guildford 1845, 132; Richmond Ry 1846, 168-9; Bishopstoke to Salisbury 1847, 56; Brighton & Chichester to Havant 1847, 139; Rouen to Havre 1847, 202; Southampton to Dorchester 1847, 62; Havant to Portsmouth 1847, 139; Weybridge to Chertsey 1848, 180-1; Nine Elms to Waterloo 1848, 160; Portcreek/Farlington/Cosham Juncs 1848, 140; Barnstaple to Fremington 1848, 113; Richmond to Datchet 1848, 173; Fareham to Cosham 1848, 140; Hampton Court branch 1849, 181; Reading, Guildford & Reigate 1849, 185; Barnes to Smallberry Green 1849, 175; GWR Windsor branch 1849, 174; Guildford to Farnham 1849, 184; Guildford to Godalming

1849, 141; Datchet to Windsor 1849, 174; Smallberry Green to main line 1850, 175; Crediton to Cowley Bridge 1851, 115; Farnham to Alton 1852, 184; North & South-Western Jcn 1853, 177; Basingstoke to Andover 1854, 85; Crediton to Barnstaple 1854, 117; Highbridge to Glastonbury 1854, 193; Barnstaple to Bideford 1855, 117-18; Staines to Ascot 1856, 182; Ascot to Wokingham 1856, 182; West End & Crystal Palace Ry 1856, 166; Andover to Salisbury 1857, 86; Highbridge to Burnham 1858, 193; Lymington Ry 1858, 98; Reading Junction Line 1858, 186; Godalming to Havant 1859, 146; Epsom to Leatherhead 1859, 153; Milford Jcn to Fisherton Jcn 1859, 89; Salisbury to Gillingham 1859, 89; Farlington Jcn to Cosham Jcn (reopening) 1860, 149; Gillingham to Sherborne 1860, 91; Sherborne to Yeovil 1860, 91; Yeovil to Exeter 1860, 92; Wimborne to Blandford 1860, 193; Exeter to Exmouth 1861, 97; Kew and Barnes curves 1862, 179; Glastonbury to Cole 1862, 195; Cole to Templecombe 1862, 195; West London Extension 1863, 166, 167; Chard Railway 1863, 97-8; Kingston branch 1863, 180; Blandford to Templecombe 1863, 195; Andover to Redbridge 1865, 192
Operating, 45-7, 236-42

Padstow, 100, 101
Palmers of Newcastle, 213
Palmerston, Lord, 108, 188
Paris, 201, 209
Paris to Havre line, 42, 200-2, 205
Parliamentary trains, 224, 233-5, **234**
Passenger arrangements, 44, 222-5, 233-5
Passenger statistics, 168, 179, 181, 233
Passes, 156, 217, 219, 231
Peel, Sir Robert, 69
Peninsular & Oriental Steam Navigation Co, 85, 200

Petersfield, 142, 156
Phillipe, King Louis, 211, 249-50
'Pines Express', 193
Pirbright, 172, 181, 183
Plymouth, 99, 100, 101, 113-14, 118-19
Pointsmen, 229
Police, 45, 228, 232
Poole, 57, 58, 60, 61, 193, 194, 196
Portal, Wyndham, 189
Porters, 45, 229, 232
Portsmouth, 27, 120, 121, 124, 125, 127, 133, 138, 139, 144, 150, 202, 209, 243, 250, **148**
Portsmouth & Ryde Steam Packet Co, 124
Prosser, W., 125, 129
Puncher, Mr, 80, 85, 232, 242
Punctuality, 241-2

Rails, 22, 35, 101, 245, 246, **23**
Railways (built): Andover & Redbridge, 188-92; Bideford Extension, 117-18; Birmingham, Bristol & Thames Jcn, see West London; Bodmin & Wadebridge, 100, 101-6, 114-5, **plates 7, 8, 9, 10, 11, 12, 13, 14**; Brighton & Chichester, 125, 129, 130, 132, 133, 135, 138, 139; Bristol & Exeter, 54, 59, 67, 71, 91, 92, 96, 97, 98, 107, 108, 109, 110, 115, 193, 195; Central Western, see Salisbury & Yeovil; Chard, 97; Cornwall, 100; Dorset Central, 65, 193, 194, 195; Dublin & Kingstown, 126; Eastern Counties, 222; Epsom & Leatherhead, 143, 151, 152, 153-4, 238, **155**; Exeter & Crediton, 107, 110-1, 112-13, 115-16; Exeter & Exmouth, 96-7; Great Western, 20, 24, 25, 51, 52-3, 60, 66, 67-9, 73, 166, 171, 172-3, 174, 185, 186, 188-91, 225-6; Guildford, Chichester, Portsmouth & Fareham, 132, 133, 135, 136, 137, 138; Guildford Junction, 125, 126, 128-9, 129, 132, 138; London & Birmingham, 17, 166; London & Brighton, 121, 125, 127-8, 129-30, 133, 135, 136, 137, 138; London & Croydon, 126, 133; London & North Western, 166, 167, 175, 176, 177, 178, 209, 225-6; Lon-

INDEX

don & Southampton, *see* main entry; London & South Western, *see* main entry; London, Brighton & South Coast, 135, 137, 138, 139, 141, 143-9, 150-1, 152, 153, 154, 156-7, 161, 165-7; London, Chatham & Dover, 166; Longmoor Military, 150; Lymington, 98; Mid-Sussex, 152, 156; North & South Western Junction, 175-80; North Devon Railway & Dock, 116, 117; North Kent, 161; North London, 177, 178, 180, 236; Oxford, Worcester & Wolverhampton, 185; Portsmouth, 141-50, 153, 157, 165-6; Reading, Guildford & Reigate, 136, 182-3, 184-6; Richmond, 127, 158, 167-70, 171, 172, 233; Richmond West End Junction, *see* Richmond; Salisbury & Yeovil, 83-5, 87-91, 96, 194-5, 238; Salisbury Railway & Market House, 96; Somerset & Dorset, 192-6; Somerset Central, 193, 195; Southampton & Dorchester, 57-8, 59, 60-6, 68-9, 74, 187, **63;** South Devon, 71, 96-7, 99, 118, 126; South Eastern, 127, 133, 142-3, 161, 185, 186, 209, 211, 250; Southampton & London, *see* London & Southampton; Staines, Wokingham & Woking Jcn, 181-2, 185-6; Surrey Iron, 127, 128, 130, 132, 150, 168; Taw Vale, alias, Taw Vale Railway Extension & Dock, 101, 107-9, 110, 111, 112, 113, 114, 116-7; Victoria Station & Pimlico, 166; West End of London & Crystal Palace, 165-6, 167; West London Extension, 166-7; West London, 166; Wilts, Somerset & Weymouth, 58-9, 60, 61, 65, 67, 71, 72, 73, 76, 85, 226; Wimbledon & Croydon, 150-1, 156; Wimbledon & Dorking, 151, 152, 153, 154-6; Windsor, Staines & South Western, 172-3, 174, 175, 181, 226

Railways (not built): Basing & Bath, 25, 48-52, **50;** Basingstoke & Didcot Jcn, 59; Basingstoke & Salisbury, 75; Basingstoke, London & Southampton, 52; Brentford & Richmond, 178, 179; Central (Salisbury & Exeter Extension), 77; Cornish, 99; Cornwall & Devon Central, 67, 69, 70, 71, 99, 100; Cornwall & Devon Central, and Plymouth, 111-2, 119; Devon & Dorset, 77, 79, 80; Direct London & Portsmouth Atmospheric, *see* Direct Portsmouth; Direct Portsmouth, 127, 129, 130, 132, 133, 137, 138, 141; Dorchester & Exeter Coast Extension, 74, 75; Dorking, Brighton & Arundel, 138; Exeter & Cowley Bridge Junction, 114; Exeter Great Western, 67, 69-70, 71; Exeter, Yeovil & Dorchester, 66, 67, 69, 70, 71, 72, 97, 100, 114; Kingston, 179; Leatherhead & Dorking, 153; London & Portsmouth, 132; London, Hounslow & Western, 171; London, Salisbury & Yeovil, 66-7, 68, 69, 70-1, 100; Manchester & Southampton, 175, 186-8; Middlesex & Surrey Grand Junction, 176; Mitcham & South Western, 150; North Devon, 108; North London, Paddington, Richmond, Hampton Court & Kingston, 179; Portsmouth Junction, 27, 120, 121; Richmond & Kew Extension, 178; Salisbury & Dorsetshire, 58, 59; Salisbury, Yeovil & Exeter, 73-4; Southampton, London & Branch, 11, **13**; Southampton, London & Branch Railway & Dock, 16, 17; South Midland Union, 193; South Western, 54; Staines & Richmond Junction, 171-2; Wandsworth & Croydon, 150; Windsor, Slough & Staines Atmospheric, 171-2

Railways, Commissioners of, 111, 112, 113
Railway Mania, 69, 71-2, 216
Railway Times, 169
Reading, 72-3, 182, 185-6
Reading Junction Line, 186
Receiving Houses, 222
Redbridge, 187, 188
Reed, William, 25, 74, 75, 76, 82, 151, 186, 200, 201
Rees, Dr Abraham, 120

Refreshments, 233
Regulation of Railways Act, 1844, 53
Remington, R. F., 154, 156
Richmond, 168-9, 178
River steamers, 36, 158-9
Robin's brake, 240
Romsey, 187, 188, 191
Roping-in of trains, 46, 160
Rouen, 42, 200-2, 205
Royal carriages, 163, 248-50
Royal Mail Steam Packet Co, 200
Royal patronage, 123, 163, 248-50
Royal Road, A, 24, 37, 45-6, 242, 255
Royal stations: Farnborough, 175, 180; Gosport, 124; Nine Elms, 163; Windsor, 175, 180
Royal trains, 239, 248, 249, 250
Ruegg, Louis H., 69
Rules, 45, 227, 228, 229, 238
Russell, C., 52-3, 68, 187
Ruthern Bridge, 101, 102, **plate 11**

St Georges Hill cutting, 22, 24, 26, 32
Salisbury, 54-56, 66, 69, 70-1, 72, 73, 74, 85-6, 89, **90**
Saunders, C., 49, 67, 68
Schuster, L., 143, 144, 146, 147, 151-2, 153
Scott, Archibald, 145, 146, 220-1, 239
Scott, Hon Francis, 75-6, 77, 78-9, 79-82
Season tickets, 223
Seaward & Capel, 211, 213
Seymour, Alfred, 85
Seymour, H. Danby, 85
Shaftesbury, 71, 72
Sherborne, meeting, 69-70
Shipping, 202-14, **203, 204, 212**
Ships: *Alliance*, 209, 210, 211-3, **212**; *Ariadne*, 202, 206, 207-8; *Atalanta*, 202, 206, 207-8, 210; *Bridegroom*, 158; *Calpe*, 202, 207-8, 209; *Camilla*, 202, 206, 207-8; *Citizen*, 158; *Courier*, 206, 207-8, 211; *Dispatch*, 206, 207-8, 211; *Express*, 206, 207-8, 211; *George IV*, 202; *Glasgow*, 202; *Grand Turk*, 202, 207-8, 209, 210, 211; *Havre*, 209, 210, 213; *Kent*, 202; *Lady de Saumarez*, 202, 207-8, 209; *Monarch*, 202, 206, 207-8, 209; *Princess Victoria*, 210; *Red Lion*, 98; *Robert Burns*, 207, 208, 209; *Solent*, 98; *Southampton*, 213; *South Western*, 205-6, 207-8, 209; *Transit*, 202, 206, 207-8, 209, 210; *Union*, 124; *William IV*, 202; *Wonder*, 206, 207-8, 209, 210, 211
Shipwrecks, 211, 213
Signals and signalling, 47, 237-40, **237**
Simmons, Capt., 160
Simpson, T. B., 169
Sleepers, 22, 246
Slip carriages, 240
Slough, 171, 172, 173
Smallberry Green, 175
Smith, Sir Frederick, 237
Snell, A., 79, 80, 81, 85
Solent Sea Steam Packet Co, 98
Southampton, 11, 14, 26, 38, 40, 42, 61, 74, 157, 186, 188, 189, 199-200, 209-10, 248
Southampton Central, 62
Southampton Docks, 15-16, 17, 27, 199-200, 207
Southampton Royal Pier, 187, 188, 209, 210
Southampton Terminus, 26, 38, 40, 61, 65, 233, **41, plate 2, frontispiece**
Southampton West, 66
South Molton, 109, 111, 116
South of England Steam Navigation Co, 202, 206, **204**
South Western Friendly Society, 231, 232
South Western Steam Packet Co, 202, 205-9
Special trains, 239
Speeds, 242
Staff, 42, 123-4, 220, 227-32
Staines, 171, 172, 180, 181, **plate 25**
Stations: Barnes, 168; Barnstaple Jcn, 233, **plate 16**; Beaulieu Road, 64; Bishopstoke, 122, **55**; Bletchynden, 61, 62; Chiswick, 172; Clapham, 167; Clapham Junction, 167, **plate 17**; Crediton, **plate 15**; Dorchester, 65; Epsom, 154; Fareham, 122; Farncombe, 150; Godalming, 150, **plates 21 and 22**; Gosport, 122, 123, 124, **plates 18 and 19**; Guildford, **plate 20**; Hampton Court, 181; Hampton Wick, 180; Hounslow,

INDEX

175; Isleworth, 175; Kew, 177, 179; Micheldever, 42, 229, 233, **plate 3;** Nine Elms, 14, 17, 36, 40, 163, **162, plate 1;** Portsmouth Joint, 138, 139, 144, **148;** Putney, 168; Richmond, 169-70; Salisbury, 89, **90;** Salisbury, Milford, 89; Smallberry Green, 175; Southampton Central, or West, 62, 66; Southampton Terminus, 38, 40, 61, 233, **41, plate 2, frontispiece;** Twickenham, 165, 170; Vauxhall, 159; Victoria, 166; Wandsworth, 167; Waterloo, 159, 160-1, 163-4, **164;** Weybridge, **plate 4;** Windsor, 174-5, **plates 23, 24;** Yeovil Town, 91
Stephenson, G., 24, 121
Stokers, *see* Enginemen
Stovin, C., 158, 185, 219-20, 221, 222, 238
Suburban traffic, 222-3
Sunday trains, 224-5
Superannuation, 231
Sutton Pool Harbour, 101, 118-19

Tavistock, 100, 101, 118
Taw, river, 107
Templecombe, 194-5, **194**
Territorial agreements: LSW and GWR, 53, 60, 66, 67-8; LSW and L & B, 130, 156-7
Thorne, Mr, 108, 110-11, 113, 116
Ticket platforms, 160, 235
Tickets, 43-4, 160, 235; season, 223; residential, 223, excursion, 223-4; **plate 12**
Times, The, 82, 187, 224, 244
Tite, William, 38, 159, 160, 233
Tongham, 183
Tootal, H., 151, 176, 177
Topsham, 96, 97
Track, 246-7, **plate 8;** defects, 64, 147, 169
Traffic: Ale, 183, 184; Livestock, 19, 49, 70, 209, 221; Racing, 36-7, 154
Train running, 236-43
Train services, 56, 92-5, 117, 123, 149, 160, 167, 173-4, 175, 177, 178, 181, 192, 223, 224, **43, 63, 93, 155**
Tunnel failures: Fareham, 122-3; Guildford, 141; Southampton, 62; Wallers Ash, 246-7

Tunnels: Black Boy, 91; Buckhorn Weston, 91; Buriton, 142; Crewkerne, 91; Fareham, 122-3; Guildford, 141; Honiton, 91; Litchfield, 32, 33; Popham, 18, 25-6, 32, 33; Wallers Ash, 32, 33
Twickenham, 165, 170, 171, 172, 178, 179
Twickenham Lines, 165

Uniforms, 45, 228, 229
Uzielli, M., 71, 72, 77, 156

Vandalism, 235
Vauxhall, 125, 159
Victoria, Queen, 172, 173, 205, 239-40, 248-50

Wadebridge, 101, 102, 103, 105
Wagons, 242-3
Wandsworth, 127, 128, 130, 133, 137, 138, 150-1, 161, 235
Waterloo, 127, 128, 137-8, 154, 159-61 165-6, 232, **164**
Wellington, Duke of, 52, 248, 250
Wenford, 101, 102, **plate 14**
West India Steam Packet Co, 200
Weybridge, 180-1, 240, **plate 4**
Weymouth, 57, 58, 59, 64, 209, 210
Weymouth & Channel Islands Steam Packet Co, 210
Wheatstone & Cooke, 243
Widenings, Nine Elms, 163, 165
Wimbledon, 150-1, 156
Wimborne, 57, 58, 68, 193, 194, 196
Windsor, 172-175, 225, 226, 232, **plates 23, 24;** N & SWJ trains, 177-8
Woking, 35-6, 125, 126, 182
Wokingham, 181-2, 185
Wood, Vice-Chancellor, 146, 147
Wooden railway, 125
Woods & Forest, Commissioners of, 61, 171, 172-3
Woods, J., 47, 216
Workshops staff, 229, 231
Wright & Bain, 243

Yeovil, 59, 60, 66, 67, 70, 71, 73, 74, 85, 86, 91-2, 95-6, **94;** Pen Mill, 72; Joint station, 91
Yolland, Colonel, 97